PIP$ PROFIT$ & POWER JOURNAL

GENIE CRAFF

authorHOUSE®

AuthorHouse™
1663 Liberty Drive
Bloomington, IN 47403
www.authorhouse.com
Phone: 1 (800) 839-8640

Published by AuthorHouse 01/15/2020

ISBN: 978-1-7283-4352-5 (sc)

"*"It's possible", said Pride. "It's Risky," said Experience.
"It's pointless", said Reason. "Give it a try", whispered the Heart."* ~~Anonymous

This work is dedicated to all FOREX traders who desire MINDSET
MASTERY. Traders prepare their minds for consistently profitable trades with
enduring focus, planned trading and regular journaling. With full confidence,
FOREX traders incorporate daily knowledge and wisdom for a prosperous
lifestyle of Abundant Gratitude.

"I Made Money"

"I made money!! Carly announced so proudly... I thought she was going to show me
her first corporate paycheck... "Well it is a whole lot of green...." My voice trailed off
as I examined the full spectrum of "the giant greenback" I held in my hands. "Tell me
about your money!" I said noticing this was indeed the most unusual "dollar bill" ever.
"It is lots of money on one paper! It is a $26 dollar bill!"
"A $26 dollar bill?" I questioned. "Yes! It is the best idea ever!! Now people won't have
to have lots of those little dollars. They can have all their dollars in one big dollar!"
"I guess that is kind of a good idea." I smiled silently to
myself, thinking about adults who would agree....
Some things just seem right...
..."I am going to keep it and take it to the bank. That is
where you keep your money." ~~ Carly age 10
HOLD MY HAND Remedy for My Destiny p. 150
By Genie Craff

CONTENTS

"Life is not measured by the number of breaths we take,
but by the moments that take our breath away."
--Anonymous

PART 1: JOYFUL FOREX TRADE JOURNALING

"Simplicity is the ultimate sophistication."
~~Leonardo da Vinci

Practice does not make us perfect, but it does allow us to realize what we want to stop doing. This is a basic that many wish they could skip. Few of us continue to do things that make us feel worse or miserable, unless we understand how those things will benefit us. You will get better with each trade and as you journal and record your story, the numbers will not lie. You will become more confident. You will know when getting into a FOREX trade is a great idea, and better yet, when to get out of a trade is a great idea.

Those who are newer to the FOREX trading journey will be more successful when this Journal is paired with PIP$ PROFIT$ & POWER FOREX MINDSET MASTERY. This companion book was written to be used to mold and shape the mindset of the FOREX trader while incorporating personal values, beliefs and experiences. Journaling your FOREX trading story can become a very inspiring and educational experience. Joyful journaling will provide the answers you need to become a more successful trader.

"Success is no accident. It is hard work perseverance, learning, studying,
sacrifice, and most of all, love of what you are doing."
~~Pele

Using a Trading Journal should be used on a regular basis for all traders who wish to do back checking and define how they actually place trades to improve the PIP$ & the PROFIT$. The trading journal will provide you answers that you need to become a more successful trader.

PROSPERITY AFFIRMATIONS

Prosperity affirmations are used for motivation, inspiration and a part of the Mindset Mastery needed for FOREX trading.

I AM:

ADMIRABLE	ABUNDANT	APPRECIATED	ACTION
BLESSED	BEAUTIFUL	BOUNDLESS	BREATH
CONSISTANT	CONFIDENCE	CELEBATION	CALM
DESIRABLE	DISCIPLINE	DANCING	DARING
ENERGY	EXPRESSIVE	ESSENTIAL	ENRICH
FINE	FOCUSED	FULFILLED	FAITH
GRATEFUL	GIVING	GALLIANT	GOOD
HONEST	HAPPY	HARMONY	HERO
INSPIRED	INTUTION	INCLUSION	IDEAS
JOYFUL	JOURNALING	JUDGEMENT	JOLLY
KIND	KNOWLEDGE	K.I.S.S.	KINDLE
LOVE	LISTENING	LIMITLESS	LIFE
MINDSET	MASTERED	MEANINGFUL	MIRACLE
NEW	NICE	NOURISHED	NEAT
ORIGINAL	ONGOING	OBVIOUS	OPINION
POWERFUL	PURPOSEFUL	PROSPERITY	PEACE
QUERY	QUESTIONING	QUEST	QUIZ
RECOGNIZED	RESOURCEFUL	READY	RICH
STRONG	SUCCESSFUL	SHARING	SAVVY
TALENTED	TENACITY	TRUST	TRADER
UNIQUE	UNDEFEATABLE	UNDENIABLE	URGENT
VALUABLE	VISIONS	VENTURE	VICTORY
WEALTHY	WISDOM	WINDFALL	WILLING
Y.E.S.	YOURSELF	YOUTHFUL	YELL
ZEAL	ZAZZY	ZANY	ZONE

CONGRATULATIONS!! You will feel the thrill of success when you see the increase in our bank account and better yet, increase your confidence and skill level!

HOW TO USE THE PIP$ PORIFT$ POWER JOURNAL

This is a description of each of the fields in your TRADING JOURNAL.

ACCOUNT:			DATE:	SESSION:		TIME:	
PAIR:	START EMOJI:	ENTRY TIME FRAME:	TRADE TYPE:	RISK TO REWARD RATIO:	RISK % LEVEL (%/$1000)	BALANCE:	
ENTRY CONFIRMATIONS: 1. 2. 3.		ENTRY: 1. 2. 3.	STOP LOSS: 1. 2. 3.	TAKE PROFIT: 1. 2. 3.	TRADE GOAL:		
POWER POINTS: (WHAT WORKED) 1. 2. 3.			END EMOJI:	+, - PIP$/ PROFIT$	ACTUAL LOSS/PROFITS		

ACCOUNT: The account you are using. As you become more experienced, you may have more than just a demo account. Some traders have many live accounts with different account balances.

DATE: The original date the trade is being place.

SESSION: The session being traded. I.e. Asian, European, North American

Session	Major Market	(GMT) Hours
Asian	Tokyo	11 p.m. – 8 a.m.
European	London	7 a.m. – 4 p.m.
North American	New York	Noon – 8 p.m.

TIME: The time the trade is being placed. So important depending on how the market moves.

PAIR: The pair being traded. This could also include commodities like oil or metals like gold or silver.

START EMOJI: The emoji of how you feel going into the trade. Try to capture your actual feelings, excited, happy, nervous, scared, unhappy etc.

ENTRY TIME FRAME: The time frame or clock you are trading on. I.e. Monthly, Weekly, Daily, 4Hour, 1Hour, 30Minutes, 15Minutes, 5Minutes, 1Minute.

TRADE TYPE: Market Execution, Buy Limit, Sell Limit, Buy Stop, or Sell Stop.

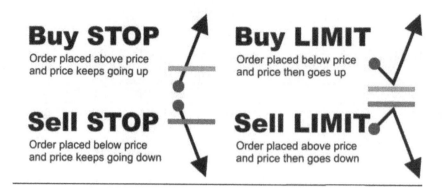

RISK TO REWARD RATIO: This is the ratio of PIP$ risked compared to the number of PIP$ you are expecting to gain. A ratio of 1:3 or better is always recommended. A ratio of 1:1 is never recommended.

RISK % LEVEL (%/1000): Also known as RISK MANAGEMENT. This is the amount of money paid for each PIP or fraction of a PIP. See the chart below.

Most successful traders risk no more than 2% of their account per day for each trade and 5% per day overall. Some traders shared that these levels were way too high with a new account with less than $1000. The decision is up to you!

The following is a guide for Risk Management.

$100	.01 - .02
$200 - $300	.02 - .04
$400 - $500	.04 - .06
$600 - $700	.06 -.08
$800 - $900	.08 - 1.00
$1000 - $2000	.10 - .15
$3000 - $4000	.30 - .35
$5000 – 6,000	.50 - .55
$7000 - $8000	.70 - .75
$8000 - $10000	.90 – 1.0

The lack of understanding appropriate risk management can come with a cost. Every trade that is entered will require a lot size (or risk) when converted to dollars, that you are personally comfortable losing. This is based on the pips. A pip is the movement found in the fourth decimal of the exchange rate. Pips are how trades are measured. Pips are divided into MICRO LOTS, MINI LOTS, and STANDARD LOTS to create the lot size (or risk).

It looks like this:

Exchange rate for EURUSD	1.1234 + 2 pips	= 1.1236
MICRO LOT	.01 -.09	$.10 cents to $.90 cents per PIP
MINI LOT	.1 - .9	$1 to $9 per PIP
STANDARD LOT	1.00	$10 per PIP

As a general guideline, it is not wise to risk high lot sizes with a relatively low account balance. You will risk blowing your account and potentially losing all the money in your account, whether you have made gains or simply just added funds. Practice appropriate risk management. This is crucial.

BALANCE: The balance in your account prior to placing a trade. This is also the number that appears at the top of your MT4/MT5 trading page with your Positions or trades.

ENTRY CONFIRMATIONS: These are the confirmations that confirm the entry to the trade. See the Sample to follow.

ENTRY: These are the price points for the trade upon your entry. There is room for three trades on each pair for those who like to twin trade or triple trade. Make sure your account can handle multiple trades before setting multiple positions on the same pair, in other words, ensure that the TOTAL of all your positions does not add up to more than 2% of your account balance.

STOP LOSS: These are the stop loss points for each trade position you have entered. There is room for a stop loss for each of three trades if you choose and if your account can handle it.

TAKE PROFIT/LOSS: This is to document the result of each of the trading positions that were set once the trade was exited.

TRADING GOAL: This is the monetary trading goal you have set for this trading session.

POWER POINTS (WHAT WORKED): This is the observation of what worked as you traded during the session. Recognizing what works means there is a greater chance you will repeat those points during future trades.

END EMOJI: Important to note your feelings and thoughts after the trade. Ecstatic joy or devastation? Jot down how your body feels with these emotions. Tight lips, sick tummy, smiles, tingles all over? Take time to recover before the next trade.

+ or – PIP$/PROFIT$: Note how many PIP$ were gained or lost. This is very important depending on the type of trader you are. The amount of PROFIT$ works with your compounding sheet to keep you on track.

ACTUAL PROFIT$: This is the amount of actual PROFIT$ you made during the trading session. Subtract any losses from your gains. Are you on track to meet your Prosperity Plan Goals?

Below is a sample of a real trade and how it was journaled. This real trade was on a live account.

SAMPLE TRADE for this JOURNAL

ACCOUNT: PIPS N PROFITS			DATE: 6/27	SESSION: WEDNESDAY LONDON INTO NY		TIME: 5:24 AM
PAIR: EURJPY	START EMOJI: ☺	ENTRY TIME DAILY FRAME: 4H	TRADE TYPE: BUY LIMIT	RISK TO REWARD RATIO: 1:3	RISK % LEVEL .02 (%/$1000)	BALANCE: $7,000+
ENTRY CONFIRMATIONS: 1. PRICE CONFIRMED BEFORE ENTRY 2. PRICE TOUCHED SUPPORT 3. PRICE FOLLOWING TREND		ENTRY: 1. 127.625 2. 3.	STOP LOSS: 1. 127.950 2. 3.	TAKE PROFIT: 1. 127.639 2. 3.		TRADE GOAL: $280.
POWER POINTS: (WHAT WORKED) 1. FOLLOWED ENTRY CONFIRMATIONS 2. APPROPRIATE RISK MANAGEMENT 3. TRADE GOAL MET			END EMOJI: ☺	+, - PIP$/PROFIT$ +14 PIPS/$294.77		ACTUAL PROFITS: $285.04

FOREX TRADING JOURNAL

"Do not go where the path may lead, go instead where there is no path and leave a trail."
~~Ralph Waldo Emerson

TRADING JOURNAL

ACCOUNT:			DATE:	SESSION:			TIME:
PAIR:	START EMOJI:	ENTRY TIME FRAME:	TRADE TYPE:	RISK TO REWARD RATIO:	RISK % LEVEL (%/$1000)		BALANCE:
ENTRY CONFIRMATIONS: 1. 2. 3.		ENTRY: 1. 2. 3.	STOP LOSS: 1. 2. 3.			TAKE PROFIT: 1. 2. 3.	TRADE GOAL:
POWER POINTS: (WHAT WORKED) 1. 2. 3.			END EMOJI:	+, - PIP$/PROFIT$			ACTUAL LOSS/PROFITS

ACCOUNT:			DATE:	SESSION:			TIME:
PAIR:	START EMOJI:	ENTRY TIME FRAME:	TRADE TYPE:	RISK TO REWARD RATIO:	RISK % LEVEL (%/$1000)		BALANCE:
ENTRY CONFIRMATIONS: 1. 2. 3.		ENTRY: 1. 2. 3.	STOP LOSS: 1. 2. 3.			TAKE PROFIT: 1. 2. 3.	TRADE GOAL:
POWER POINTS: (WHAT WORKED) 1. 2. 3.			END EMOJI:	+, - PIP$/PROFIT$			ACTUAL LOSS/PROFITS

TRADING JOURNAL

ACCOUNT:			DATE:	SESSION:		TIME:	
PAIR:	START EMOJI:	ENTRY TIME FRAME:	TRADE TYPE:	RISK TO REWARD RATIO:	RISK % LEVEL (%/$1000)	BALANCE:	
ENTRY CONFIRMATIONS: 1. 2. 3.		ENTRY: 1. 2. 3.	STOP LOSS: 1. 2. 3.		TAKE PROFIT: 1. 2. 3.	TRADE GOAL:	
POWER POINTS: (WHAT WORKED) 1. 2. 3.			END EMOJI:	+, - PIP$/PROFIT$		ACTUAL LOSS/PROFITS	

ACCOUNT:			DATE:	SESSION:		TIME:	
PAIR:	START EMOJI:	ENTRY TIME FRAME:	TRADE TYPE:	RISK TO REWARD RATIO:	RISK % LEVEL (%/$1000)	BALANCE:	
ENTRY CONFIRMATIONS: 1. 2. 3.		ENTRY: 1. 2. 3.	STOP LOSS: 1. 2. 3.		TAKE PROFIT: 1. 2. 3.	TRADE GOAL:	
POWER POINTS: (WHAT WORKED) 1. 2. 3.			END EMOJI:	+, - PIP$/PROFIT$		ACTUAL LOSS/PROFITS	

ACCOUNT:			DATE:	SESSION:		TIME:	
PAIR:	START EMOJI:	ENTRY TIME FRAME:	TRADE TYPE:	RISK TO REWARD RATIO:	RISK % LEVEL (%/$1000)	BALANCE:	
ENTRY CONFIRMATIONS: 1. 2. 3.		ENTRY: 1. 2. 3.	STOP LOSS: 1. 2. 3.		TAKE PROFIT: 1. 2. 3.	TRADE GOAL:	
POWER POINTS: (WHAT WORKED) 1. 2. 3.			END EMOJI:	+, - PIP$/PROFIT$		ACTUAL LOSS/PROFITS	

TRADING JOURNAL

ACCOUNT:			DATE:	SESSION:			TIME:
PAIR:	START EMOJI:	ENTRY TIME FRAME:	TRADE TYPE:	RISK TO REWARD RATIO:	RISK % LEVEL (%/$1000)		BALANCE:
ENTRY CONFIRMATIONS: 1. 2. 3.		ENTRY: 1. 2. 3.	STOP LOSS: 1. 2. 3.			TAKE PROFIT: 1. 2. 3.	TRADE GOAL:
POWER POINTS: (WHAT WORKED) 1. 2. 3.			END EMOJI:	+, - PIP$/PROFIT$			ACTUAL LOSS/PROFITS

ACCOUNT:			DATE:	SESSION:			TIME:
PAIR:	START EMOJI:	ENTRY TIME FRAME:	TRADE TYPE:	RISK TO REWARD RATIO:	RISK % LEVEL (%/$1000)		BALANCE:
ENTRY CONFIRMATIONS: 1. 2. 3.		ENTRY: 1. 2. 3.	STOP LOSS: 1. 2. 3.			TAKE PROFIT: 1. 2. 3.	TRADE GOAL:
POWER POINTS: (WHAT WORKED) 1. 2. 3.			END EMOJI:	+, - PIP$/PROFIT$			ACTUAL LOSS/PROFITS

ACCOUNT:			DATE:	SESSION:			TIME:
PAIR:	START EMOJI:	ENTRY TIME FRAME:	TRADE TYPE:	RISK TO REWARD RATIO:	RISK % LEVEL (%/$1000)		BALANCE:
ENTRY CONFIRMATIONS: 1. 2. 3.		ENTRY: 1. 2. 3.	STOP LOSS: 1. 2. 3.			TAKE PROFIT: 1. 2. 3.	TRADE GOAL:
POWER POINTS: (WHAT WORKED) 1. 2. 3.			END EMOJI:	+, - PIP$/PROFIT$			ACTUAL LOSS/PROFITS

TRADING JOURNAL

ACCOUNT:			DATE:	SESSION:			TIME:	
PAIR:	START EMOJI:	ENTRY TIME FRAME:	TRADE TYPE:	RISK TO REWARD RATIO:	RISK % LEVEL (%/$1000)		BALANCE:	
ENTRY CONFIRMATIONS: 1. 2. 3.		ENTRY: 1. 2. 3.	STOP LOSS: 1. 2. 3.			TAKE PROFIT: 1. 2. 3.	TRADE GOAL:	
POWER POINTS: (WHAT WORKED) 1. 2. 3.			END EMOJI:	+, - PIP$/PROFIT$			ACTUAL LOSS/PROFITS	

ACCOUNT:			DATE:	SESSION:			TIME:	
PAIR:	START EMOJI:	ENTRY TIME FRAME:	TRADE TYPE:	RISK TO REWARD RATIO:	RISK % LEVEL (%/$1000)		BALANCE:	
ENTRY CONFIRMATIONS: 1. 2. 3.		ENTRY: 1. 2. 3.	STOP LOSS: 1. 2. 3.			TAKE PROFIT: 1. 2. 3.	TRADE GOAL:	
POWER POINTS: (WHAT WORKED) 1. 2. 3.			END EMOJI:	+, - PIP$/PROFIT$			ACTUAL LOSS/PROFITS	

ACCOUNT:			DATE:	SESSION:			TIME:	
PAIR:	START EMOJI:	ENTRY TIME FRAME:	TRADE TYPE:	RISK TO REWARD RATIO:	RISK % LEVEL (%/$1000)		BALANCE:	
ENTRY CONFIRMATIONS: 1. 2. 3.		ENTRY: 1. 2. 3.	STOP LOSS: 1. 2. 3.			TAKE PROFIT: 1. 2. 3.	TRADE GOAL:	
POWER POINTS: (WHAT WORKED) 1. 2. 3.			END EMOJI:	+, - PIP$/PROFIT$			ACTUAL LOSS/PROFITS	

TRADING JOURNAL

ACCOUNT:			DATE:	SESSION:		TIME:	
PAIR:	START EMOJI:	ENTRY TIME FRAME:	TRADE TYPE:	RISK TO REWARD RATIO:	RISK % LEVEL (%/$1000)	BALANCE:	
ENTRY CONFIRMATIONS: 1. 2. 3.		ENTRY: 1. 2. 3.	STOP LOSS: 1. 2. 3.		TAKE PROFIT: 1. 2. 3.	TRADE GOAL:	
POWER POINTS: (WHAT WORKED) 1. 2. 3.			END EMOJI:	+, - PIP$/PROFIT$		ACTUAL LOSS/PROFITS	

ACCOUNT:			DATE:	SESSION:		TIME:	
PAIR:	START EMOJI:	ENTRY TIME FRAME:	TRADE TYPE:	RISK TO REWARD RATIO:	RISK % LEVEL (%/$1000)	BALANCE:	
ENTRY CONFIRMATIONS: 1. 2. 3.		ENTRY: 1. 2. 3.	STOP LOSS: 1. 2. 3.		TAKE PROFIT: 1. 2. 3.	TRADE GOAL:	
POWER POINTS: (WHAT WORKED) 1. 2. 3.			END EMOJI:	+, - PIP$/PROFIT$		ACTUAL LOSS/PROFITS	

ACCOUNT:			DATE:	SESSION:		TIME:	
PAIR:	START EMOJI:	ENTRY TIME FRAME:	TRADE TYPE:	RISK TO REWARD RATIO:	RISK % LEVEL (%/$1000)	BALANCE:	
ENTRY CONFIRMATIONS: 1. 2. 3.		ENTRY: 1. 2. 3.	STOP LOSS: 1. 2. 3.		TAKE PROFIT: 1. 2. 3.	TRADE GOAL:	
POWER POINTS: (WHAT WORKED) 1. 2. 3.			END EMOJI:	+, - PIP$/PROFIT$		ACTUAL LOSS/PROFITS	

Genie Craff

TRADING JOURNAL

ACCOUNT:			DATE:	SESSION:			TIME:
PAIR:	START EMOJI:	ENTRY TIME FRAME:	TRADE TYPE:	RISK TO REWARD RATIO:	RISK % LEVEL (%/$1000)		BALANCE:
ENTRY CONFIRMATIONS: 1. 2. 3.		ENTRY: 1. 2. 3.	STOP LOSS: 1. 2. 3.		TAKE PROFIT: 1. 2. 3.		TRADE GOAL:
POWER POINTS: (WHAT WORKED) 1. 2. 3.			END EMOJI:	+, - PIP$/PROFIT$			ACTUAL LOSS/PROFITS

ACCOUNT:			DATE:	SESSION:			TIME:
PAIR:	START EMOJI:	ENTRY TIME FRAME:	TRADE TYPE:	RISK TO REWARD RATIO:	RISK % LEVEL (%/$1000)		BALANCE:
ENTRY CONFIRMATIONS: 1. 2. 3.		ENTRY: 1. 2. 3.	STOP LOSS: 1. 2. 3.		TAKE PROFIT: 1. 2. 3.		TRADE GOAL:
POWER POINTS: (WHAT WORKED) 1. 2. 3.			END EMOJI:	+, - PIP$/PROFIT$			ACTUAL LOSS/PROFITS

ACCOUNT:			DATE:	SESSION:			TIME:
PAIR:	START EMOJI:	ENTRY TIME FRAME:	TRADE TYPE:	RISK TO REWARD RATIO:	RISK % LEVEL (%/$1000)		BALANCE:
ENTRY CONFIRMATIONS: 1. 2. 3.		ENTRY: 1. 2. 3.	STOP LOSS: 1. 2. 3.		TAKE PROFIT: 1. 2. 3.		TRADE GOAL:
POWER POINTS: (WHAT WORKED) 1. 2. 3.			END EMOJI:	+, - PIP$/PROFIT$			ACTUAL LOSS/PROFITS

TRADING JOURNAL

ACCOUNT:			DATE:	SESSION:			TIME:
PAIR:	START EMOJI:	ENTRY TIME FRAME:	TRADE TYPE:	RISK TO REWARD RATIO:	RISK % LEVEL (%/$1000)		BALANCE:
ENTRY CONFIRMATIONS: 1. 2. 3.		ENTRY: 1. 2. 3.	STOP LOSS: 1. 2. 3.		TAKE PROFIT: 1. 2. 3.		TRADE GOAL:
POWER POINTS: (WHAT WORKED) 1. 2. 3.			END EMOJI:	+, - PIP$/PROFIT$			ACTUAL LOSS/PROFITS

ACCOUNT:			DATE:	SESSION:			TIME:
PAIR:	START EMOJI:	ENTRY TIME FRAME:	TRADE TYPE:	RISK TO REWARD RATIO:	RISK % LEVEL (%/$1000)		BALANCE:
ENTRY CONFIRMATIONS: 1. 2. 3.		ENTRY: 1. 2. 3.	STOP LOSS: 1. 2. 3.		TAKE PROFIT: 1. 2. 3.		TRADE GOAL:
POWER POINTS: (WHAT WORKED) 1. 2. 3.			END EMOJI:	+, - PIP$/PROFIT$			ACTUAL LOSS/PROFITS

ACCOUNT:			DATE:	SESSION:			TIME:
PAIR:	START EMOJI:	ENTRY TIME FRAME:	TRADE TYPE:	RISK TO REWARD RATIO:	RISK % LEVEL (%/$1000)		BALANCE:
ENTRY CONFIRMATIONS: 1. 2. 3.		ENTRY: 1. 2. 3.	STOP LOSS: 1. 2. 3.		TAKE PROFIT: 1. 2. 3.		TRADE GOAL:
POWER POINTS: (WHAT WORKED) 1. 2. 3.			END EMOJI:	+, - PIP$/PROFIT$			ACTUAL LOSS/PROFITS

TRADING JOURNAL

ACCOUNT:			DATE:	SESSION:		TIME:	
PAIR:	START EMOJI:	ENTRY TIME FRAME:	TRADE TYPE:	RISK TO REWARD RATIO:	RISK % LEVEL (%/$1000)	BALANCE:	
ENTRY CONFIRMATIONS: 1. 2. 3.		ENTRY: 1. 2. 3.	STOP LOSS: 1. 2. 3.		TAKE PROFIT: 1. 2. 3.	TRADE GOAL:	
POWER POINTS: (WHAT WORKED) 1. 2. 3.			END EMOJI:	+, - PIP$/PROFIT$		ACTUAL LOSS/PROFITS	

ACCOUNT:			DATE:	SESSION:		TIME:	
PAIR:	START EMOJI:	ENTRY TIME FRAME:	TRADE TYPE:	RISK TO REWARD RATIO:	RISK % LEVEL (%/$1000)	BALANCE:	
ENTRY CONFIRMATIONS: 1. 2. 3.		ENTRY: 1. 2. 3.	STOP LOSS: 1. 2. 3.		TAKE PROFIT: 1. 2. 3.	TRADE GOAL:	
POWER POINTS: (WHAT WORKED) 1. 2. 3.			END EMOJI:	+, - PIP$/PROFIT$		ACTUAL LOSS/PROFITS	

ACCOUNT:			DATE:	SESSION:		TIME:	
PAIR:	START EMOJI:	ENTRY TIME FRAME:	TRADE TYPE:	RISK TO REWARD RATIO:	RISK % LEVEL (%/$1000)	BALANCE:	
ENTRY CONFIRMATIONS: 1. 2. 3.		ENTRY: 1. 2. 3.	STOP LOSS: 1. 2. 3.		TAKE PROFIT: 1. 2. 3.	TRADE GOAL:	
POWER POINTS: (WHAT WORKED) 1. 2. 3.			END EMOJI:	+, - PIP$/PROFIT$		ACTUAL LOSS/PROFITS	

TRADING JOURNAL

ACCOUNT:			DATE:	SESSION:			TIME:
PAIR:	START EMOJI:	ENTRY TIME FRAME:	TRADE TYPE:	RISK TO REWARD RATIO:	RISK % LEVEL (%/$1000)		BALANCE:
ENTRY CONFIRMATIONS: 1. 2. 3.		ENTRY: 1. 2. 3.	STOP LOSS: 1. 2. 3.		TAKE PROFIT: 1. 2. 3.		TRADE GOAL:
POWER POINTS: (WHAT WORKED) 1. 2. 3.			END EMOJI:	+, - PIP$/PROFIT$			ACTUAL LOSS/PROFITS

ACCOUNT:			DATE:	SESSION:			TIME:
PAIR:	START EMOJI:	ENTRY TIME FRAME:	TRADE TYPE:	RISK TO REWARD RATIO:	RISK % LEVEL (%/$1000)		BALANCE:
ENTRY CONFIRMATIONS: 1. 2. 3.		ENTRY: 1. 2. 3.	STOP LOSS: 1. 2. 3.		TAKE PROFIT: 1. 2. 3.		TRADE GOAL:
POWER POINTS: (WHAT WORKED) 1. 2. 3.			END EMOJI:	+, - PIP$/PROFIT$			ACTUAL LOSS/PROFITS

ACCOUNT:			DATE:	SESSION:			TIME:
PAIR:	START EMOJI:	ENTRY TIME FRAME:	TRADE TYPE:	RISK TO REWARD RATIO:	RISK % LEVEL (%/$1000)		BALANCE:
ENTRY CONFIRMATIONS: 1. 2. 3.		ENTRY: 1. 2. 3.	STOP LOSS: 1. 2. 3.		TAKE PROFIT: 1. 2. 3.		TRADE GOAL:
POWER POINTS: (WHAT WORKED) 1. 2. 3.			END EMOJI:	+, - PIP$/PROFIT$			ACTUAL LOSS/PROFITS

TRADING JOURNAL

ACCOUNT:			DATE:	SESSION:		TIME:	
PAIR:	START EMOJI:	ENTRY TIME FRAME:	TRADE TYPE:	RISK TO REWARD RATIO:	RISK % LEVEL (%/$1000)	BALANCE:	
ENTRY CONFIRMATIONS: 1. 2. 3.		ENTRY: 1. 2. 3.	STOP LOSS: 1. 2. 3.		TAKE PROFIT: 1. 2. 3.	TRADE GOAL:	
POWER POINTS: (WHAT WORKED) 1. 2. 3.			END EMOJI:	+, - PIP$/PROFIT$		ACTUAL LOSS/PROFITS	

ACCOUNT:			DATE:	SESSION:		TIME:	
PAIR:	START EMOJI:	ENTRY TIME FRAME:	TRADE TYPE:	RISK TO REWARD RATIO:	RISK % LEVEL (%/$1000)	BALANCE:	
ENTRY CONFIRMATIONS: 1. 2. 3.		ENTRY: 1. 2. 3.	STOP LOSS: 1. 2. 3.		TAKE PROFIT: 1. 2. 3.	TRADE GOAL:	
POWER POINTS: (WHAT WORKED) 1. 2. 3.			END EMOJI:	+, - PIP$/PROFIT$		ACTUAL LOSS/PROFITS	

ACCOUNT:			DATE:	SESSION:		TIME:	
PAIR:	START EMOJI:	ENTRY TIME FRAME:	TRADE TYPE:	RISK TO REWARD RATIO:	RISK % LEVEL (%/$1000)	BALANCE:	
ENTRY CONFIRMATIONS: 1. 2. 3.		ENTRY: 1. 2. 3.	STOP LOSS: 1. 2. 3.		TAKE PROFIT: 1. 2. 3.	TRADE GOAL:	
POWER POINTS: (WHAT WORKED) 1. 2. 3.			END EMOJI:	+, - PIP$/PROFIT$		ACTUAL LOSS/PROFITS	

TRADING JOURNAL

ACCOUNT:			DATE:	SESSION:		TIME:	
PAIR:	START EMOJI:	ENTRY TIME FRAME:	TRADE TYPE:	RISK TO REWARD RATIO:	RISK % LEVEL (%/$1000)	BALANCE:	
ENTRY CONFIRMATIONS: 1. 2. 3.		ENTRY: 1. 2. 3.	STOP LOSS: 1. 2. 3.		TAKE PROFIT: 1. 2. 3.	TRADE GOAL:	
POWER POINTS: (WHAT WORKED) 1. 2. 3.			END EMOJI:	+, - PIP$/PROFIT$		ACTUAL LOSS/PROFITS	

ACCOUNT:			DATE:	SESSION:		TIME:	
PAIR:	START EMOJI:	ENTRY TIME FRAME:	TRADE TYPE:	RISK TO REWARD RATIO:	RISK % LEVEL (%/$1000)	BALANCE:	
ENTRY CONFIRMATIONS: 1. 2. 3.		ENTRY: 1. 2. 3.	STOP LOSS: 1. 2. 3.		TAKE PROFIT: 1. 2. 3.	TRADE GOAL:	
POWER POINTS: (WHAT WORKED) 1. 2. 3.			END EMOJI:	+, - PIP$/PROFIT$		ACTUAL LOSS/PROFITS	

ACCOUNT:			DATE:	SESSION:		TIME:	
PAIR:	START EMOJI:	ENTRY TIME FRAME:	TRADE TYPE:	RISK TO REWARD RATIO:	RISK % LEVEL (%/$1000)	BALANCE:	
ENTRY CONFIRMATIONS: 1. 2. 3.		ENTRY: 1. 2. 3.	STOP LOSS: 1. 2. 3.		TAKE PROFIT: 1. 2. 3.	TRADE GOAL:	
POWER POINTS: (WHAT WORKED) 1. 2. 3.			END EMOJI:	+, - PIP$/PROFIT$		ACTUAL LOSS/PROFITS	

TRADING JOURNAL

ACCOUNT:			DATE:	SESSION:		TIME:	
PAIR:	START EMOJI:	ENTRY TIME FRAME:	TRADE TYPE:	RISK TO REWARD RATIO:	RISK % LEVEL (%/$1000)	BALANCE:	
ENTRY CONFIRMATIONS: 1. 2. 3.		ENTRY: 1. 2. 3.	STOP LOSS: 1. 2. 3.		TAKE PROFIT: 1. 2. 3.	TRADE GOAL:	
POWER POINTS: (WHAT WORKED) 1. 2. 3.			END EMOJI:	+, - PIP$/PROFIT$		ACTUAL LOSS/PROFITS	

ACCOUNT:			DATE:	SESSION:		TIME:	
PAIR:	START EMOJI:	ENTRY TIME FRAME:	TRADE TYPE:	RISK TO REWARD RATIO:	RISK % LEVEL (%/$1000)	BALANCE:	
ENTRY CONFIRMATIONS: 1. 2. 3.		ENTRY: 1. 2. 3.	STOP LOSS: 1. 2. 3.		TAKE PROFIT: 1. 2. 3.	TRADE GOAL:	
POWER POINTS: (WHAT WORKED) 1. 2. 3.			END EMOJI:	+, - PIP$/PROFIT$		ACTUAL LOSS/PROFITS	

ACCOUNT:			DATE:	SESSION:		TIME:	
PAIR:	START EMOJI:	ENTRY TIME FRAME:	TRADE TYPE:	RISK TO REWARD RATIO:	RISK % LEVEL (%/$1000)	BALANCE:	
ENTRY CONFIRMATIONS: 1. 2. 3.		ENTRY: 1. 2. 3.	STOP LOSS: 1. 2. 3.		TAKE PROFIT: 1. 2. 3.	TRADE GOAL:	
POWER POINTS: (WHAT WORKED) 1. 2. 3.			END EMOJI:	+, - PIP$/PROFIT$		ACTUAL LOSS/PROFITS	

TRADING JOURNAL

ACCOUNT:			DATE:	SESSION:		TIME:	
PAIR:	START EMOJI:	ENTRY TIME FRAME:	TRADE TYPE:	RISK TO REWARD RATIO:	RISK % LEVEL (%/$1000)	BALANCE:	
ENTRY CONFIRMATIONS: 1. 2. 3.		ENTRY: 1. 2. 3.	STOP LOSS: 1. 2. 3.		TAKE PROFIT: 1. 2. 3.	TRADE GOAL:	
POWER POINTS: (WHAT WORKED) 1. 2. 3.			END EMOJI:	+, - PIP$/PROFIT$		ACTUAL LOSS/PROFITS	

ACCOUNT:			DATE:	SESSION:		TIME:	
PAIR:	START EMOJI:	ENTRY TIME FRAME:	TRADE TYPE:	RISK TO REWARD RATIO:	RISK % LEVEL (%/$1000)	BALANCE:	
ENTRY CONFIRMATIONS: 1. 2. 3.		ENTRY: 1. 2. 3.	STOP LOSS: 1. 2. 3.		TAKE PROFIT: 1. 2. 3.	TRADE GOAL:	
POWER POINTS: (WHAT WORKED) 1. 2. 3.			END EMOJI:	+, - PIP$/PROFIT$		ACTUAL LOSS/PROFITS	

ACCOUNT:			DATE:	SESSION:		TIME:	
PAIR:	START EMOJI:	ENTRY TIME FRAME:	TRADE TYPE:	RISK TO REWARD RATIO:	RISK % LEVEL (%/$1000)	BALANCE:	
ENTRY CONFIRMATIONS: 1. 2. 3.		ENTRY: 1. 2. 3.	STOP LOSS: 1. 2. 3.		TAKE PROFIT: 1. 2. 3.	TRADE GOAL:	
POWER POINTS: (WHAT WORKED) 1. 2. 3.			END EMOJI:	+, - PIP$/PROFIT$		ACTUAL LOSS/PROFITS	

TRADING JOURNAL

ACCOUNT:			DATE:	SESSION:			TIME:	
PAIR:	START EMOJI:	ENTRY TIME FRAME:	TRADE TYPE:	RISK TO REWARD RATIO:	RISK % LEVEL (%/$1000)		BALANCE:	
ENTRY CONFIRMATIONS: 1. 2. 3.		ENTRY: 1. 2. 3.	STOP LOSS: 1. 2. 3.			TAKE PROFIT: 1. 2. 3.	TRADE GOAL:	
POWER POINTS: (WHAT WORKED) 1. 2. 3.			END EMOJI:	+, - PIP$/PROFIT$			ACTUAL LOSS/PROFITS	

ACCOUNT:			DATE:	SESSION:			TIME:	
PAIR:	START EMOJI:	ENTRY TIME FRAME:	TRADE TYPE:	RISK TO REWARD RATIO:	RISK % LEVEL (%/$1000)		BALANCE:	
ENTRY CONFIRMATIONS: 1. 2. 3.		ENTRY: 1. 2. 3.	STOP LOSS: 1. 2. 3.			TAKE PROFIT: 1. 2. 3.	TRADE GOAL:	
POWER POINTS: (WHAT WORKED) 1. 2. 3.			END EMOJI:	+, - PIP$/PROFIT$			ACTUAL LOSS/PROFITS	

ACCOUNT:			DATE:	SESSION:			TIME:	
PAIR:	START EMOJI:	ENTRY TIME FRAME:	TRADE TYPE:	RISK TO REWARD RATIO:	RISK % LEVEL (%/$1000)		BALANCE:	
ENTRY CONFIRMATIONS: 1. 2. 3.		ENTRY: 1. 2. 3.	STOP LOSS: 1. 2. 3.			TAKE PROFIT: 1. 2. 3.	TRADE GOAL:	
POWER POINTS: (WHAT WORKED) 1. 2. 3.			END EMOJI:	+, - PIP$/PROFIT$			ACTUAL LOSS/PROFITS	

TRADING JOURNAL

ACCOUNT:			DATE:	SESSION:			TIME:
PAIR:	START EMOJI:	ENTRY TIME FRAME:	TRADE TYPE:	RISK TO REWARD RATIO:	RISK % LEVEL (%/$1000)		BALANCE:
ENTRY CONFIRMATIONS: 1. 2. 3.		ENTRY: 1. 2. 3.	STOP LOSS: 1. 2. 3.			TAKE PROFIT: 1. 2. 3.	TRADE GOAL:
POWER POINTS: (WHAT WORKED) 1. 2. 3.			END EMOJI:	+, - PIP$/PROFIT$			ACTUAL LOSS/PROFITS

ACCOUNT:			DATE:	SESSION:			TIME:
PAIR:	START EMOJI:	ENTRY TIME FRAME:	TRADE TYPE:	RISK TO REWARD RATIO:	RISK % LEVEL (%/$1000)		BALANCE:
ENTRY CONFIRMATIONS: 1. 2. 3.		ENTRY: 1. 2. 3.	STOP LOSS: 1. 2. 3.			TAKE PROFIT: 1. 2. 3.	TRADE GOAL:
POWER POINTS: (WHAT WORKED) 1. 2. 3.			END EMOJI:	+, - PIP$/PROFIT$			ACTUAL LOSS/PROFITS

ACCOUNT:			DATE:	SESSION:			TIME:
PAIR:	START EMOJI:	ENTRY TIME FRAME:	TRADE TYPE:	RISK TO REWARD RATIO:	RISK % LEVEL (%/$1000)		BALANCE:
ENTRY CONFIRMATIONS: 1. 2. 3.		ENTRY: 1. 2. 3.	STOP LOSS: 1. 2. 3.			TAKE PROFIT: 1. 2. 3.	TRADE GOAL:
POWER POINTS: (WHAT WORKED) 1. 2. 3.			END EMOJI:	+, - PIP$/PROFIT$			ACTUAL LOSS/PROFITS

TRADING JOURNAL

ACCOUNT:			DATE:	SESSION:			TIME:	
PAIR:	START EMOJI:	ENTRY TIME FRAME:	TRADE TYPE:	RISK TO REWARD RATIO:	RISK % LEVEL (%/$1000)		BALANCE:	
ENTRY CONFIRMATIONS: 1. 2. 3.		ENTRY: 1. 2. 3.	STOP LOSS: 1. 2. 3.			TAKE PROFIT: 1. 2. 3.	TRADE GOAL:	
POWER POINTS: (WHAT WORKED) 1. 2. 3.			END EMOJI:	+, - PIP$/PROFIT$			ACTUAL LOSS/PROFITS	

ACCOUNT:			DATE:	SESSION:			TIME:	
PAIR:	START EMOJI:	ENTRY TIME FRAME:	TRADE TYPE:	RISK TO REWARD RATIO:	RISK % LEVEL (%/$1000)		BALANCE:	
ENTRY CONFIRMATIONS: 1. 2. 3.		ENTRY: 1. 2. 3.	STOP LOSS: 1. 2. 3.			TAKE PROFIT: 1. 2. 3.	TRADE GOAL:	
POWER POINTS: (WHAT WORKED) 1. 2. 3.			END EMOJI:	+, - PIP$/PROFIT$			ACTUAL LOSS/PROFITS	

ACCOUNT:			DATE:	SESSION:			TIME:	
PAIR:	START EMOJI:	ENTRY TIME FRAME:	TRADE TYPE:	RISK TO REWARD RATIO:	RISK % LEVEL (%/$1000)		BALANCE:	
ENTRY CONFIRMATIONS: 1. 2. 3.		ENTRY: 1. 2. 3.	STOP LOSS: 1. 2. 3.			TAKE PROFIT: 1. 2. 3.	TRADE GOAL:	
POWER POINTS: (WHAT WORKED) 1. 2. 3.			END EMOJI:	+, - PIP$/PROFIT$			ACTUAL LOSS/PROFITS	

TRADING JOURNAL

ACCOUNT:			DATE:	SESSION:			TIME:
PAIR:	START EMOJI:	ENTRY TIME FRAME:	TRADE TYPE:	RISK TO REWARD RATIO:	RISK % LEVEL (%/$1000)		BALANCE:
ENTRY CONFIRMATIONS: 1. 2. 3.		ENTRY: 1. 2. 3.	STOP LOSS: 1. 2. 3.		TAKE PROFIT: 1. 2. 3.		TRADE GOAL:
POWER POINTS: (WHAT WORKED) 1. 2. 3.			END EMOJI:	+, - PIP$/PROFIT$			ACTUAL LOSS/PROFITS

ACCOUNT:			DATE:	SESSION:			TIME:
PAIR:	START EMOJI:	ENTRY TIME FRAME:	TRADE TYPE:	RISK TO REWARD RATIO:	RISK % LEVEL (%/$1000)		BALANCE:
ENTRY CONFIRMATIONS: 1. 2. 3.		ENTRY: 1. 2. 3.	STOP LOSS: 1. 2. 3.		TAKE PROFIT: 1. 2. 3.		TRADE GOAL:
POWER POINTS: (WHAT WORKED) 1. 2. 3.			END EMOJI:	+, - PIP$/PROFIT$			ACTUAL LOSS/PROFITS

ACCOUNT:			DATE:	SESSION:			TIME:
PAIR:	START EMOJI:	ENTRY TIME FRAME:	TRADE TYPE:	RISK TO REWARD RATIO:	RISK % LEVEL (%/$1000)		BALANCE:
ENTRY CONFIRMATIONS: 1. 2. 3.		ENTRY: 1. 2. 3.	STOP LOSS: 1. 2. 3.		TAKE PROFIT: 1. 2. 3.		TRADE GOAL:
POWER POINTS: (WHAT WORKED) 1. 2. 3.			END EMOJI:	+, - PIP$/PROFIT$			ACTUAL LOSS/PROFITS

TRADING JOURNAL

ACCOUNT:			DATE:	SESSION:		TIME:	
PAIR:	START EMOJI:	ENTRY TIME FRAME:	TRADE TYPE:	RISK TO REWARD RATIO:	RISK % LEVEL (%/$1000)	BALANCE:	
ENTRY CONFIRMATIONS: 1. 2. 3.		ENTRY: 1. 2. 3.	STOP LOSS: 1. 2. 3.		TAKE PROFIT: 1. 2. 3.	TRADE GOAL:	
POWER POINTS: (WHAT WORKED) 1. 2. 3.			END EMOJI:	+, - PIP$/PROFIT$		ACTUAL LOSS/PROFITS	

ACCOUNT:			DATE:	SESSION:		TIME:	
PAIR:	START EMOJI:	ENTRY TIME FRAME:	TRADE TYPE:	RISK TO REWARD RATIO:	RISK % LEVEL (%/$1000)	BALANCE:	
ENTRY CONFIRMATIONS: 1. 2. 3.		ENTRY: 1. 2. 3.	STOP LOSS: 1. 2. 3.		TAKE PROFIT: 1. 2. 3.	TRADE GOAL:	
POWER POINTS: (WHAT WORKED) 1. 2. 3.			END EMOJI:	+, - PIP$/PROFIT$		ACTUAL LOSS/PROFITS	

ACCOUNT:			DATE:	SESSION:		TIME:	
PAIR:	START EMOJI:	ENTRY TIME FRAME:	TRADE TYPE:	RISK TO REWARD RATIO:	RISK % LEVEL (%/$1000)	BALANCE:	
ENTRY CONFIRMATIONS: 1. 2. 3.		ENTRY: 1. 2. 3.	STOP LOSS: 1. 2. 3.		TAKE PROFIT: 1. 2. 3.	TRADE GOAL:	
POWER POINTS: (WHAT WORKED) 1. 2. 3.			END EMOJI:	+, - PIP$/PROFIT$		ACTUAL LOSS/PROFITS	

TRADING JOURNAL

ACCOUNT:			DATE:	SESSION:			TIME:
PAIR:	START EMOJI:	ENTRY TIME FRAME:	TRADE TYPE:	RISK TO REWARD RATIO:	RISK % LEVEL (%/$1000)		BALANCE:
ENTRY CONFIRMATIONS: 1. 2. 3.		ENTRY: 1. 2. 3.	STOP LOSS: 1. 2. 3.		TAKE PROFIT: 1. 2. 3.		TRADE GOAL:
POWER POINTS: (WHAT WORKED) 1. 2. 3.			END EMOJI:	+, - PIP$/PROFIT$		ACTUAL LOSS/PROFITS	

ACCOUNT:			DATE:	SESSION:			TIME:
PAIR:	START EMOJI:	ENTRY TIME FRAME:	TRADE TYPE:	RISK TO REWARD RATIO:	RISK % LEVEL (%/$1000)		BALANCE:
ENTRY CONFIRMATIONS: 1. 2. 3.		ENTRY: 1. 2. 3.	STOP LOSS: 1. 2. 3.		TAKE PROFIT: 1. 2. 3.		TRADE GOAL:
POWER POINTS: (WHAT WORKED) 1. 2. 3.			END EMOJI:	+, - PIP$/PROFIT$		ACTUAL LOSS/PROFITS	

ACCOUNT:			DATE:	SESSION:			TIME:
PAIR:	START EMOJI:	ENTRY TIME FRAME:	TRADE TYPE:	RISK TO REWARD RATIO:	RISK % LEVEL (%/$1000)		BALANCE:
ENTRY CONFIRMATIONS: 1. 2. 3.		ENTRY: 1. 2. 3.	STOP LOSS: 1. 2. 3.		TAKE PROFIT: 1. 2. 3.		TRADE GOAL:
POWER POINTS: (WHAT WORKED) 1. 2. 3.			END EMOJI:	+, - PIP$/PROFIT$		ACTUAL LOSS/PROFITS	

TRADING JOURNAL

ACCOUNT:			DATE:	SESSION:			TIME:
PAIR:	START EMOJI:	ENTRY TIME FRAME:	TRADE TYPE:	RISK TO REWARD RATIO:	RISK % LEVEL (%/$1000)		BALANCE:
ENTRY CONFIRMATIONS: 1. 2. 3.		ENTRY: 1. 2. 3.	STOP LOSS: 1. 2. 3.		TAKE PROFIT: 1. 2. 3.		TRADE GOAL:
POWER POINTS: (WHAT WORKED) 1. 2. 3.			END EMOJI:	+, - PIP$/PROFIT$			ACTUAL LOSS/PROFITS

ACCOUNT:			DATE:	SESSION:			TIME:
PAIR:	START EMOJI:	ENTRY TIME FRAME:	TRADE TYPE:	RISK TO REWARD RATIO:	RISK % LEVEL (%/$1000)		BALANCE:
ENTRY CONFIRMATIONS: 1. 2. 3.		ENTRY: 1. 2. 3.	STOP LOSS: 1. 2. 3.		TAKE PROFIT: 1. 2. 3.		TRADE GOAL:
POWER POINTS: (WHAT WORKED) 1. 2. 3.			END EMOJI:	+, - PIP$/PROFIT$			ACTUAL LOSS/PROFITS

ACCOUNT:			DATE:	SESSION:			TIME:
PAIR:	START EMOJI:	ENTRY TIME FRAME:	TRADE TYPE:	RISK TO REWARD RATIO:	RISK % LEVEL (%/$1000)		BALANCE:
ENTRY CONFIRMATIONS: 1. 2. 3.		ENTRY: 1. 2. 3.	STOP LOSS: 1. 2. 3.		TAKE PROFIT: 1. 2. 3.		TRADE GOAL:
POWER POINTS: (WHAT WORKED) 1. 2. 3.			END EMOJI:	+, - PIP$/PROFIT$			ACTUAL LOSS/PROFITS

TRADING JOURNAL

ACCOUNT:			DATE:	SESSION:			TIME:
PAIR:	START EMOJI:	ENTRY TIME FRAME:	TRADE TYPE:	RISK TO REWARD RATIO:	RISK % LEVEL (%/$1000)		BALANCE:
ENTRY CONFIRMATIONS: 1. 2. 3.		ENTRY: 1. 2. 3.	STOP LOSS: 1. 2. 3.		TAKE PROFIT: 1. 2. 3.		TRADE GOAL:
POWER POINTS: (WHAT WORKED) 1. 2. 3.			END EMOJI:	+, - PIP$/PROFIT$		ACTUAL LOSS/PROFITS	

ACCOUNT:			DATE:	SESSION:			TIME:
PAIR:	START EMOJI:	ENTRY TIME FRAME:	TRADE TYPE:	RISK TO REWARD RATIO:	RISK % LEVEL (%/$1000)		BALANCE:
ENTRY CONFIRMATIONS: 1. 2. 3.		ENTRY: 1. 2. 3.	STOP LOSS: 1. 2. 3.		TAKE PROFIT: 1. 2. 3.		TRADE GOAL:
POWER POINTS: (WHAT WORKED) 1. 2. 3.			END EMOJI:	+, - PIP$/PROFIT$		ACTUAL LOSS/PROFITS	

ACCOUNT:			DATE:	SESSION:			TIME:
PAIR:	START EMOJI:	ENTRY TIME FRAME:	TRADE TYPE:	RISK TO REWARD RATIO:	RISK % LEVEL (%/$1000)		BALANCE:
ENTRY CONFIRMATIONS: 1. 2. 3.		ENTRY: 1. 2. 3.	STOP LOSS: 1. 2. 3.		TAKE PROFIT: 1. 2. 3.		TRADE GOAL:
POWER POINTS: (WHAT WORKED) 1. 2. 3.			END EMOJI:	+, - PIP$/PROFIT$		ACTUAL LOSS/PROFITS	

TRADING JOURNAL

ACCOUNT:			DATE:	SESSION:			TIME:
PAIR:	START EMOJI:	ENTRY TIME FRAME:	TRADE TYPE:	RISK TO REWARD RATIO:	RISK % LEVEL (%/$1000)		BALANCE:
ENTRY CONFIRMATIONS: 1. 2. 3.		ENTRY: 1. 2. 3.	STOP LOSS: 1. 2. 3.		TAKE PROFIT: 1. 2. 3.		TRADE GOAL:
POWER POINTS: (WHAT WORKED) 1. 2. 3.			END EMOJI:	+, - PIP$/PROFIT$			ACTUAL LOSS/PROFITS

ACCOUNT:			DATE:	SESSION:			TIME:
PAIR:	START EMOJI:	ENTRY TIME FRAME:	TRADE TYPE:	RISK TO REWARD RATIO:	RISK % LEVEL (%/$1000)		BALANCE:
ENTRY CONFIRMATIONS: 1. 2. 3.		ENTRY: 1. 2. 3.	STOP LOSS: 1. 2. 3.		TAKE PROFIT: 1. 2. 3.		TRADE GOAL:
POWER POINTS: (WHAT WORKED) 1. 2. 3.			END EMOJI:	+, - PIP$/PROFIT$			ACTUAL LOSS/PROFITS

ACCOUNT:			DATE:	SESSION:			TIME:
PAIR:	START EMOJI:	ENTRY TIME FRAME:	TRADE TYPE:	RISK TO REWARD RATIO:	RISK % LEVEL (%/$1000)		BALANCE:
ENTRY CONFIRMATIONS: 1. 2. 3.		ENTRY: 1. 2. 3.	STOP LOSS: 1. 2. 3.		TAKE PROFIT: 1. 2. 3.		TRADE GOAL:
POWER POINTS: (WHAT WORKED) 1. 2. 3.			END EMOJI:	+, - PIP$/PROFIT$			ACTUAL LOSS/PROFITS

TRADING JOURNAL

ACCOUNT:			DATE:	SESSION:			TIME:	
PAIR:	START EMOJI:	ENTRY TIME FRAME:	TRADE TYPE:	RISK TO REWARD RATIO:	RISK % LEVEL (%/$1000)		BALANCE:	
ENTRY CONFIRMATIONS: 1. 2. 3.		ENTRY: 1. 2. 3.	STOP LOSS: 1. 2. 3.			TAKE PROFIT: 1. 2. 3.	TRADE GOAL:	
POWER POINTS: (WHAT WORKED) 1. 2. 3.			END EMOJI:	+, - PIP$/PROFIT$			ACTUAL LOSS/PROFITS	

ACCOUNT:			DATE:	SESSION:			TIME:	
PAIR:	START EMOJI:	ENTRY TIME FRAME:	TRADE TYPE:	RISK TO REWARD RATIO:	RISK % LEVEL (%/$1000)		BALANCE:	
ENTRY CONFIRMATIONS: 1. 2. 3.		ENTRY: 1. 2. 3.	STOP LOSS: 1. 2. 3.			TAKE PROFIT: 1. 2. 3.	TRADE GOAL:	
POWER POINTS: (WHAT WORKED) 1. 2. 3.			END EMOJI:	+, - PIP$/PROFIT$			ACTUAL LOSS/PROFITS	

ACCOUNT:			DATE:	SESSION:			TIME:	
PAIR:	START EMOJI:	ENTRY TIME FRAME:	TRADE TYPE:	RISK TO REWARD RATIO:	RISK % LEVEL (%/$1000)		BALANCE:	
ENTRY CONFIRMATIONS: 1. 2. 3.		ENTRY: 1. 2. 3.	STOP LOSS: 1. 2. 3.			TAKE PROFIT: 1. 2. 3.	TRADE GOAL:	
POWER POINTS: (WHAT WORKED) 1. 2. 3.			END EMOJI:	+, - PIP$/PROFIT$			ACTUAL LOSS/PROFITS	

TRADING JOURNAL

ACCOUNT:			DATE:	SESSION:			TIME:	
PAIR:	START EMOJI:	ENTRY TIME FRAME:	TRADE TYPE:	RISK TO REWARD RATIO:	RISK % LEVEL (%/$1000)		BALANCE:	
ENTRY CONFIRMATIONS: 1. 2. 3.		ENTRY: 1. 2. 3.	STOP LOSS: 1. 2. 3.			TAKE PROFIT: 1. 2. 3.	TRADE GOAL:	
POWER POINTS: (WHAT WORKED) 1. 2. 3.			END EMOJI:	+, - PIP$/PROFIT$			ACTUAL LOSS/PROFITS	

ACCOUNT:			DATE:	SESSION:			TIME:	
PAIR:	START EMOJI:	ENTRY TIME FRAME:	TRADE TYPE:	RISK TO REWARD RATIO:	RISK % LEVEL (%/$1000)		BALANCE:	
ENTRY CONFIRMATIONS: 1. 2. 3.		ENTRY: 1. 2. 3.	STOP LOSS: 1. 2. 3.			TAKE PROFIT: 1. 2. 3.	TRADE GOAL:	
POWER POINTS: (WHAT WORKED) 1. 2. 3.			END EMOJI:	+, - PIP$/PROFIT$			ACTUAL LOSS/PROFITS	

ACCOUNT:			DATE:	SESSION:			TIME:	
PAIR:	START EMOJI:	ENTRY TIME FRAME:	TRADE TYPE:	RISK TO REWARD RATIO:	RISK % LEVEL (%/$1000)		BALANCE:	
ENTRY CONFIRMATIONS: 1. 2. 3.		ENTRY: 1. 2. 3.	STOP LOSS: 1. 2. 3.			TAKE PROFIT: 1. 2. 3.	TRADE GOAL:	
POWER POINTS: (WHAT WORKED) 1. 2. 3.			END EMOJI:	+, - PIP$/PROFIT$			ACTUAL LOSS/PROFITS	

TRADING JOURNAL

ACCOUNT:			DATE:	SESSION:			TIME:
PAIR:	START EMOJI:	ENTRY TIME FRAME:	TRADE TYPE:	RISK TO REWARD RATIO:	RISK % LEVEL (%/$1000)		BALANCE:
ENTRY CONFIRMATIONS: 1. 2. 3.		ENTRY: 1. 2. 3.	STOP LOSS: 1. 2. 3.		TAKE PROFIT: 1. 2. 3.		TRADE GOAL:
POWER POINTS: (WHAT WORKED) 1. 2. 3.			END EMOJI:	+, - PIP$/PROFIT$			ACTUAL LOSS/PROFITS

ACCOUNT:			DATE:	SESSION:			TIME:
PAIR:	START EMOJI:	ENTRY TIME FRAME:	TRADE TYPE:	RISK TO REWARD RATIO:	RISK % LEVEL (%/$1000)		BALANCE:
ENTRY CONFIRMATIONS: 1. 2. 3.		ENTRY: 1. 2. 3.	STOP LOSS: 1. 2. 3.		TAKE PROFIT: 1. 2. 3.		TRADE GOAL:
POWER POINTS: (WHAT WORKED) 1. 2. 3.			END EMOJI:	+, - PIP$/PROFIT$			ACTUAL LOSS/PROFITS

ACCOUNT:			DATE:	SESSION:			TIME:
PAIR:	START EMOJI:	ENTRY TIME FRAME:	TRADE TYPE:	RISK TO REWARD RATIO:	RISK % LEVEL (%/$1000)		BALANCE:
ENTRY CONFIRMATIONS: 1. 2. 3.		ENTRY: 1. 2. 3.	STOP LOSS: 1. 2. 3.		TAKE PROFIT: 1. 2. 3.		TRADE GOAL:
POWER POINTS: (WHAT WORKED) 1. 2. 3.			END EMOJI:	+, - PIP$/PROFIT$			ACTUAL LOSS/PROFITS

TRADING JOURNAL

ACCOUNT:			DATE:	SESSION:		TIME:	
PAIR:	START EMOJI:	ENTRY TIME FRAME:	TRADE TYPE:	RISK TO REWARD RATIO:	RISK % LEVEL (%/$1000)	BALANCE:	
ENTRY CONFIRMATIONS: 1. 2. 3.		ENTRY: 1. 2. 3.	STOP LOSS: 1. 2. 3.		TAKE PROFIT: 1. 2. 3.	TRADE GOAL:	
POWER POINTS: (WHAT WORKED) 1. 2. 3.			END EMOJI:	+, - PIP$/PROFIT$		ACTUAL LOSS/PROFITS	

ACCOUNT:			DATE:	SESSION:		TIME:	
PAIR:	START EMOJI:	ENTRY TIME FRAME:	TRADE TYPE:	RISK TO REWARD RATIO:	RISK % LEVEL (%/$1000)	BALANCE:	
ENTRY CONFIRMATIONS: 1. 2. 3.		ENTRY: 1. 2. 3.	STOP LOSS: 1. 2. 3.		TAKE PROFIT: 1. 2. 3.	TRADE GOAL:	
POWER POINTS: (WHAT WORKED) 1. 2. 3.			END EMOJI:	+, - PIP$/PROFIT$		ACTUAL LOSS/PROFITS	

ACCOUNT:			DATE:	SESSION:		TIME:	
PAIR:	START EMOJI:	ENTRY TIME FRAME:	TRADE TYPE:	RISK TO REWARD RATIO:	RISK % LEVEL (%/$1000)	BALANCE:	
ENTRY CONFIRMATIONS: 1. 2. 3.		ENTRY: 1. 2. 3.	STOP LOSS: 1. 2. 3.		TAKE PROFIT: 1. 2. 3.	TRADE GOAL:	
POWER POINTS: (WHAT WORKED) 1. 2. 3.			END EMOJI:	+, - PIP$/PROFIT$		ACTUAL LOSS/PROFITS	

TRADING JOURNAL

ACCOUNT:			DATE:	SESSION:			TIME:
PAIR:	START EMOJI:	ENTRY TIME FRAME:	TRADE TYPE:	RISK TO REWARD RATIO:	RISK % LEVEL (%/$1000)		BALANCE:
ENTRY CONFIRMATIONS: 1. 2. 3.		ENTRY: 1. 2. 3.	STOP LOSS: 1. 2. 3.		TAKE PROFIT: 1. 2. 3.		TRADE GOAL:
POWER POINTS: (WHAT WORKED) 1. 2. 3.			END EMOJI:	+, - PIP$/PROFIT$		ACTUAL LOSS/PROFITS	

ACCOUNT:			DATE:	SESSION:			TIME:
PAIR:	START EMOJI:	ENTRY TIME FRAME:	TRADE TYPE:	RISK TO REWARD RATIO:	RISK % LEVEL (%/$1000)		BALANCE:
ENTRY CONFIRMATIONS: 1. 2. 3.		ENTRY: 1. 2. 3.	STOP LOSS: 1. 2. 3.		TAKE PROFIT: 1. 2. 3.		TRADE GOAL:
POWER POINTS: (WHAT WORKED) 1. 2. 3.			END EMOJI:	+, - PIP$/PROFIT$		ACTUAL LOSS/PROFITS	

ACCOUNT:			DATE:	SESSION:			TIME:
PAIR:	START EMOJI:	ENTRY TIME FRAME:	TRADE TYPE:	RISK TO REWARD RATIO:	RISK % LEVEL (%/$1000)		BALANCE:
ENTRY CONFIRMATIONS: 1. 2. 3.		ENTRY: 1. 2. 3.	STOP LOSS: 1. 2. 3.		TAKE PROFIT: 1. 2. 3.		TRADE GOAL:
POWER POINTS: (WHAT WORKED) 1. 2. 3.			END EMOJI:	+, - PIP$/PROFIT$		ACTUAL LOSS/PROFITS	

TRADING JOURNAL

ACCOUNT:			DATE:	SESSION:			TIME:	
PAIR:	START EMOJI:	ENTRY TIME FRAME:	TRADE TYPE:	RISK TO REWARD RATIO:	RISK % LEVEL (%/$1000)		BALANCE:	
ENTRY CONFIRMATIONS: 1. 2. 3.		ENTRY: 1. 2. 3.	STOP LOSS: 1. 2. 3.		TAKE PROFIT: 1. 2. 3.		TRADE GOAL:	
POWER POINTS: (WHAT WORKED) 1. 2. 3.			END EMOJI:	+, - PIP$/PROFIT$		ACTUAL LOSS/PROFITS		

ACCOUNT:			DATE:	SESSION:			TIME:	
PAIR:	START EMOJI:	ENTRY TIME FRAME:	TRADE TYPE:	RISK TO REWARD RATIO:	RISK % LEVEL (%/$1000)		BALANCE:	
ENTRY CONFIRMATIONS: 1. 2. 3.		ENTRY: 1. 2. 3.	STOP LOSS: 1. 2. 3.		TAKE PROFIT: 1. 2. 3.		TRADE GOAL:	
POWER POINTS: (WHAT WORKED) 1. 2. 3.			END EMOJI:	+, - PIP$/PROFIT$		ACTUAL LOSS/PROFITS		

ACCOUNT:			DATE:	SESSION:			TIME:	
PAIR:	START EMOJI:	ENTRY TIME FRAME:	TRADE TYPE:	RISK TO REWARD RATIO:	RISK % LEVEL (%/$1000)		BALANCE:	
ENTRY CONFIRMATIONS: 1. 2. 3.		ENTRY: 1. 2. 3.	STOP LOSS: 1. 2. 3.		TAKE PROFIT: 1. 2. 3.		TRADE GOAL:	
POWER POINTS: (WHAT WORKED) 1. 2. 3.			END EMOJI:	+, - PIP$/PROFIT$		ACTUAL LOSS/PROFITS		

TRADING JOURNAL

ACCOUNT:			DATE:	SESSION:		TIME:	
PAIR:	START EMOJI:	ENTRY TIME FRAME:	TRADE TYPE:	RISK TO REWARD RATIO:	RISK % LEVEL (%/$1000)	BALANCE:	
ENTRY CONFIRMATIONS: 1. 2. 3.		ENTRY: 1. 2. 3.	STOP LOSS: 1. 2. 3.		TAKE PROFIT: 1. 2. 3.	TRADE GOAL:	
POWER POINTS: (WHAT WORKED) 1. 2. 3.			END EMOJI:	+, - PIP$/PROFIT$		ACTUAL LOSS/PROFITS	

ACCOUNT:			DATE:	SESSION:		TIME:	
PAIR:	START EMOJI:	ENTRY TIME FRAME:	TRADE TYPE:	RISK TO REWARD RATIO:	RISK % LEVEL (%/$1000)	BALANCE:	
ENTRY CONFIRMATIONS: 1. 2. 3.		ENTRY: 1. 2. 3.	STOP LOSS: 1. 2. 3.		TAKE PROFIT: 1. 2. 3.	TRADE GOAL:	
POWER POINTS: (WHAT WORKED) 1. 2. 3.			END EMOJI:	+, - PIP$/PROFIT$		ACTUAL LOSS/PROFITS	

ACCOUNT:			DATE:	SESSION:		TIME:	
PAIR:	START EMOJI:	ENTRY TIME FRAME:	TRADE TYPE:	RISK TO REWARD RATIO:	RISK % LEVEL (%/$1000)	BALANCE:	
ENTRY CONFIRMATIONS: 1. 2. 3.		ENTRY: 1. 2. 3.	STOP LOSS: 1. 2. 3.		TAKE PROFIT: 1. 2. 3.	TRADE GOAL:	
POWER POINTS: (WHAT WORKED) 1. 2. 3.			END EMOJI:	+, - PIP$/PROFIT$		ACTUAL LOSS/PROFITS	

TRADING JOURNAL

ACCOUNT:			DATE:	SESSION:		TIME:	
PAIR:	START EMOJI:	ENTRY TIME FRAME:	TRADE TYPE:	RISK TO REWARD RATIO:	RISK % LEVEL (%/$1000)	BALANCE:	
ENTRY CONFIRMATIONS: 1. 2. 3.		ENTRY: 1. 2. 3.	STOP LOSS: 1. 2. 3.		TAKE PROFIT: 1. 2. 3.	TRADE GOAL:	
POWER POINTS: (WHAT WORKED) 1. 2. 3.			END EMOJI:	+, - PIP$/PROFIT$		ACTUAL LOSS/PROFITS	

ACCOUNT:			DATE:	SESSION:		TIME:	
PAIR:	START EMOJI:	ENTRY TIME FRAME:	TRADE TYPE:	RISK TO REWARD RATIO:	RISK % LEVEL (%/$1000)	BALANCE:	
ENTRY CONFIRMATIONS: 1. 2. 3.		ENTRY: 1. 2. 3.	STOP LOSS: 1. 2. 3.		TAKE PROFIT: 1. 2. 3.	TRADE GOAL:	
POWER POINTS: (WHAT WORKED) 1. 2. 3.			END EMOJI:	+, - PIP$/PROFIT$		ACTUAL LOSS/PROFITS	

ACCOUNT:			DATE:	SESSION:		TIME:	
PAIR:	START EMOJI:	ENTRY TIME FRAME:	TRADE TYPE:	RISK TO REWARD RATIO:	RISK % LEVEL (%/$1000)	BALANCE:	
ENTRY CONFIRMATIONS: 1. 2. 3.		ENTRY: 1. 2. 3.	STOP LOSS: 1. 2. 3.		TAKE PROFIT: 1. 2. 3.	TRADE GOAL:	
POWER POINTS: (WHAT WORKED) 1. 2. 3.			END EMOJI:	+, - PIP$/PROFIT$		ACTUAL LOSS/PROFITS	

TRADING JOURNAL

ACCOUNT:			DATE:	SESSION:			TIME:
PAIR:	START EMOJI:	ENTRY TIME FRAME:	TRADE TYPE:	RISK TO REWARD RATIO:	RISK % LEVEL (%/$1000)		BALANCE:
ENTRY CONFIRMATIONS: 1. 2. 3.		ENTRY: 1. 2. 3.	STOP LOSS: 1. 2. 3.		TAKE PROFIT: 1. 2. 3.		TRADE GOAL:
POWER POINTS: (WHAT WORKED) 1. 2. 3.			END EMOJI:	+, - PIP$/PROFIT$			ACTUAL LOSS/PROFITS

ACCOUNT:			DATE:	SESSION:			TIME:
PAIR:	START EMOJI:	ENTRY TIME FRAME:	TRADE TYPE:	RISK TO REWARD RATIO:	RISK % LEVEL (%/$1000)		BALANCE:
ENTRY CONFIRMATIONS: 1. 2. 3.		ENTRY: 1. 2. 3.	STOP LOSS: 1. 2. 3.		TAKE PROFIT: 1. 2. 3.		TRADE GOAL:
POWER POINTS: (WHAT WORKED) 1. 2. 3.			END EMOJI:	+, - PIP$/PROFIT$			ACTUAL LOSS/PROFITS

ACCOUNT:			DATE:	SESSION:			TIME:
PAIR:	START EMOJI:	ENTRY TIME FRAME:	TRADE TYPE:	RISK TO REWARD RATIO:	RISK % LEVEL (%/$1000)		BALANCE:
ENTRY CONFIRMATIONS: 1. 2. 3.		ENTRY: 1. 2. 3.	STOP LOSS: 1. 2. 3.		TAKE PROFIT: 1. 2. 3.		TRADE GOAL:
POWER POINTS: (WHAT WORKED) 1. 2. 3.			END EMOJI:	+, - PIP$/PROFIT$			ACTUAL LOSS/PROFITS

TRADING JOURNAL

ACCOUNT:			DATE:	SESSION:		TIME:	
PAIR:	START EMOJI:	ENTRY TIME FRAME:	TRADE TYPE:	RISK TO REWARD RATIO:	RISK % LEVEL (%/$1000)	BALANCE:	
ENTRY CONFIRMATIONS: 1. 2. 3.		ENTRY: 1. 2. 3.	STOP LOSS: 1. 2. 3.		TAKE PROFIT: 1. 2. 3.	TRADE GOAL:	
POWER POINTS: (WHAT WORKED) 1. 2. 3.			END EMOJI:	+, - PIP$/PROFIT$		ACTUAL LOSS/PROFITS	

ACCOUNT:			DATE:	SESSION:		TIME:	
PAIR:	START EMOJI:	ENTRY TIME FRAME:	TRADE TYPE:	RISK TO REWARD RATIO:	RISK % LEVEL (%/$1000)	BALANCE:	
ENTRY CONFIRMATIONS: 1. 2. 3.		ENTRY: 1. 2. 3.	STOP LOSS: 1. 2. 3.		TAKE PROFIT: 1. 2. 3.	TRADE GOAL:	
POWER POINTS: (WHAT WORKED) 1. 2. 3.			END EMOJI:	+, - PIP$/PROFIT$		ACTUAL LOSS/PROFITS	

ACCOUNT:			DATE:	SESSION:		TIME:	
PAIR:	START EMOJI:	ENTRY TIME FRAME:	TRADE TYPE:	RISK TO REWARD RATIO:	RISK % LEVEL (%/$1000)	BALANCE:	
ENTRY CONFIRMATIONS: 1. 2. 3.		ENTRY: 1. 2. 3.	STOP LOSS: 1. 2. 3.		TAKE PROFIT: 1. 2. 3.	TRADE GOAL:	
POWER POINTS: (WHAT WORKED) 1. 2. 3.			END EMOJI:	+, - PIP$/PROFIT$		ACTUAL LOSS/PROFITS	

TRADING JOURNAL

ACCOUNT:			DATE:	SESSION:			TIME:	
PAIR:	START EMOJI:	ENTRY TIME FRAME:	TRADE TYPE:	RISK TO REWARD RATIO:	RISK % LEVEL (%/$1000)		BALANCE:	
ENTRY CONFIRMATIONS: 1. 2. 3.		ENTRY: 1. 2. 3.	STOP LOSS: 1. 2. 3.			TAKE PROFIT: 1. 2. 3.	TRADE GOAL:	
POWER POINTS: (WHAT WORKED) 1. 2. 3.			END EMOJI:	+, - PIP$/PROFIT$			ACTUAL LOSS/PROFITS	

ACCOUNT:			DATE:	SESSION:			TIME:	
PAIR:	START EMOJI:	ENTRY TIME FRAME:	TRADE TYPE:	RISK TO REWARD RATIO:	RISK % LEVEL (%/$1000)		BALANCE:	
ENTRY CONFIRMATIONS: 1. 2. 3.		ENTRY: 1. 2. 3.	STOP LOSS: 1. 2. 3.			TAKE PROFIT: 1. 2. 3.	TRADE GOAL:	
POWER POINTS: (WHAT WORKED) 1. 2. 3.			END EMOJI:	+, - PIP$/PROFIT$			ACTUAL LOSS/PROFITS	

ACCOUNT:			DATE:	SESSION:			TIME:	
PAIR:	START EMOJI:	ENTRY TIME FRAME:	TRADE TYPE:	RISK TO REWARD RATIO:	RISK % LEVEL (%/$1000)		BALANCE:	
ENTRY CONFIRMATIONS: 1. 2. 3.		ENTRY: 1. 2. 3.	STOP LOSS: 1. 2. 3.			TAKE PROFIT: 1. 2. 3.	TRADE GOAL:	
POWER POINTS: (WHAT WORKED) 1. 2. 3.			END EMOJI:	+, - PIP$/PROFIT$			ACTUAL LOSS/PROFITS	

TRADING JOURNAL

ACCOUNT:			DATE:	SESSION:			TIME:	
PAIR:	START EMOJI:	ENTRY TIME FRAME:	TRADE TYPE:	RISK TO REWARD RATIO:	RISK % LEVEL (%/$1000)		BALANCE:	
ENTRY CONFIRMATIONS: 1. 2. 3.		ENTRY: 1. 2. 3.	STOP LOSS: 1. 2. 3.			TAKE PROFIT: 1. 2. 3.	TRADE GOAL:	
POWER POINTS: (WHAT WORKED) 1. 2. 3.			END EMOJI:	+, - PIP$/PROFIT$			ACTUAL LOSS/PROFITS	

ACCOUNT:			DATE:	SESSION:			TIME:	
PAIR:	START EMOJI:	ENTRY TIME FRAME:	TRADE TYPE:	RISK TO REWARD RATIO:	RISK % LEVEL (%/$1000)		BALANCE:	
ENTRY CONFIRMATIONS: 1. 2. 3.		ENTRY: 1. 2. 3.	STOP LOSS: 1. 2. 3.			TAKE PROFIT: 1. 2. 3.	TRADE GOAL:	
POWER POINTS: (WHAT WORKED) 1. 2. 3.			END EMOJI:	+, - PIP$/PROFIT$			ACTUAL LOSS/PROFITS	

ACCOUNT:			DATE:	SESSION:			TIME:	
PAIR:	START EMOJI:	ENTRY TIME FRAME:	TRADE TYPE:	RISK TO REWARD RATIO:	RISK % LEVEL (%/$1000)		BALANCE:	
ENTRY CONFIRMATIONS: 1. 2. 3.		ENTRY: 1. 2. 3.	STOP LOSS: 1. 2. 3.			TAKE PROFIT: 1. 2. 3.	TRADE GOAL:	
POWER POINTS: (WHAT WORKED) 1. 2. 3.			END EMOJI:	+, - PIP$/PROFIT$			ACTUAL LOSS/PROFITS	

TRADING JOURNAL

ACCOUNT:			DATE:	SESSION:			TIME:	
PAIR:	START EMOJI:	ENTRY TIME FRAME:	TRADE TYPE:	RISK TO REWARD RATIO:	RISK % LEVEL (%/$1000)		BALANCE:	
ENTRY CONFIRMATIONS: 1. 2. 3.		ENTRY: 1. 2. 3.	STOP LOSS: 1. 2. 3.			TAKE PROFIT: 1. 2. 3.	TRADE GOAL:	
POWER POINTS: (WHAT WORKED) 1. 2. 3.			END EMOJI:	+, - PIP$/PROFIT$			ACTUAL LOSS/PROFITS	

ACCOUNT:			DATE:	SESSION:			TIME:	
PAIR:	START EMOJI:	ENTRY TIME FRAME:	TRADE TYPE:	RISK TO REWARD RATIO:	RISK % LEVEL (%/$1000)		BALANCE:	
ENTRY CONFIRMATIONS: 1. 2. 3.		ENTRY: 1. 2. 3.	STOP LOSS: 1. 2. 3.			TAKE PROFIT: 1. 2. 3.	TRADE GOAL:	
POWER POINTS: (WHAT WORKED) 1. 2. 3.			END EMOJI:	+, - PIP$/PROFIT$			ACTUAL LOSS/PROFITS	

ACCOUNT:			DATE:	SESSION:			TIME:	
PAIR:	START EMOJI:	ENTRY TIME FRAME:	TRADE TYPE:	RISK TO REWARD RATIO:	RISK % LEVEL (%/$1000)		BALANCE:	
ENTRY CONFIRMATIONS: 1. 2. 3.		ENTRY: 1. 2. 3.	STOP LOSS: 1. 2. 3.			TAKE PROFIT: 1. 2. 3.	TRADE GOAL:	
POWER POINTS: (WHAT WORKED) 1. 2. 3.			END EMOJI:	+, - PIP$/PROFIT$			ACTUAL LOSS/PROFITS	

TRADING JOURNAL

ACCOUNT:			DATE:	SESSION:			TIME:
PAIR:	START EMOJI:	ENTRY TIME FRAME:	TRADE TYPE:	RISK TO REWARD RATIO:	RISK % LEVEL (%/$1000)		BALANCE:
ENTRY CONFIRMATIONS: 1. 2. 3.		ENTRY: 1. 2. 3.	STOP LOSS: 1. 2. 3.		TAKE PROFIT: 1. 2. 3.		TRADE GOAL:
POWER POINTS: (WHAT WORKED) 1. 2. 3.			END EMOJI:	+, - PIP$/PROFIT$			ACTUAL LOSS/PROFITS

ACCOUNT:			DATE:	SESSION:			TIME:
PAIR:	START EMOJI:	ENTRY TIME FRAME:	TRADE TYPE:	RISK TO REWARD RATIO:	RISK % LEVEL (%/$1000)		BALANCE:
ENTRY CONFIRMATIONS: 1. 2. 3.		ENTRY: 1. 2. 3.	STOP LOSS: 1. 2. 3.		TAKE PROFIT: 1. 2. 3.		TRADE GOAL:
POWER POINTS: (WHAT WORKED) 1. 2. 3.			END EMOJI:	+, - PIP$/PROFIT$			ACTUAL LOSS/PROFITS

ACCOUNT:			DATE:	SESSION:			TIME:
PAIR:	START EMOJI:	ENTRY TIME FRAME:	TRADE TYPE:	RISK TO REWARD RATIO:	RISK % LEVEL (%/$1000)		BALANCE:
ENTRY CONFIRMATIONS: 1. 2. 3.		ENTRY: 1. 2. 3.	STOP LOSS: 1. 2. 3.		TAKE PROFIT: 1. 2. 3.		TRADE GOAL:
POWER POINTS: (WHAT WORKED) 1. 2. 3.			END EMOJI:	+, - PIP$/PROFIT$			ACTUAL LOSS/PROFITS

TRADING JOURNAL

ACCOUNT:			DATE:	SESSION:			TIME:	
PAIR:	START EMOJI:	ENTRY TIME FRAME:	TRADE TYPE:	RISK TO REWARD RATIO:	RISK % LEVEL (%/$1000)		BALANCE:	
ENTRY CONFIRMATIONS: 1. 2. 3.		ENTRY: 1. 2. 3.	STOP LOSS: 1. 2. 3.		TAKE PROFIT: 1. 2. 3.		TRADE GOAL:	
POWER POINTS: (WHAT WORKED) 1. 2. 3.			END EMOJI:	+, - PIP$/PROFIT$			ACTUAL LOSS/PROFITS	

ACCOUNT:			DATE:	SESSION:			TIME:	
PAIR:	START EMOJI:	ENTRY TIME FRAME:	TRADE TYPE:	RISK TO REWARD RATIO:	RISK % LEVEL (%/$1000)		BALANCE:	
ENTRY CONFIRMATIONS: 1. 2. 3.		ENTRY: 1. 2. 3.	STOP LOSS: 1. 2. 3.		TAKE PROFIT: 1. 2. 3.		TRADE GOAL:	
POWER POINTS: (WHAT WORKED) 1. 2. 3.			END EMOJI:	+, - PIP$/PROFIT$			ACTUAL LOSS/PROFITS	

ACCOUNT:			DATE:	SESSION:			TIME:	
PAIR:	START EMOJI:	ENTRY TIME FRAME:	TRADE TYPE:	RISK TO REWARD RATIO:	RISK % LEVEL (%/$1000)		BALANCE:	
ENTRY CONFIRMATIONS: 1. 2. 3.		ENTRY: 1. 2. 3.	STOP LOSS: 1. 2. 3.		TAKE PROFIT: 1. 2. 3.		TRADE GOAL:	
POWER POINTS: (WHAT WORKED) 1. 2. 3.			END EMOJI:	+, - PIP$/PROFIT$			ACTUAL LOSS/PROFITS	

TRADING JOURNAL

ACCOUNT:			DATE:	SESSION:		TIME:	
PAIR:	START EMOJI:	ENTRY TIME FRAME:	TRADE TYPE:	RISK TO REWARD RATIO:	RISK % LEVEL (%/$1000)	BALANCE:	
ENTRY CONFIRMATIONS: 1. 2. 3.		ENTRY: 1. 2. 3.	STOP LOSS: 1. 2. 3.		TAKE PROFIT: 1. 2. 3.	TRADE GOAL:	
POWER POINTS: (WHAT WORKED) 1. 2. 3.			END EMOJI:	+, - PIP$/PROFIT$		ACTUAL LOSS/PROFITS	

ACCOUNT:			DATE:	SESSION:		TIME:	
PAIR:	START EMOJI:	ENTRY TIME FRAME:	TRADE TYPE:	RISK TO REWARD RATIO:	RISK % LEVEL (%/$1000)	BALANCE:	
ENTRY CONFIRMATIONS: 1. 2. 3.		ENTRY: 1. 2. 3.	STOP LOSS: 1. 2. 3.		TAKE PROFIT: 1. 2. 3.	TRADE GOAL:	
POWER POINTS: (WHAT WORKED) 1. 2. 3.			END EMOJI:	+, - PIP$/PROFIT$		ACTUAL LOSS/PROFITS	

ACCOUNT:			DATE:	SESSION:		TIME:	
PAIR:	START EMOJI:	ENTRY TIME FRAME:	TRADE TYPE:	RISK TO REWARD RATIO:	RISK % LEVEL (%/$1000)	BALANCE:	
ENTRY CONFIRMATIONS: 1. 2. 3.		ENTRY: 1. 2. 3.	STOP LOSS: 1. 2. 3.		TAKE PROFIT: 1. 2. 3.	TRADE GOAL:	
POWER POINTS: (WHAT WORKED) 1. 2. 3.			END EMOJI:	+, - PIP$/PROFIT$		ACTUAL LOSS/PROFITS	

TRADING JOURNAL

ACCOUNT:			DATE:	SESSION:			TIME:	
PAIR:	START EMOJI:	ENTRY TIME FRAME:	TRADE TYPE:	RISK TO REWARD RATIO:	RISK % LEVEL (%/$1000)		BALANCE:	
ENTRY CONFIRMATIONS: 1. 2. 3.		ENTRY: 1. 2. 3.	STOP LOSS: 1. 2. 3.		TAKE PROFIT: 1. 2. 3.		TRADE GOAL:	
POWER POINTS: (WHAT WORKED) 1. 2. 3.			END EMOJI:	+, - PIP$/PROFIT$			ACTUAL LOSS/PROFITS	

ACCOUNT:			DATE:	SESSION:			TIME:	
PAIR:	START EMOJI:	ENTRY TIME FRAME:	TRADE TYPE:	RISK TO REWARD RATIO:	RISK % LEVEL (%/$1000)		BALANCE:	
ENTRY CONFIRMATIONS: 1. 2. 3.		ENTRY: 1. 2. 3.	STOP LOSS: 1. 2. 3.		TAKE PROFIT: 1. 2. 3.		TRADE GOAL:	
POWER POINTS: (WHAT WORKED) 1. 2. 3.			END EMOJI:	+, - PIP$/PROFIT$			ACTUAL LOSS/PROFITS	

ACCOUNT:			DATE:	SESSION:			TIME:	
PAIR:	START EMOJI:	ENTRY TIME FRAME:	TRADE TYPE:	RISK TO REWARD RATIO:	RISK % LEVEL (%/$1000)		BALANCE:	
ENTRY CONFIRMATIONS: 1. 2. 3.		ENTRY: 1. 2. 3.	STOP LOSS: 1. 2. 3.		TAKE PROFIT: 1. 2. 3.		TRADE GOAL:	
POWER POINTS: (WHAT WORKED) 1. 2. 3.			END EMOJI:	+, - PIP$/PROFIT$			ACTUAL LOSS/PROFITS	

TRADING JOURNAL

ACCOUNT:			DATE:	SESSION:			TIME:	
PAIR:	START EMOJI:	ENTRY TIME FRAME:	TRADE TYPE:	RISK TO REWARD RATIO:		RISK % LEVEL (%/$1000)	BALANCE:	
ENTRY CONFIRMATIONS: 1. 2. 3.		ENTRY: 1. 2. 3.	STOP LOSS: 1. 2. 3.			TAKE PROFIT: 1. 2. 3.	TRADE GOAL:	
POWER POINTS: (WHAT WORKED) 1. 2. 3.			END EMOJI:	+, - PIP$/PROFIT$			ACTUAL LOSS/PROFITS	

ACCOUNT:			DATE:	SESSION:			TIME:	
PAIR:	START EMOJI:	ENTRY TIME FRAME:	TRADE TYPE:	RISK TO REWARD RATIO:		RISK % LEVEL (%/$1000)	BALANCE:	
ENTRY CONFIRMATIONS: 1. 2. 3.		ENTRY: 1. 2. 3.	STOP LOSS: 1. 2. 3.			TAKE PROFIT: 1. 2. 3.	TRADE GOAL:	
POWER POINTS: (WHAT WORKED) 1. 2. 3.			END EMOJI:	+, - PIP$/PROFIT$			ACTUAL LOSS/PROFITS	

ACCOUNT:			DATE:	SESSION:			TIME:	
PAIR:	START EMOJI:	ENTRY TIME FRAME:	TRADE TYPE:	RISK TO REWARD RATIO:		RISK % LEVEL (%/$1000)	BALANCE:	
ENTRY CONFIRMATIONS: 1. 2. 3.		ENTRY: 1. 2. 3.	STOP LOSS: 1. 2. 3.			TAKE PROFIT: 1. 2. 3.	TRADE GOAL:	
POWER POINTS: (WHAT WORKED) 1. 2. 3.			END EMOJI:	+, - PIP$/PROFIT$			ACTUAL LOSS/PROFITS	

TRADING JOURNAL

ACCOUNT:			DATE:	SESSION:		TIME:	
PAIR:	START EMOJI:	ENTRY TIME FRAME:	TRADE TYPE:	RISK TO REWARD RATIO:	RISK % LEVEL (%/$1000)	BALANCE:	
ENTRY CONFIRMATIONS: 1. 2. 3.		ENTRY: 1. 2. 3.	STOP LOSS: 1. 2. 3.		TAKE PROFIT: 1. 2. 3.	TRADE GOAL:	
POWER POINTS: (WHAT WORKED) 1. 2. 3.			END EMOJI:	+, - PIP$/PROFIT$		ACTUAL LOSS/PROFITS	

ACCOUNT:			DATE:	SESSION:		TIME:	
PAIR:	START EMOJI:	ENTRY TIME FRAME:	TRADE TYPE:	RISK TO REWARD RATIO:	RISK % LEVEL (%/$1000)	BALANCE:	
ENTRY CONFIRMATIONS: 1. 2. 3.		ENTRY: 1. 2. 3.	STOP LOSS: 1. 2. 3.		TAKE PROFIT: 1. 2. 3.	TRADE GOAL:	
POWER POINTS: (WHAT WORKED) 1. 2. 3.			END EMOJI:	+, - PIP$/PROFIT$		ACTUAL LOSS/PROFITS	

ACCOUNT:			DATE:	SESSION:		TIME:	
PAIR:	START EMOJI:	ENTRY TIME FRAME:	TRADE TYPE:	RISK TO REWARD RATIO:	RISK % LEVEL (%/$1000)	BALANCE:	
ENTRY CONFIRMATIONS: 1. 2. 3.		ENTRY: 1. 2. 3.	STOP LOSS: 1. 2. 3.		TAKE PROFIT: 1. 2. 3.	TRADE GOAL:	
POWER POINTS: (WHAT WORKED) 1. 2. 3.			END EMOJI:	+, - PIP$/PROFIT$		ACTUAL LOSS/PROFITS	

TRADING JOURNAL

ACCOUNT:			DATE:	SESSION:			TIME:
PAIR:	START EMOJI:	ENTRY TIME FRAME:	TRADE TYPE:	RISK TO REWARD RATIO:	RISK % LEVEL (%/$1000)		BALANCE:
ENTRY CONFIRMATIONS: 1. 2. 3.		ENTRY: 1. 2. 3.	STOP LOSS: 1. 2. 3.		TAKE PROFIT: 1. 2. 3.		TRADE GOAL:
POWER POINTS: (WHAT WORKED) 1. 2. 3.			END EMOJI:	+, - PIP$/PROFIT$		ACTUAL LOSS/PROFITS	

ACCOUNT:			DATE:	SESSION:			TIME:
PAIR:	START EMOJI:	ENTRY TIME FRAME:	TRADE TYPE:	RISK TO REWARD RATIO:	RISK % LEVEL (%/$1000)		BALANCE:
ENTRY CONFIRMATIONS: 1. 2. 3.		ENTRY: 1. 2. 3.	STOP LOSS: 1. 2. 3.		TAKE PROFIT: 1. 2. 3.		TRADE GOAL:
POWER POINTS: (WHAT WORKED) 1. 2. 3.			END EMOJI:	+, - PIP$/PROFIT$		ACTUAL LOSS/PROFITS	

ACCOUNT:			DATE:	SESSION:			TIME:
PAIR:	START EMOJI:	ENTRY TIME FRAME:	TRADE TYPE:	RISK TO REWARD RATIO:	RISK % LEVEL (%/$1000)		BALANCE:
ENTRY CONFIRMATIONS: 1. 2. 3.		ENTRY: 1. 2. 3.	STOP LOSS: 1. 2. 3.		TAKE PROFIT: 1. 2. 3.		TRADE GOAL:
POWER POINTS: (WHAT WORKED) 1. 2. 3.			END EMOJI:	+, - PIP$/PROFIT$		ACTUAL LOSS/PROFITS	

TRADING JOURNAL

ACCOUNT:			DATE:	SESSION:			TIME:	
PAIR:	START EMOJI:	ENTRY TIME FRAME:	TRADE TYPE:	RISK TO REWARD RATIO:	RISK % LEVEL (%/$1000)		BALANCE:	
ENTRY CONFIRMATIONS: 1. 2. 3.		ENTRY: 1. 2. 3.	STOP LOSS: 1. 2. 3.			TAKE PROFIT: 1. 2. 3.	TRADE GOAL:	
POWER POINTS: (WHAT WORKED) 1. 2. 3.			END EMOJI:	+, - PIP$/PROFIT$			ACTUAL LOSS/PROFITS	

ACCOUNT:			DATE:	SESSION:			TIME:	
PAIR:	START EMOJI:	ENTRY TIME FRAME:	TRADE TYPE:	RISK TO REWARD RATIO:	RISK % LEVEL (%/$1000)		BALANCE:	
ENTRY CONFIRMATIONS: 1. 2. 3.		ENTRY: 1. 2. 3.	STOP LOSS: 1. 2. 3.			TAKE PROFIT: 1. 2. 3.	TRADE GOAL:	
POWER POINTS: (WHAT WORKED) 1. 2. 3.			END EMOJI:	+, - PIP$/PROFIT$			ACTUAL LOSS/PROFITS	

ACCOUNT:			DATE:	SESSION:			TIME:	
PAIR:	START EMOJI:	ENTRY TIME FRAME:	TRADE TYPE:	RISK TO REWARD RATIO:	RISK % LEVEL (%/$1000)		BALANCE:	
ENTRY CONFIRMATIONS: 1. 2. 3.		ENTRY: 1. 2. 3.	STOP LOSS: 1. 2. 3.			TAKE PROFIT: 1. 2. 3.	TRADE GOAL:	
POWER POINTS: (WHAT WORKED) 1. 2. 3.			END EMOJI:	+, - PIP$/PROFIT$			ACTUAL LOSS/PROFITS	

TRADING JOURNAL

ACCOUNT:			DATE:	SESSION:			TIME:	
PAIR:	START EMOJI:	ENTRY TIME FRAME:	TRADE TYPE:	RISK TO REWARD RATIO:		RISK % LEVEL (%/$1000)	BALANCE:	
ENTRY CONFIRMATIONS: 1. 2. 3.		ENTRY: 1. 2. 3.	STOP LOSS: 1. 2. 3.			TAKE PROFIT: 1. 2. 3.	TRADE GOAL:	
POWER POINTS: (WHAT WORKED) 1. 2. 3.			END EMOJI:	+, - PIP$/PROFIT$			ACTUAL LOSS/PROFITS	

ACCOUNT:			DATE:	SESSION:			TIME:	
PAIR:	START EMOJI:	ENTRY TIME FRAME:	TRADE TYPE:	RISK TO REWARD RATIO:		RISK % LEVEL (%/$1000)	BALANCE:	
ENTRY CONFIRMATIONS: 1. 2. 3.		ENTRY: 1. 2. 3.	STOP LOSS: 1. 2. 3.			TAKE PROFIT: 1. 2. 3.	TRADE GOAL:	
POWER POINTS: (WHAT WORKED) 1. 2. 3.			END EMOJI:	+, - PIP$/PROFIT$			ACTUAL LOSS/PROFITS	

ACCOUNT:			DATE:	SESSION:			TIME:	
PAIR:	START EMOJI:	ENTRY TIME FRAME:	TRADE TYPE:	RISK TO REWARD RATIO:		RISK % LEVEL (%/$1000)	BALANCE:	
ENTRY CONFIRMATIONS: 1. 2. 3.		ENTRY: 1. 2. 3.	STOP LOSS: 1. 2. 3.			TAKE PROFIT: 1. 2. 3.	TRADE GOAL:	
POWER POINTS: (WHAT WORKED) 1. 2. 3.			END EMOJI:	+, - PIP$/PROFIT$			ACTUAL LOSS/PROFITS	

TRADING JOURNAL

ACCOUNT:			DATE:	SESSION:			TIME:	
PAIR:	START EMOJI:	ENTRY TIME FRAME:	TRADE TYPE:	RISK TO REWARD RATIO:	RISK % LEVEL (%/$1000)		BALANCE:	
ENTRY CONFIRMATIONS: 1. 2. 3.		ENTRY: 1. 2. 3.	STOP LOSS: 1. 2. 3.		TAKE PROFIT: 1. 2. 3.		TRADE GOAL:	
POWER POINTS: (WHAT WORKED) 1. 2. 3.			END EMOJI:	+, - PIP$/PROFIT$			ACTUAL LOSS/PROFITS	

ACCOUNT:			DATE:	SESSION:			TIME:	
PAIR:	START EMOJI:	ENTRY TIME FRAME:	TRADE TYPE:	RISK TO REWARD RATIO:	RISK % LEVEL (%/$1000)		BALANCE:	
ENTRY CONFIRMATIONS: 1. 2. 3.		ENTRY: 1. 2. 3.	STOP LOSS: 1. 2. 3.		TAKE PROFIT: 1. 2. 3.		TRADE GOAL:	
POWER POINTS: (WHAT WORKED) 1. 2. 3.			END EMOJI:	+, - PIP$/PROFIT$			ACTUAL LOSS/PROFITS	

ACCOUNT:			DATE:	SESSION:			TIME:	
PAIR:	START EMOJI:	ENTRY TIME FRAME:	TRADE TYPE:	RISK TO REWARD RATIO:	RISK % LEVEL (%/$1000)		BALANCE:	
ENTRY CONFIRMATIONS: 1. 2. 3.		ENTRY: 1. 2. 3.	STOP LOSS: 1. 2. 3.		TAKE PROFIT: 1. 2. 3.		TRADE GOAL:	
POWER POINTS: (WHAT WORKED) 1. 2. 3.			END EMOJI:	+, - PIP$/PROFIT$			ACTUAL LOSS/PROFITS	

TRADING JOURNAL

ACCOUNT:			DATE:	SESSION:			TIME:
PAIR:	START EMOJI:	ENTRY TIME FRAME:	TRADE TYPE:	RISK TO REWARD RATIO:	RISK % LEVEL (%/$1000)		BALANCE:
ENTRY CONFIRMATIONS: 1. 2. 3.		ENTRY: 1. 2. 3.	STOP LOSS: 1. 2. 3.			TAKE PROFIT: 1. 2. 3.	TRADE GOAL:
POWER POINTS: (WHAT WORKED) 1. 2. 3.			END EMOJI:	+, - PIP$/PROFIT$			ACTUAL LOSS/PROFITS

ACCOUNT:			DATE:	SESSION:			TIME:
PAIR:	START EMOJI:	ENTRY TIME FRAME:	TRADE TYPE:	RISK TO REWARD RATIO:	RISK % LEVEL (%/$1000)		BALANCE:
ENTRY CONFIRMATIONS: 1. 2. 3.		ENTRY: 1. 2. 3.	STOP LOSS: 1. 2. 3.			TAKE PROFIT: 1. 2. 3.	TRADE GOAL:
POWER POINTS: (WHAT WORKED) 1. 2. 3.			END EMOJI:	+, - PIP$/PROFIT$			ACTUAL LOSS/PROFITS

ACCOUNT:			DATE:	SESSION:			TIME:
PAIR:	START EMOJI:	ENTRY TIME FRAME:	TRADE TYPE:	RISK TO REWARD RATIO:	RISK % LEVEL (%/$1000)		BALANCE:
ENTRY CONFIRMATIONS: 1. 2. 3.		ENTRY: 1. 2. 3.	STOP LOSS: 1. 2. 3.			TAKE PROFIT: 1. 2. 3.	TRADE GOAL:
POWER POINTS: (WHAT WORKED) 1. 2. 3.			END EMOJI:	+, - PIP$/PROFIT$			ACTUAL LOSS/PROFITS

TRADING JOURNAL

ACCOUNT:			DATE:	SESSION:			TIME:
PAIR:	START EMOJI:	ENTRY TIME FRAME:	TRADE TYPE:	RISK TO REWARD RATIO:	RISK % LEVEL (%/$1000)		BALANCE:
ENTRY CONFIRMATIONS: 1. 2. 3.		ENTRY: 1. 2. 3.	STOP LOSS: 1. 2. 3.		TAKE PROFIT: 1. 2. 3.		TRADE GOAL:
POWER POINTS: (WHAT WORKED) 1. 2. 3.			END EMOJI:	+, - PIP$/PROFIT$			ACTUAL LOSS/PROFITS

ACCOUNT:			DATE:	SESSION:			TIME:
PAIR:	START EMOJI:	ENTRY TIME FRAME:	TRADE TYPE:	RISK TO REWARD RATIO:	RISK % LEVEL (%/$1000)		BALANCE:
ENTRY CONFIRMATIONS: 1. 2. 3.		ENTRY: 1. 2. 3.	STOP LOSS: 1. 2. 3.		TAKE PROFIT: 1. 2. 3.		TRADE GOAL:
POWER POINTS: (WHAT WORKED) 1. 2. 3.			END EMOJI:	+, - PIP$/PROFIT$			ACTUAL LOSS/PROFITS

ACCOUNT:			DATE:	SESSION:			TIME:
PAIR:	START EMOJI:	ENTRY TIME FRAME:	TRADE TYPE:	RISK TO REWARD RATIO:	RISK % LEVEL (%/$1000)		BALANCE:
ENTRY CONFIRMATIONS: 1. 2. 3.		ENTRY: 1. 2. 3.	STOP LOSS: 1. 2. 3.		TAKE PROFIT: 1. 2. 3.		TRADE GOAL:
POWER POINTS: (WHAT WORKED) 1. 2. 3.			END EMOJI:	+, - PIP$/PROFIT$			ACTUAL LOSS/PROFITS

TRADING JOURNAL

ACCOUNT:			DATE:	SESSION:			TIME:	
PAIR:	START EMOJI:	ENTRY TIME FRAME:	TRADE TYPE:	RISK TO REWARD RATIO:	RISK % LEVEL (%/$1000)		BALANCE:	
ENTRY CONFIRMATIONS: 1. 2. 3.		ENTRY: 1. 2. 3.	STOP LOSS: 1. 2. 3.			TAKE PROFIT: 1. 2. 3.	TRADE GOAL:	
POWER POINTS: (WHAT WORKED) 1. 2. 3.			END EMOJI:	+, - PIP$/PROFIT$			ACTUAL LOSS/PROFITS	

ACCOUNT:			DATE:	SESSION:			TIME:	
PAIR:	START EMOJI:	ENTRY TIME FRAME:	TRADE TYPE:	RISK TO REWARD RATIO:	RISK % LEVEL (%/$1000)		BALANCE:	
ENTRY CONFIRMATIONS: 1. 2. 3.		ENTRY: 1. 2. 3.	STOP LOSS: 1. 2. 3.			TAKE PROFIT: 1. 2. 3.	TRADE GOAL:	
POWER POINTS: (WHAT WORKED) 1. 2. 3.			END EMOJI:	+, - PIP$/PROFIT$			ACTUAL LOSS/PROFITS	

ACCOUNT:			DATE:	SESSION:			TIME:	
PAIR:	START EMOJI:	ENTRY TIME FRAME:	TRADE TYPE:	RISK TO REWARD RATIO:	RISK % LEVEL (%/$1000)		BALANCE:	
ENTRY CONFIRMATIONS: 1. 2. 3.		ENTRY: 1. 2. 3.	STOP LOSS: 1. 2. 3.			TAKE PROFIT: 1. 2. 3.	TRADE GOAL:	
POWER POINTS: (WHAT WORKED) 1. 2. 3.			END EMOJI:	+, - PIP$/PROFIT$			ACTUAL LOSS/PROFITS	

TRADING JOURNAL

ACCOUNT:			DATE:	SESSION:		TIME:	
PAIR:	START EMOJI:	ENTRY TIME FRAME:	TRADE TYPE:	RISK TO REWARD RATIO:	RISK % LEVEL (%/$1000)	BALANCE:	
ENTRY CONFIRMATIONS: 1. 2. 3.		ENTRY: 1. 2. 3.	STOP LOSS: 1. 2. 3.		TAKE PROFIT: 1. 2. 3.	TRADE GOAL:	
POWER POINTS: (WHAT WORKED) 1. 2. 3.			END EMOJI:	+, - PIP$/PROFIT$		ACTUAL LOSS/PROFITS	

ACCOUNT:			DATE:	SESSION:		TIME:	
PAIR:	START EMOJI:	ENTRY TIME FRAME:	TRADE TYPE:	RISK TO REWARD RATIO:	RISK % LEVEL (%/$1000)	BALANCE:	
ENTRY CONFIRMATIONS: 1. 2. 3.		ENTRY: 1. 2. 3.	STOP LOSS: 1. 2. 3.		TAKE PROFIT: 1. 2. 3.	TRADE GOAL:	
POWER POINTS: (WHAT WORKED) 1. 2. 3.			END EMOJI:	+, - PIP$/PROFIT$		ACTUAL LOSS/PROFITS	

ACCOUNT:			DATE:	SESSION:		TIME:	
PAIR:	START EMOJI:	ENTRY TIME FRAME:	TRADE TYPE:	RISK TO REWARD RATIO:	RISK % LEVEL (%/$1000)	BALANCE:	
ENTRY CONFIRMATIONS: 1. 2. 3.		ENTRY: 1. 2. 3.	STOP LOSS: 1. 2. 3.		TAKE PROFIT: 1. 2. 3.	TRADE GOAL:	
POWER POINTS: (WHAT WORKED) 1. 2. 3.			END EMOJI:	+, - PIP$/PROFIT$		ACTUAL LOSS/PROFITS	

TRADING JOURNAL

ACCOUNT:			DATE:	SESSION:			TIME:
PAIR:	START EMOJI:	ENTRY TIME FRAME:	TRADE TYPE:	RISK TO REWARD RATIO:	RISK % LEVEL (%/$1000)		BALANCE:
ENTRY CONFIRMATIONS: 1. 2. 3.		ENTRY: 1. 2. 3.	STOP LOSS: 1. 2. 3.		TAKE PROFIT: 1. 2. 3.		TRADE GOAL:
POWER POINTS: (WHAT WORKED) 1. 2. 3.			END EMOJI:	+, - PIP$/PROFIT$		ACTUAL LOSS/PROFITS	

ACCOUNT:			DATE:	SESSION:			TIME:
PAIR:	START EMOJI:	ENTRY TIME FRAME:	TRADE TYPE:	RISK TO REWARD RATIO:	RISK % LEVEL (%/$1000)		BALANCE:
ENTRY CONFIRMATIONS: 1. 2. 3.		ENTRY: 1. 2. 3.	STOP LOSS: 1. 2. 3.		TAKE PROFIT: 1. 2. 3.		TRADE GOAL:
POWER POINTS: (WHAT WORKED) 1. 2. 3.			END EMOJI:	+, - PIP$/PROFIT$		ACTUAL LOSS/PROFITS	

ACCOUNT:			DATE:	SESSION:			TIME:
PAIR:	START EMOJI:	ENTRY TIME FRAME:	TRADE TYPE:	RISK TO REWARD RATIO:	RISK % LEVEL (%/$1000)		BALANCE:
ENTRY CONFIRMATIONS: 1. 2. 3.		ENTRY: 1. 2. 3.	STOP LOSS: 1. 2. 3.		TAKE PROFIT: 1. 2. 3.		TRADE GOAL:
POWER POINTS: (WHAT WORKED) 1. 2. 3.			END EMOJI:	+, - PIP$/PROFIT$		ACTUAL LOSS/PROFITS	

TRADING JOURNAL

ACCOUNT:			DATE:	SESSION:			TIME:
PAIR:	START EMOJI:	ENTRY TIME FRAME:	TRADE TYPE:	RISK TO REWARD RATIO:	RISK % LEVEL (%/$1000)		BALANCE:
ENTRY CONFIRMATIONS: 1. 2. 3.		ENTRY: 1. 2. 3.	STOP LOSS: 1. 2. 3.		TAKE PROFIT: 1. 2. 3.		TRADE GOAL:
POWER POINTS: (WHAT WORKED) 1. 2. 3.			END EMOJI:	+, - PIP$/PROFIT$			ACTUAL LOSS/PROFITS

ACCOUNT:			DATE:	SESSION:			TIME:
PAIR:	START EMOJI:	ENTRY TIME FRAME:	TRADE TYPE:	RISK TO REWARD RATIO:	RISK % LEVEL (%/$1000)		BALANCE:
ENTRY CONFIRMATIONS: 1. 2. 3.		ENTRY: 1. 2. 3.	STOP LOSS: 1. 2. 3.		TAKE PROFIT: 1. 2. 3.		TRADE GOAL:
POWER POINTS: (WHAT WORKED) 1. 2. 3.			END EMOJI:	+, - PIP$/PROFIT$			ACTUAL LOSS/PROFITS

ACCOUNT:			DATE:	SESSION:			TIME:
PAIR:	START EMOJI:	ENTRY TIME FRAME:	TRADE TYPE:	RISK TO REWARD RATIO:	RISK % LEVEL (%/$1000)		BALANCE:
ENTRY CONFIRMATIONS: 1. 2. 3.		ENTRY: 1. 2. 3.	STOP LOSS: 1. 2. 3.		TAKE PROFIT: 1. 2. 3.		TRADE GOAL:
POWER POINTS: (WHAT WORKED) 1. 2. 3.			END EMOJI:	+, - PIP$/PROFIT$			ACTUAL LOSS/PROFITS

TRADING JOURNAL

ACCOUNT:			DATE:	SESSION:			TIME:	
PAIR:	START EMOJI:	ENTRY TIME FRAME:	TRADE TYPE:	RISK TO REWARD RATIO:		RISK % LEVEL (%/$1000)	BALANCE:	
ENTRY CONFIRMATIONS: 1. 2. 3.		ENTRY: 1. 2. 3.	STOP LOSS: 1. 2. 3.		TAKE PROFIT: 1. 2. 3.		TRADE GOAL:	
POWER POINTS: (WHAT WORKED) 1. 2. 3.			END EMOJI:	+, - PIP$/PROFIT$			ACTUAL LOSS/PROFITS	

ACCOUNT:			DATE:	SESSION:			TIME:	
PAIR:	START EMOJI:	ENTRY TIME FRAME:	TRADE TYPE:	RISK TO REWARD RATIO:		RISK % LEVEL (%/$1000)	BALANCE:	
ENTRY CONFIRMATIONS: 1. 2. 3.		ENTRY: 1. 2. 3.	STOP LOSS: 1. 2. 3.		TAKE PROFIT: 1. 2. 3.		TRADE GOAL:	
POWER POINTS: (WHAT WORKED) 1. 2. 3.			END EMOJI:	+, - PIP$/PROFIT$			ACTUAL LOSS/PROFITS	

ACCOUNT:			DATE:	SESSION:			TIME:	
PAIR:	START EMOJI:	ENTRY TIME FRAME:	TRADE TYPE:	RISK TO REWARD RATIO:		RISK % LEVEL (%/$1000)	BALANCE:	
ENTRY CONFIRMATIONS: 1. 2. 3.		ENTRY: 1. 2. 3.	STOP LOSS: 1. 2. 3.		TAKE PROFIT: 1. 2. 3.		TRADE GOAL:	
POWER POINTS: (WHAT WORKED) 1. 2. 3.			END EMOJI:	+, - PIP$/PROFIT$			ACTUAL LOSS/PROFITS	

TRADING JOURNAL

ACCOUNT:			DATE:	SESSION:		TIME:	
PAIR:	START EMOJI:	ENTRY TIME FRAME:	TRADE TYPE:	RISK TO REWARD RATIO:	RISK % LEVEL (%/$1000)	BALANCE:	
ENTRY CONFIRMATIONS: 1. 2. 3.		ENTRY: 1. 2. 3.	STOP LOSS: 1. 2. 3.		TAKE PROFIT: 1. 2. 3.	TRADE GOAL:	
POWER POINTS: (WHAT WORKED) 1. 2. 3.			END EMOJI:	+, - PIP$/PROFIT$		ACTUAL LOSS/PROFITS	

ACCOUNT:			DATE:	SESSION:		TIME:	
PAIR:	START EMOJI:	ENTRY TIME FRAME:	TRADE TYPE:	RISK TO REWARD RATIO:	RISK % LEVEL (%/$1000)	BALANCE:	
ENTRY CONFIRMATIONS: 1. 2. 3.		ENTRY: 1. 2. 3.	STOP LOSS: 1. 2. 3.		TAKE PROFIT: 1. 2. 3.	TRADE GOAL:	
POWER POINTS: (WHAT WORKED) 1. 2. 3.			END EMOJI:	+, - PIP$/PROFIT$		ACTUAL LOSS/PROFITS	

ACCOUNT:			DATE:	SESSION:		TIME:	
PAIR:	START EMOJI:	ENTRY TIME FRAME:	TRADE TYPE:	RISK TO REWARD RATIO:	RISK % LEVEL (%/$1000)	BALANCE:	
ENTRY CONFIRMATIONS: 1. 2. 3.		ENTRY: 1. 2. 3.	STOP LOSS: 1. 2. 3.		TAKE PROFIT: 1. 2. 3.	TRADE GOAL:	
POWER POINTS: (WHAT WORKED) 1. 2. 3.			END EMOJI:	+, - PIP$/PROFIT$		ACTUAL LOSS/PROFITS	

TRADING JOURNAL

ACCOUNT:			DATE:	SESSION:			TIME:
PAIR:	START EMOJI:	ENTRY TIME FRAME:	TRADE TYPE:	RISK TO REWARD RATIO:	RISK % LEVEL (%/$1000)		BALANCE:
ENTRY CONFIRMATIONS: 1. 2. 3.		ENTRY: 1. 2. 3.	STOP LOSS: 1. 2. 3.		TAKE PROFIT: 1. 2. 3.		TRADE GOAL:
POWER POINTS: (WHAT WORKED) 1. 2. 3.			END EMOJI:	+, - PIP$/PROFIT$			ACTUAL LOSS/PROFITS

ACCOUNT:			DATE:	SESSION:			TIME:
PAIR:	START EMOJI:	ENTRY TIME FRAME:	TRADE TYPE:	RISK TO REWARD RATIO:	RISK % LEVEL (%/$1000)		BALANCE:
ENTRY CONFIRMATIONS: 1. 2. 3.		ENTRY: 1. 2. 3.	STOP LOSS: 1. 2. 3.		TAKE PROFIT: 1. 2. 3.		TRADE GOAL:
POWER POINTS: (WHAT WORKED) 1. 2. 3.			END EMOJI:	+, - PIP$/PROFIT$			ACTUAL LOSS/PROFITS

ACCOUNT:			DATE:	SESSION:			TIME:
PAIR:	START EMOJI:	ENTRY TIME FRAME:	TRADE TYPE:	RISK TO REWARD RATIO:	RISK % LEVEL (%/$1000)		BALANCE:
ENTRY CONFIRMATIONS: 1. 2. 3.		ENTRY: 1. 2. 3.	STOP LOSS: 1. 2. 3.		TAKE PROFIT: 1. 2. 3.		TRADE GOAL:
POWER POINTS: (WHAT WORKED) 1. 2. 3.			END EMOJI:	+, - PIP$/PROFIT$			ACTUAL LOSS/PROFITS

TRADING JOURNAL

ACCOUNT:			DATE:	SESSION:		TIME:	
PAIR:	START EMOJI:	ENTRY TIME FRAME:	TRADE TYPE:	RISK TO REWARD RATIO:	RISK % LEVEL (%/$1000)	BALANCE:	
ENTRY CONFIRMATIONS: 1. 2. 3.		ENTRY: 1. 2. 3.	STOP LOSS: 1. 2. 3.		TAKE PROFIT: 1. 2. 3.	TRADE GOAL:	
POWER POINTS: (WHAT WORKED) 1. 2. 3.			END EMOJI:	+, - PIP$/PROFIT$		ACTUAL LOSS/PROFITS	

ACCOUNT:			DATE:	SESSION:		TIME:	
PAIR:	START EMOJI:	ENTRY TIME FRAME:	TRADE TYPE:	RISK TO REWARD RATIO:	RISK % LEVEL (%/$1000)	BALANCE:	
ENTRY CONFIRMATIONS: 1. 2. 3.		ENTRY: 1. 2. 3.	STOP LOSS: 1. 2. 3.		TAKE PROFIT: 1. 2. 3.	TRADE GOAL:	
POWER POINTS: (WHAT WORKED) 1. 2. 3.			END EMOJI:	+, - PIP$/PROFIT$		ACTUAL LOSS/PROFITS	

ACCOUNT:			DATE:	SESSION:		TIME:	
PAIR:	START EMOJI:	ENTRY TIME FRAME:	TRADE TYPE:	RISK TO REWARD RATIO:	RISK % LEVEL (%/$1000)	BALANCE:	
ENTRY CONFIRMATIONS: 1. 2. 3.		ENTRY: 1. 2. 3.	STOP LOSS: 1. 2. 3.		TAKE PROFIT: 1. 2. 3.	TRADE GOAL:	
POWER POINTS: (WHAT WORKED) 1. 2. 3.			END EMOJI:	+, - PIP$/PROFIT$		ACTUAL LOSS/PROFITS	

TRADING JOURNAL

ACCOUNT:			DATE:	SESSION:			TIME:	
PAIR:	START EMOJI:	ENTRY TIME FRAME:	TRADE TYPE:	RISK TO REWARD RATIO:	RISK % LEVEL (%/$1000)		BALANCE:	
ENTRY CONFIRMATIONS: 1. 2. 3.		ENTRY: 1. 2. 3.	STOP LOSS: 1. 2. 3.		TAKE PROFIT: 1. 2. 3.		TRADE GOAL:	
POWER POINTS: (WHAT WORKED) 1. 2. 3.			END EMOJI:	+, - PIP$/PROFIT$			ACTUAL LOSS/PROFITS	

ACCOUNT:			DATE:	SESSION:			TIME:	
PAIR:	START EMOJI:	ENTRY TIME FRAME:	TRADE TYPE:	RISK TO REWARD RATIO:	RISK % LEVEL (%/$1000)		BALANCE:	
ENTRY CONFIRMATIONS: 1. 2. 3.		ENTRY: 1. 2. 3.	STOP LOSS: 1. 2. 3.		TAKE PROFIT: 1. 2. 3.		TRADE GOAL:	
POWER POINTS: (WHAT WORKED) 1. 2. 3.			END EMOJI:	+, - PIP$/PROFIT$			ACTUAL LOSS/PROFITS	

ACCOUNT:			DATE:	SESSION:			TIME:	
PAIR:	START EMOJI:	ENTRY TIME FRAME:	TRADE TYPE:	RISK TO REWARD RATIO:	RISK % LEVEL (%/$1000)		BALANCE:	
ENTRY CONFIRMATIONS: 1. 2. 3.		ENTRY: 1. 2. 3.	STOP LOSS: 1. 2. 3.		TAKE PROFIT: 1. 2. 3.		TRADE GOAL:	
POWER POINTS: (WHAT WORKED) 1. 2. 3.			END EMOJI:	+, - PIP$/PROFIT$			ACTUAL LOSS/PROFITS	

TRADING JOURNAL

ACCOUNT:			DATE:	SESSION:			TIME:
PAIR:	START EMOJI:	ENTRY TIME FRAME:	TRADE TYPE:	RISK TO REWARD RATIO:	RISK % LEVEL (%/$1000)		BALANCE:
ENTRY CONFIRMATIONS: 1. 2. 3.		ENTRY: 1. 2. 3.	STOP LOSS: 1. 2. 3.		TAKE PROFIT: 1. 2. 3.		TRADE GOAL:
POWER POINTS: (WHAT WORKED) 1. 2. 3.			END EMOJI:	+, - PIP$/PROFIT$			ACTUAL LOSS/PROFITS

ACCOUNT:			DATE:	SESSION:			TIME:
PAIR:	START EMOJI:	ENTRY TIME FRAME:	TRADE TYPE:	RISK TO REWARD RATIO:	RISK % LEVEL (%/$1000)		BALANCE:
ENTRY CONFIRMATIONS: 1. 2. 3.		ENTRY: 1. 2. 3.	STOP LOSS: 1. 2. 3.		TAKE PROFIT: 1. 2. 3.		TRADE GOAL:
POWER POINTS: (WHAT WORKED) 1. 2. 3.			END EMOJI:	+, - PIP$/PROFIT$			ACTUAL LOSS/PROFITS

ACCOUNT:			DATE:	SESSION:			TIME:
PAIR:	START EMOJI:	ENTRY TIME FRAME:	TRADE TYPE:	RISK TO REWARD RATIO:	RISK % LEVEL (%/$1000)		BALANCE:
ENTRY CONFIRMATIONS: 1. 2. 3.		ENTRY: 1. 2. 3.	STOP LOSS: 1. 2. 3.		TAKE PROFIT: 1. 2. 3.		TRADE GOAL:
POWER POINTS: (WHAT WORKED) 1. 2. 3.			END EMOJI:	+, - PIP$/PROFIT$			ACTUAL LOSS/PROFITS

TRADING JOURNAL

ACCOUNT:			DATE:	SESSION:		TIME:	
PAIR:	START EMOJI:	ENTRY TIME FRAME:	TRADE TYPE:	RISK TO REWARD RATIO:	RISK % LEVEL (%/$1000)	BALANCE:	
ENTRY CONFIRMATIONS: 1. 2. 3.		ENTRY: 1. 2. 3.	STOP LOSS: 1. 2. 3.		TAKE PROFIT: 1. 2. 3.	TRADE GOAL:	
POWER POINTS: (WHAT WORKED) 1. 2. 3.			END EMOJI:	+, - PIP$/PROFIT$		ACTUAL LOSS/PROFITS	

ACCOUNT:			DATE:	SESSION:		TIME:	
PAIR:	START EMOJI:	ENTRY TIME FRAME:	TRADE TYPE:	RISK TO REWARD RATIO:	RISK % LEVEL (%/$1000)	BALANCE:	
ENTRY CONFIRMATIONS: 1. 2. 3.		ENTRY: 1. 2. 3.	STOP LOSS: 1. 2. 3.		TAKE PROFIT: 1. 2. 3.	TRADE GOAL:	
POWER POINTS: (WHAT WORKED) 1. 2. 3.			END EMOJI:	+, - PIP$/PROFIT$		ACTUAL LOSS/PROFITS	

ACCOUNT:			DATE:	SESSION:		TIME:	
PAIR:	START EMOJI:	ENTRY TIME FRAME:	TRADE TYPE:	RISK TO REWARD RATIO:	RISK % LEVEL (%/$1000)	BALANCE:	
ENTRY CONFIRMATIONS: 1. 2. 3.		ENTRY: 1. 2. 3.	STOP LOSS: 1. 2. 3.		TAKE PROFIT: 1. 2. 3.	TRADE GOAL:	
POWER POINTS: (WHAT WORKED) 1. 2. 3.			END EMOJI:	+, - PIP$/PROFIT$		ACTUAL LOSS/PROFITS	

TRADING JOURNAL

ACCOUNT:			DATE:	SESSION:		TIME:	
PAIR:	START EMOJI:	ENTRY TIME FRAME:	TRADE TYPE:	RISK TO REWARD RATIO:	RISK % LEVEL (%/$1000)	BALANCE:	
ENTRY CONFIRMATIONS: 1. 2. 3.		ENTRY: 1. 2. 3.	STOP LOSS: 1. 2. 3.		TAKE PROFIT: 1. 2. 3.	TRADE GOAL:	
POWER POINTS: (WHAT WORKED) 1. 2. 3.			END EMOJI:	+, - PIP$/PROFIT$		ACTUAL LOSS/PROFITS	

ACCOUNT:			DATE:	SESSION:		TIME:	
PAIR:	START EMOJI:	ENTRY TIME FRAME:	TRADE TYPE:	RISK TO REWARD RATIO:	RISK % LEVEL (%/$1000)	BALANCE:	
ENTRY CONFIRMATIONS: 1. 2. 3.		ENTRY: 1. 2. 3.	STOP LOSS: 1. 2. 3.		TAKE PROFIT: 1. 2. 3.	TRADE GOAL:	
POWER POINTS: (WHAT WORKED) 1. 2. 3.			END EMOJI:	+, - PIP$/PROFIT$		ACTUAL LOSS/PROFITS	

ACCOUNT:			DATE:	SESSION:		TIME:	
PAIR:	START EMOJI:	ENTRY TIME FRAME:	TRADE TYPE:	RISK TO REWARD RATIO:	RISK % LEVEL (%/$1000)	BALANCE:	
ENTRY CONFIRMATIONS: 1. 2. 3.		ENTRY: 1. 2. 3.	STOP LOSS: 1. 2. 3.		TAKE PROFIT: 1. 2. 3.	TRADE GOAL:	
POWER POINTS: (WHAT WORKED) 1. 2. 3.			END EMOJI:	+, - PIP$/PROFIT$		ACTUAL LOSS/PROFITS	

TRADING JOURNAL

ACCOUNT:			DATE:	SESSION:			TIME:	
PAIR:	START EMOJI:	ENTRY TIME FRAME:	TRADE TYPE:	RISK TO REWARD RATIO:	RISK % LEVEL (%/$1000)		BALANCE:	
ENTRY CONFIRMATIONS: 1. 2. 3.		ENTRY: 1. 2. 3.	STOP LOSS: 1. 2. 3.			TAKE PROFIT: 1. 2. 3.	TRADE GOAL:	
POWER POINTS: (WHAT WORKED) 1. 2. 3.			END EMOJI:	+, - PIP$/PROFIT$			ACTUAL LOSS/PROFITS	

ACCOUNT:			DATE:	SESSION:			TIME:	
PAIR:	START EMOJI:	ENTRY TIME FRAME:	TRADE TYPE:	RISK TO REWARD RATIO:	RISK % LEVEL (%/$1000)		BALANCE:	
ENTRY CONFIRMATIONS: 1. 2. 3.		ENTRY: 1. 2. 3.	STOP LOSS: 1. 2. 3.			TAKE PROFIT: 1. 2. 3.	TRADE GOAL:	
POWER POINTS: (WHAT WORKED) 1. 2. 3.			END EMOJI:	+, - PIP$/PROFIT$			ACTUAL LOSS/PROFITS	

ACCOUNT:			DATE:	SESSION:			TIME:	
PAIR:	START EMOJI:	ENTRY TIME FRAME:	TRADE TYPE	RISK TO REWARD RATIO:	RISK % LEVEL (%/$1000)		BALANCE:	
ENTRY CONFIRMATIONS: 1. 2. 3.		ENTRY: 1. 2. 3.	STOP LOSS: 1. 2. 3.			TAKE PROFIT: 1. 2. 3.	TRADE GOAL:	
POWER POINTS: (WHAT WORKED) 1. 2. 3.			END EMOJI:	+, - PIP$/PROFIT$			ACTUAL LOSS/PROFITS	

TRADING JOURNAL

ACCOUNT:			DATE:	SESSION:			TIME:	
PAIR:	START EMOJI:	ENTRY TIME FRAME:	TRADE TYPE:	RISK TO REWARD RATIO:	RISK % LEVEL (%/$1000)		BALANCE:	
ENTRY CONFIRMATIONS: 1. 2. 3.		ENTRY: 1. 2. 3.	STOP LOSS: 1. 2. 3.		TAKE PROFIT: 1. 2. 3.		TRADE GOAL:	
POWER POINTS: (WHAT WORKED) 1. 2. 3.			END EMOJI:	+, - PIP$/PROFIT$			ACTUAL LOSS/PROFITS	

ACCOUNT:			DATE:	SESSION:			TIME:	
PAIR:	START EMOJI:	ENTRY TIME FRAME:	TRADE TYPE:	RISK TO REWARD RATIO:	RISK % LEVEL (%/$1000)		BALANCE:	
ENTRY CONFIRMATIONS: 1. 2. 3.		ENTRY: 1. 2. 3.	STOP LOSS: 1. 2. 3.		TAKE PROFIT: 1. 2. 3.		TRADE GOAL:	
POWER POINTS: (WHAT WORKED) 1. 2. 3.			END EMOJI:	+, - PIP$/PROFIT$			ACTUAL LOSS/PROFITS	

ACCOUNT:			DATE:	SESSION:			TIME:	
PAIR:	START EMOJI:	ENTRY TIME FRAME:	TRADE TYPE:	RISK TO REWARD RATIO:	RISK % LEVEL (%/$1000)		BALANCE:	
ENTRY CONFIRMATIONS: 1. 2. 3.		ENTRY: 1. 2. 3.	STOP LOSS: 1. 2. 3.		TAKE PROFIT: 1. 2. 3.		TRADE GOAL:	
POWER POINTS: (WHAT WORKED) 1. 2. 3.			END EMOJI:	+, - PIP$/PROFIT$			ACTUAL LOSS/PROFITS	

TRADING JOURNAL

ACCOUNT:			DATE:	SESSION:			TIME:
PAIR:	START EMOJI:	ENTRY TIME FRAME:	TRADE TYPE:	RISK TO REWARD RATIO:	RISK % LEVEL (%/$1000)		BALANCE:
ENTRY CONFIRMATIONS: 1. 2. 3.		ENTRY: 1. 2. 3.	STOP LOSS: 1. 2. 3.			TAKE PROFIT: 1. 2. 3.	TRADE GOAL:
POWER POINTS: (WHAT WORKED) 1. 2. 3.			END EMOJI:	+, - PIP$/PROFIT$			ACTUAL LOSS/PROFITS

ACCOUNT:			DATE:	SESSION:			TIME:
PAIR:	START EMOJI:	ENTRY TIME FRAME:	TRADE TYPE:	RISK TO REWARD RATIO:	RISK % LEVEL (%/$1000)		BALANCE:
ENTRY CONFIRMATIONS: 1. 2. 3.		ENTRY: 1. 2. 3.	STOP LOSS: 1. 2. 3.			TAKE PROFIT: 1. 2. 3.	TRADE GOAL:
POWER POINTS: (WHAT WORKED) 1. 2. 3.			END EMOJI:	+, - PIP$/PROFIT$			ACTUAL LOSS/PROFITS

ACCOUNT:			DATE:	SESSION:			TIME:
PAIR:	START EMOJI:	ENTRY TIME FRAME:	TRADE TYPE:	RISK TO REWARD RATIO:	RISK % LEVEL (%/$1000)		BALANCE:
ENTRY CONFIRMATIONS: 1. 2. 3.		ENTRY: 1. 2. 3.	STOP LOSS: 1. 2. 3.			TAKE PROFIT: 1. 2. 3.	TRADE GOAL:
POWER POINTS: (WHAT WORKED) 1. 2. 3.			END EMOJI:	+, - PIP$/PROFIT$			ACTUAL LOSS/PROFITS

TRADING JOURNAL

ACCOUNT:			DATE:	SESSION:		TIME:	
PAIR:	START EMOJI:	ENTRY TIME FRAME:	TRADE TYPE:	RISK TO REWARD RATIO:	RISK % LEVEL (%/$1000)	BALANCE:	
ENTRY CONFIRMATIONS: 1. 2. 3.		ENTRY: 1. 2. 3.	STOP LOSS: 1. 2. 3.		TAKE PROFIT: 1. 2. 3.	TRADE GOAL:	
POWER POINTS: (WHAT WORKED) 1. 2. 3.			END EMOJI:	+, - PIP$/PROFIT$		ACTUAL LOSS/PROFITS	

ACCOUNT:			DATE:	SESSION:		TIME:	
PAIR:	START EMOJI:	ENTRY TIME FRAME:	TRADE TYPE:	RISK TO REWARD RATIO:	RISK % LEVEL (%/$1000)	BALANCE:	
ENTRY CONFIRMATIONS: 1. 2. 3.		ENTRY: 1. 2. 3.	STOP LOSS: 1. 2. 3.		TAKE PROFIT: 1. 2. 3.	TRADE GOAL:	
POWER POINTS: (WHAT WORKED) 1. 2. 3.			END EMOJI:	+, - PIP$/PROFIT$		ACTUAL LOSS/PROFITS	

ACCOUNT:			DATE:	SESSION:		TIME:	
PAIR:	START EMOJI:	ENTRY TIME FRAME:	TRADE TYPE:	RISK TO REWARD RATIO:	RISK % LEVEL (%/$1000)	BALANCE:	
ENTRY CONFIRMATIONS: 1. 2. 3.		ENTRY: 1. 2. 3.	STOP LOSS: 1. 2. 3.		TAKE PROFIT: 1. 2. 3.	TRADE GOAL:	
POWER POINTS: (WHAT WORKED) 1. 2. 3.			END EMOJI:	+, - PIP$/PROFIT$		ACTUAL LOSS/PROFITS	

TRADING JOURNAL

ACCOUNT:			DATE:	SESSION:		TIME:	
PAIR:	START EMOJI:	ENTRY TIME FRAME:	TRADE TYPE:	RISK TO REWARD RATIO:	RISK % LEVEL (%/$1000)	BALANCE:	
ENTRY CONFIRMATIONS: 1. 2. 3.		ENTRY: 1. 2. 3.	STOP LOSS: 1. 2. 3.		TAKE PROFIT: 1. 2. 3.	TRADE GOAL:	
POWER POINTS: (WHAT WORKED) 1. 2. 3.			END EMOJI:	+, - PIP$/PROFIT$		ACTUAL LOSS/PROFITS	

ACCOUNT:			DATE:	SESSION:		TIME:	
PAIR:	START EMOJI:	ENTRY TIME FRAME:	TRADE TYPE:	RISK TO REWARD RATIO:	RISK % LEVEL (%/$1000)	BALANCE:	
ENTRY CONFIRMATIONS: 1. 2. 3.		ENTRY: 1. 2. 3.	STOP LOSS: 1. 2. 3.		TAKE PROFIT: 1. 2. 3.	TRADE GOAL:	
POWER POINTS: (WHAT WORKED) 1. 2. 3.			END EMOJI:	+, - PIP$/PROFIT$		ACTUAL LOSS/PROFITS	

ACCOUNT:			DATE:	SESSION:		TIME:	
PAIR:	START EMOJI:	ENTRY TIME FRAME:	TRADE TYPE:	RISK TO REWARD RATIO:	RISK % LEVEL (%/$1000)	BALANCE:	
ENTRY CONFIRMATIONS: 1. 2. 3.		ENTRY: 1. 2. 3.	STOP LOSS: 1. 2. 3.		TAKE PROFIT: 1. 2. 3.	TRADE GOAL:	
POWER POINTS: (WHAT WORKED) 1. 2. 3.			END EMOJI:	+, - PIP$/PROFIT$		ACTUAL LOSS/PROFITS	

TRADING JOURNAL

ACCOUNT:			DATE:	SESSION:			TIME:
PAIR:	START EMOJI:	ENTRY TIME FRAME:	TRADE TYPE:	RISK TO REWARD RATIO:	RISK % LEVEL (%/$1000)		BALANCE:
ENTRY CONFIRMATIONS: 1. 2. 3.		ENTRY: 1. 2. 3.	STOP LOSS: 1. 2. 3.		TAKE PROFIT: 1. 2. 3.		TRADE GOAL:
POWER POINTS: (WHAT WORKED) 1. 2. 3.			END EMOJI:	+, - PIP$/PROFIT$			ACTUAL LOSS/PROFITS

ACCOUNT:			DATE:	SESSION:			TIME:
PAIR:	START EMOJI:	ENTRY TIME FRAME:	TRADE TYPE:	RISK TO REWARD RATIO:	RISK % LEVEL (%/$1000)		BALANCE:
ENTRY CONFIRMATIONS: 1. 2. 3.		ENTRY: 1. 2. 3.	STOP LOSS: 1. 2. 3.		TAKE PROFIT: 1. 2. 3.		TRADE GOAL:
POWER POINTS: (WHAT WORKED) 1. 2. 3.			END EMOJI:	+, - PIP$/PROFIT$			ACTUAL LOSS/PROFITS

ACCOUNT:			DATE:	SESSION:			TIME:
PAIR:	START EMOJI:	ENTRY TIME FRAME:	TRADE TYPE:	RISK TO REWARD RATIO:	RISK % LEVEL (%/$1000)		BALANCE:
ENTRY CONFIRMATIONS: 1. 2. 3.		ENTRY: 1. 2. 3.	STOP LOSS: 1. 2. 3.		TAKE PROFIT: 1. 2. 3.		TRADE GOAL:
POWER POINTS: (WHAT WORKED) 1. 2. 3.			END EMOJI:	+, - PIP$/PROFIT$			ACTUAL LOSS/PROFITS

Genie Craff

TRADING JOURNAL

ACCOUNT:			DATE:	SESSION:		TIME:	
PAIR:	START EMOJI:	ENTRY TIME FRAME:	TRADE TYPE:	RISK TO REWARD RATIO:	RISK % LEVEL (%/$1000)	BALANCE:	
ENTRY CONFIRMATIONS: 1. 2. 3.		ENTRY: 1. 2. 3.	STOP LOSS: 1. 2. 3.		TAKE PROFIT: 1. 2. 3.	TRADE GOAL:	
POWER POINTS: (WHAT WORKED) 1. 2. 3.			END EMOJI:	+, - PIP$/PROFIT$		ACTUAL LOSS/PROFITS	

ACCOUNT:			DATE:	SESSION:		TIME:	
PAIR:	START EMOJI:	ENTRY TIME FRAME:	TRADE TYPE:	RISK TO REWARD RATIO:	RISK % LEVEL (%/$1000)	BALANCE:	
ENTRY CONFIRMATIONS: 1. 2. 3.		ENTRY: 1. 2. 3.	STOP LOSS: 1. 2. 3.		TAKE PROFIT: 1. 2. 3.	TRADE GOAL:	
POWER POINTS: (WHAT WORKED) 1. 2. 3.			END EMOJI:	+, - PIP$/PROFIT$		ACTUAL LOSS/PROFITS	

ACCOUNT:			DATE:	SESSION:		TIME:	
PAIR:	START EMOJI:	ENTRY TIME FRAME:	TRADE TYPE:	RISK TO REWARD RATIO:	RISK % LEVEL (%/$1000)	BALANCE:	
ENTRY CONFIRMATIONS: 1. 2. 3.		ENTRY: 1. 2. 3.	STOP LOSS: 1. 2. 3.		TAKE PROFIT: 1. 2. 3.	TRADE GOAL:	
POWER POINTS: (WHAT WORKED) 1. 2. 3.			END EMOJI:	+, - PIP$/PROFIT$		ACTUAL LOSS/PROFITS	

72

TRADING JOURNAL

ACCOUNT:				DATE:	SESSION:		TIME:
PAIR:	START EMOJI:	ENTRY TIME FRAME:	TRADE TYPE:	RISK TO REWARD RATIO:	RISK % LEVEL (%/$1000)		BALANCE:
ENTRY CONFIRMATIONS: 1. 2. 3.		ENTRY: 1. 2. 3.	STOP LOSS: 1. 2. 3.		TAKE PROFIT: 1. 2. 3.		TRADE GOAL:
POWER POINTS: (WHAT WORKED) 1. 2. 3.			END EMOJI:	+, - PIP$/PROFIT$		ACTUAL LOSS/PROFITS	

ACCOUNT:				DATE:	SESSION:		TIME:
PAIR:	START EMOJI:	ENTRY TIME FRAME:	TRADE TYPE:	RISK TO REWARD RATIO:	RISK % LEVEL (%/$1000)		BALANCE:
ENTRY CONFIRMATIONS: 1. 2. 3.		ENTRY: 1. 2. 3.	STOP LOSS: 1. 2. 3.		TAKE PROFIT: 1. 2. 3.		TRADE GOAL:
POWER POINTS: (WHAT WORKED) 1. 2. 3.			END EMOJI:	+, - PIP$/PROFIT$		ACTUAL LOSS/PROFITS	

ACCOUNT:				DATE:	SESSION:		TIME:
PAIR:	START EMOJI:	ENTRY TIME FRAME:	TRADE TYPE:	RISK TO REWARD RATIO:	RISK % LEVEL (%/$1000)		BALANCE:
ENTRY CONFIRMATIONS: 1. 2. 3.		ENTRY: 1. 2. 3.	STOP LOSS: 1. 2. 3.		TAKE PROFIT: 1. 2. 3.		TRADE GOAL:
POWER POINTS: (WHAT WORKED) 1. 2. 3.			END EMOJI:	+, - PIP$/PROFIT$		ACTUAL LOSS/PROFITS	

TRADING JOURNAL

ACCOUNT:			DATE:	SESSION:			TIME:	
PAIR:	START EMOJI:	ENTRY TIME FRAME:	TRADE TYPE:	RISK TO REWARD RATIO:	RISK % LEVEL (%/$1000)		BALANCE:	
ENTRY CONFIRMATIONS: 1. 2. 3.		ENTRY: 1. 2. 3.	STOP LOSS: 1. 2. 3.		TAKE PROFIT: 1. 2. 3.		TRADE GOAL:	
POWER POINTS: (WHAT WORKED) 1. 2. 3.			END EMOJI:	+, - PIP$/PROFIT$			ACTUAL LOSS/PROFITS	

ACCOUNT:			DATE:	SESSION:			TIME:	
PAIR:	START EMOJI:	ENTRY TIME FRAME:	TRADE TYPE:	RISK TO REWARD RATIO:	RISK % LEVEL (%/$1000)		BALANCE:	
ENTRY CONFIRMATIONS: 1. 2. 3.		ENTRY: 1. 2. 3.	STOP LOSS: 1. 2. 3.		TAKE PROFIT: 1. 2. 3.		TRADE GOAL:	
POWER POINTS: (WHAT WORKED) 1. 2. 3.			END EMOJI:	+, - PIP$/PROFIT$			ACTUAL LOSS/PROFITS	

ACCOUNT:			DATE:	SESSION:			TIME:	
PAIR:	START EMOJI:	ENTRY TIME FRAME:	TRADE TYPE:	RISK TO REWARD RATIO:	RISK % LEVEL (%/$1000)		BALANCE:	
ENTRY CONFIRMATIONS: 1. 2. 3.		ENTRY: 1. 2. 3.	STOP LOSS: 1. 2. 3.		TAKE PROFIT: 1. 2. 3.		TRADE GOAL:	
POWER POINTS: (WHAT WORKED) 1. 2. 3.			END EMOJI:	+, - PIP$/PROFIT$			ACTUAL LOSS/PROFITS	

TRADING JOURNAL

ACCOUNT:			DATE:	SESSION:			TIME:
PAIR:	START EMOJI:	ENTRY TIME FRAME:	TRADE TYPE:	RISK TO REWARD RATIO:	RISK % LEVEL (%/$1000)		BALANCE:
ENTRY CONFIRMATIONS: 1. 2. 3.		ENTRY: 1. 2. 3.	STOP LOSS: 1. 2. 3.			TAKE PROFIT: 1. 2. 3.	TRADE GOAL:
POWER POINTS: (WHAT WORKED) 1. 2. 3.			END EMOJI:	+, - PIP$/PROFIT$			ACTUAL LOSS/PROFITS

ACCOUNT:			DATE:	SESSION:			TIME:
PAIR:	START EMOJI:	ENTRY TIME FRAME:	TRADE TYPE:	RISK TO REWARD RATIO:	RISK % LEVEL (%/$1000)		BALANCE:
ENTRY CONFIRMATIONS: 1. 2. 3.		ENTRY: 1. 2. 3.	STOP LOSS: 1. 2. 3.			TAKE PROFIT: 1. 2. 3.	TRADE GOAL:
POWER POINTS: (WHAT WORKED) 1. 2. 3.			END EMOJI:	+, - PIP$/PROFIT$			ACTUAL LOSS/PROFITS

ACCOUNT:			DATE:	SESSION:			TIME:
PAIR:	START EMOJI:	ENTRY TIME FRAME:	TRADE TYPE:	RISK TO REWARD RATIO:	RISK % LEVEL (%/$1000)		BALANCE:
ENTRY CONFIRMATIONS: 1. 2. 3.		ENTRY: 1. 2. 3.	STOP LOSS: 1. 2. 3.			TAKE PROFIT: 1. 2. 3.	TRADE GOAL:
POWER POINTS: (WHAT WORKED) 1. 2. 3.			END EMOJI:	+, - PIP$/PROFIT$			ACTUAL LOSS/PROFITS

TRADING JOURNAL

ACCOUNT:			DATE:	SESSION:		TIME:
PAIR:	START EMOJI:	ENTRY TIME FRAME:	TRADE TYPE:	RISK TO REWARD RATIO:	RISK % LEVEL (%/$1000)	BALANCE:
ENTRY CONFIRMATIONS: 1. 2. 3.		ENTRY: 1. 2. 3.	STOP LOSS: 1. 2. 3.		TAKE PROFIT: 1. 2. 3.	TRADE GOAL:
POWER POINTS: (WHAT WORKED) 1. 2. 3.			END EMOJI:	+, - PIP$/PROFIT$		ACTUAL LOSS/PROFITS

ACCOUNT:			DATE:	SESSION:		TIME:
PAIR:	START EMOJI:	ENTRY TIME FRAME:	TRADE TYPE:	RISK TO REWARD RATIO:	RISK % LEVEL (%/$1000)	BALANCE:
ENTRY CONFIRMATIONS: 1. 2. 3.		ENTRY: 1. 2. 3.	STOP LOSS: 1. 2. 3.		TAKE PROFIT: 1. 2. 3.	TRADE GOAL:
POWER POINTS: (WHAT WORKED) 1. 2. 3.			END EMOJI:	+, - PIP$/PROFIT$		ACTUAL LOSS/PROFITS

ACCOUNT:			DATE:	SESSION:		TIME:
PAIR:	START EMOJI:	ENTRY TIME FRAME:	TRADE TYPE:	RISK TO REWARD RATIO:	RISK % LEVEL (%/$1000)	BALANCE:
ENTRY CONFIRMATIONS: 1. 2. 3.		ENTRY: 1. 2. 3.	STOP LOSS: 1. 2. 3.		TAKE PROFIT: 1. 2. 3.	TRADE GOAL:
POWER POINTS: (WHAT WORKED) 1. 2. 3.			END EMOJI:	+, - PIP$/PROFIT$		ACTUAL LOSS/PROFITS

TRADING JOURNAL

ACCOUNT:			DATE:	SESSION:			TIME:
PAIR:	START EMOJI:	ENTRY TIME FRAME:	TRADE TYPE:	RISK TO REWARD RATIO:	RISK % LEVEL (%/$1000)		BALANCE:
ENTRY CONFIRMATIONS: 1. 2. 3.		ENTRY: 1. 2. 3.	STOP LOSS: 1. 2. 3.		TAKE PROFIT: 1. 2. 3.		TRADE GOAL:
POWER POINTS: (WHAT WORKED) 1. 2. 3.			END EMOJI:	+, - PIP$/PROFIT$			ACTUAL LOSS/PROFITS

ACCOUNT:			DATE:	SESSION:			TIME:
PAIR:	START EMOJI:	ENTRY TIME FRAME:	TRADE TYPE:	RISK TO REWARD RATIO:	RISK % LEVEL (%/$1000)		BALANCE:
ENTRY CONFIRMATIONS: 1. 2. 3.		ENTRY: 1. 2. 3.	STOP LOSS: 1. 2. 3.		TAKE PROFIT: 1. 2. 3.		TRADE GOAL:
POWER POINTS: (WHAT WORKED) 1. 2. 3.			END EMOJI:	+, - PIP$/PROFIT$			ACTUAL LOSS/PROFITS

ACCOUNT:			DATE:	SESSION:			TIME:
PAIR:	START EMOJI:	ENTRY TIME FRAME:	TRADE TYPE:	RISK TO REWARD RATIO:	RISK % LEVEL (%/$1000)		BALANCE:
ENTRY CONFIRMATIONS: 1. 2. 3.		ENTRY: 1. 2. 3.	STOP LOSS: 1. 2. 3.		TAKE PROFIT: 1. 2. 3.		TRADE GOAL:
POWER POINTS: (WHAT WORKED) 1. 2. 3.			END EMOJI:	+, - PIP$/PROFIT$			ACTUAL LOSS/PROFITS

TRADING JOURNAL

ACCOUNT:			DATE:	SESSION:			TIME:	
PAIR:	START EMOJI:	ENTRY TIME FRAME:	TRADE TYPE:	RISK TO REWARD RATIO:	RISK % LEVEL (%/$1000)		BALANCE:	
ENTRY CONFIRMATIONS: 1. 2. 3.		ENTRY: 1. 2. 3.	STOP LOSS: 1. 2. 3.			TAKE PROFIT: 1. 2. 3.	TRADE GOAL:	
POWER POINTS: (WHAT WORKED) 1. 2. 3.			END EMOJI:	+, - PIP$/PROFIT$			ACTUAL LOSS/PROFITS	

ACCOUNT:			DATE:	SESSION:			TIME:	
PAIR:	START EMOJI:	ENTRY TIME FRAME:	TRADE TYPE:	RISK TO REWARD RATIO:	RISK % LEVEL (%/$1000)		BALANCE:	
ENTRY CONFIRMATIONS: 1. 2. 3.		ENTRY: 1. 2. 3.	STOP LOSS: 1. 2. 3.			TAKE PROFIT: 1. 2. 3.	TRADE GOAL:	
POWER POINTS: (WHAT WORKED) 1. 2. 3.			END EMOJI:	+, - PIP$/PROFIT$			ACTUAL LOSS/PROFITS	

ACCOUNT:			DATE:	SESSION:			TIME:	
PAIR:	START EMOJI:	ENTRY TIME FRAME:	TRADE TYPE:	RISK TO REWARD RATIO:	RISK % LEVEL (%/$1000)		BALANCE:	
ENTRY CONFIRMATIONS: 1. 2. 3.		ENTRY: 1. 2. 3.	STOP LOSS: 1. 2. 3.			TAKE PROFIT: 1. 2. 3.	TRADE GOAL:	
POWER POINTS: (WHAT WORKED) 1. 2. 3.			END EMOJI:	+, - PIP$/PROFIT$			ACTUAL LOSS/PROFITS	

TRADING JOURNAL

ACCOUNT:			DATE:	SESSION:		TIME:	
PAIR:	START EMOJI:	ENTRY TIME FRAME:	TRADE TYPE:	RISK TO REWARD RATIO:	RISK % LEVEL (%/$1000)	BALANCE:	
ENTRY CONFIRMATIONS: 1. 2. 3.		ENTRY: 1. 2. 3.	STOP LOSS: 1. 2. 3.		TAKE PROFIT: 1. 2. 3.	TRADE GOAL:	
POWER POINTS: (WHAT WORKED) 1. 2. 3.			END EMOJI:	+, - PIP$/PROFIT$		ACTUAL LOSS/PROFITS	

ACCOUNT:			DATE:	SESSION:		TIME:	
PAIR:	START EMOJI:	ENTRY TIME FRAME:	TRADE TYPE:	RISK TO REWARD RATIO:	RISK % LEVEL (%/$1000)	BALANCE:	
ENTRY CONFIRMATIONS: 1. 2. 3.		ENTRY: 1. 2. 3.	STOP LOSS: 1. 2. 3.		TAKE PROFIT: 1. 2. 3.	TRADE GOAL:	
POWER POINTS: (WHAT WORKED) 1. 2. 3.			END EMOJI:	+, - PIP$/PROFIT$		ACTUAL LOSS/PROFITS	

ACCOUNT:			DATE:	SESSION:		TIME:	
PAIR:	START EMOJI:	ENTRY TIME FRAME:	TRADE TYPE:	RISK TO REWARD RATIO:	RISK % LEVEL (%/$1000)	BALANCE:	
ENTRY CONFIRMATIONS: 1. 2. 3.		ENTRY: 1. 2. 3.	STOP LOSS: 1. 2. 3.		TAKE PROFIT: 1. 2. 3.	TRADE GOAL:	
POWER POINTS: (WHAT WORKED) 1. 2. 3.			END EMOJI:	+, - PIP$/PROFIT$		ACTUAL LOSS/PROFITS	

TRADING JOURNAL

ACCOUNT:			DATE:	SESSION:		TIME:	
PAIR:	START EMOJI:	ENTRY TIME FRAME:	TRADE TYPE:	RISK TO REWARD RATIO:	RISK % LEVEL (%/$1000)	BALANCE:	
ENTRY CONFIRMATIONS: 1. 2. 3.		ENTRY: 1. 2. 3.	STOP LOSS: 1. 2. 3.		TAKE PROFIT: 1. 2. 3.	TRADE GOAL:	
POWER POINTS: (WHAT WORKED) 1. 2. 3.			END EMOJI:	+, - PIP$/PROFIT$		ACTUAL LOSS/PROFITS	

ACCOUNT:			DATE:	SESSION:		TIME:	
PAIR:	START EMOJI:	ENTRY TIME FRAME:	TRADE TYPE:	RISK TO REWARD RATIO:	RISK % LEVEL (%/$1000)	BALANCE:	
ENTRY CONFIRMATIONS: 1. 2. 3.		ENTRY: 1. 2. 3.	STOP LOSS: 1. 2. 3.		TAKE PROFIT: 1. 2. 3.	TRADE GOAL:	
POWER POINTS: (WHAT WORKED) 1. 2. 3.			END EMOJI:	+, - PIP$/PROFIT$		ACTUAL LOSS/PROFITS	

ACCOUNT:			DATE:	SESSION:		TIME:	
PAIR:	START EMOJI:	ENTRY TIME FRAME:	TRADE TYPE:	RISK TO REWARD RATIO:	RISK % LEVEL (%/$1000)	BALANCE:	
ENTRY CONFIRMATIONS: 1. 2. 3.		ENTRY: 1. 2. 3.	STOP LOSS: 1. 2. 3.		TAKE PROFIT: 1. 2. 3.	TRADE GOAL:	
POWER POINTS: (WHAT WORKED) 1. 2. 3.			END EMOJI:	+, - PIP$/PROFIT$		ACTUAL LOSS/PROFITS	

TRADING JOURNAL

ACCOUNT:			DATE:	SESSION:			TIME:	
PAIR:	START EMOJI:	ENTRY TIME FRAME:	TRADE TYPE:	RISK TO REWARD RATIO:	RISK % LEVEL (%/$1000)		BALANCE:	
ENTRY CONFIRMATIONS: 1. 2. 3.		ENTRY: 1. 2. 3.	STOP LOSS: 1. 2. 3.			TAKE PROFIT: 1. 2. 3.	TRADE GOAL:	
POWER POINTS: (WHAT WORKED) 1. 2. 3.			END EMOJI:	+, - PIP$/PROFIT$			ACTUAL LOSS/PROFITS	

ACCOUNT:			DATE:	SESSION:			TIME:	
PAIR:	START EMOJI:	ENTRY TIME FRAME:	TRADE TYPE:	RISK TO REWARD RATIO:	RISK % LEVEL (%/$1000)		BALANCE:	
ENTRY CONFIRMATIONS: 1. 2. 3.		ENTRY: 1. 2. 3.	STOP LOSS: 1. 2. 3.			TAKE PROFIT: 1. 2. 3.	TRADE GOAL:	
POWER POINTS: (WHAT WORKED) 1. 2. 3.			END EMOJI:	+, - PIP$/PROFIT$			ACTUAL LOSS/PROFITS	

ACCOUNT:			DATE:	SESSION:			TIME:	
PAIR:	START EMOJI:	ENTRY TIME FRAME:	TRADE TYPE:	RISK TO REWARD RATIO:	RISK % LEVEL (%/$1000)		BALANCE:	
ENTRY CONFIRMATIONS: 1. 2. 3.		ENTRY: 1. 2. 3.	STOP LOSS: 1. 2. 3.			TAKE PROFIT: 1. 2. 3.	TRADE GOAL:	
POWER POINTS: (WHAT WORKED) 1. 2. 3.			END EMOJI:	+, - PIP$/PROFIT$			ACTUAL LOSS/PROFITS	

TRADING JOURNAL

ACCOUNT:			DATE:	SESSION:			TIME:
PAIR:	START EMOJI:	ENTRY TIME FRAME:	TRADE TYPE:	RISK TO REWARD RATIO:	RISK % LEVEL (%/$1000)		BALANCE:
ENTRY CONFIRMATIONS: 1. 2. 3.		ENTRY: 1. 2. 3.	STOP LOSS: 1. 2. 3.			TAKE PROFIT: 1. 2. 3.	TRADE GOAL:
POWER POINTS: (WHAT WORKED) 1. 2. 3.			END EMOJI:	+, - PIP$/PROFIT$			ACTUAL LOSS/PROFITS

ACCOUNT:			DATE:	SESSION:			TIME:
PAIR:	START EMOJI:	ENTRY TIME FRAME:	TRADE TYPE:	RISK TO REWARD RATIO:	RISK % LEVEL (%/$1000)		BALANCE:
ENTRY CONFIRMATIONS: 1. 2. 3.		ENTRY: 1. 2. 3.	STOP LOSS: 1. 2. 3.			TAKE PROFIT: 1. 2. 3.	TRADE GOAL:
POWER POINTS: (WHAT WORKED) 1. 2. 3.			END EMOJI:	+, - PIP$/PROFIT$			ACTUAL LOSS/PROFITS

ACCOUNT:			DATE:	SESSION:			TIME:
PAIR:	START EMOJI:	ENTRY TIME FRAME:	TRADE TYPE:	RISK TO REWARD RATIO:	RISK % LEVEL (%/$1000)		BALANCE:
ENTRY CONFIRMATIONS: 1. 2. 3.		ENTRY: 1. 2. 3.	STOP LOSS: 1. 2. 3.			TAKE PROFIT: 1. 2. 3.	TRADE GOAL:
POWER POINTS: (WHAT WORKED) 1. 2. 3.			END EMOJI:	+, - PIP$/PROFIT$			ACTUAL LOSS/PROFITS

TRADING JOURNAL

ACCOUNT:			DATE:	SESSION:		TIME:	
PAIR:	START EMOJI:	ENTRY TIME FRAME:	TRADE TYPE:	RISK TO REWARD RATIO:	RISK % LEVEL (%/$1000)	BALANCE:	
ENTRY CONFIRMATIONS: 1. 2. 3.		ENTRY: 1. 2. 3.	STOP LOSS: 1. 2. 3.		TAKE PROFIT: 1. 2. 3.	TRADE GOAL:	
POWER POINTS: (WHAT WORKED) 1. 2. 3.			END EMOJI:	+, - PIP$/PROFIT$		ACTUAL LOSS/PROFITS	

ACCOUNT:			DATE:	SESSION:		TIME:	
PAIR:	START EMOJI:	ENTRY TIME FRAME:	TRADE TYPE:	RISK TO REWARD RATIO:	RISK % LEVEL (%/$1000)	BALANCE:	
ENTRY CONFIRMATIONS: 1. 2. 3.		ENTRY: 1. 2. 3.	STOP LOSS: 1. 2. 3.		TAKE PROFIT: 1. 2. 3.	TRADE GOAL:	
POWER POINTS: (WHAT WORKED) 1. 2. 3.			END EMOJI:	+, - PIP$/PROFIT$		ACTUAL LOSS/PROFITS	

ACCOUNT:			DATE:	SESSION:		TIME:	
PAIR:	START EMOJI:	ENTRY TIME FRAME:	TRADE TYPE:	RISK TO REWARD RATIO:	RISK % LEVEL (%/$1000)	BALANCE:	
ENTRY CONFIRMATIONS: 1. 2. 3.		ENTRY: 1. 2. 3.	STOP LOSS: 1. 2. 3.		TAKE PROFIT: 1. 2. 3.	TRADE GOAL:	
POWER POINTS: (WHAT WORKED) 1. 2. 3.			END EMOJI:	+, - PIP$/PROFIT$		ACTUAL LOSS/PROFITS	

TRADING JOURNAL

ACCOUNT:			DATE:	SESSION:			TIME:
PAIR:	START EMOJI:	ENTRY TIME FRAME:	TRADE TYPE:	RISK TO REWARD RATIO:	RISK % LEVEL (%/$1000)		BALANCE:
ENTRY CONFIRMATIONS: 1. 2. 3.		ENTRY: 1. 2. 3.	STOP LOSS: 1. 2. 3.		TAKE PROFIT: 1. 2. 3.		TRADE GOAL:
POWER POINTS: (WHAT WORKED) 1. 2. 3.			END EMOJI:	+, - PIP$/PROFIT$			ACTUAL LOSS/PROFITS

ACCOUNT:			DATE:	SESSION:			TIME:
PAIR:	START EMOJI:	ENTRY TIME FRAME:	TRADE TYPE:	RISK TO REWARD RATIO:	RISK % LEVEL (%/$1000)		BALANCE:
ENTRY CONFIRMATIONS: 1. 2. 3.		ENTRY: 1. 2. 3.	STOP LOSS: 1. 2. 3.		TAKE PROFIT: 1. 2. 3.		TRADE GOAL:
POWER POINTS: (WHAT WORKED) 1. 2. 3.			END EMOJI:	+, - PIP$/PROFIT$			ACTUAL LOSS/PROFITS

ACCOUNT:			DATE:	SESSION:			TIME:
PAIR:	START EMOJI:	ENTRY TIME FRAME:	TRADE TYPE:	RISK TO REWARD RATIO:	RISK % LEVEL (%/$1000)		BALANCE:
ENTRY CONFIRMATIONS: 1. 2. 3.		ENTRY: 1. 2. 3.	STOP LOSS: 1. 2. 3.		TAKE PROFIT: 1. 2. 3.		TRADE GOAL:
POWER POINTS: (WHAT WORKED) 1. 2. 3.			END EMOJI:	+, - PIP$/PROFIT$			ACTUAL LOSS/PROFITS

TRADING JOURNAL

ACCOUNT:			DATE:	SESSION:			TIME:
PAIR:	START EMOJI:	ENTRY TIME FRAME:	TRADE TYPE:	RISK TO REWARD RATIO:	RISK % LEVEL (%/$1000)		BALANCE:
ENTRY CONFIRMATIONS: 1. 2. 3.		ENTRY: 1. 2. 3.	STOP LOSS: 1. 2. 3.		TAKE PROFIT: 1. 2. 3.		TRADE GOAL:
POWER POINTS: (WHAT WORKED) 1. 2. 3.			END EMOJI:	+, - PIP$/PROFIT$			ACTUAL LOSS/PROFITS

ACCOUNT:			DATE:	SESSION:			TIME:
PAIR:	START EMOJI:	ENTRY TIME FRAME:	TRADE TYPE:	RISK TO REWARD RATIO:	RISK % LEVEL (%/$1000)		BALANCE:
ENTRY CONFIRMATIONS: 1. 2. 3.		ENTRY: 1. 2. 3.	STOP LOSS: 1. 2. 3.		TAKE PROFIT: 1. 2. 3.		TRADE GOAL:
POWER POINTS: (WHAT WORKED) 1. 2. 3.			END EMOJI:	+, - PIP$/PROFIT$			ACTUAL LOSS/PROFITS

ACCOUNT:			DATE:	SESSION:			TIME:
PAIR:	START EMOJI:	ENTRY TIME FRAME:	TRADE TYPE:	RISK TO REWARD RATIO:	RISK % LEVEL (%/$1000)		BALANCE:
ENTRY CONFIRMATIONS: 1. 2. 3.		ENTRY: 1. 2. 3.	STOP LOSS: 1. 2. 3.		TAKE PROFIT: 1. 2. 3.		TRADE GOAL:
POWER POINTS: (WHAT WORKED) 1. 2. 3.			END EMOJI:	+, - PIP$/PROFIT$			ACTUAL LOSS/PROFITS

TRADING JOURNAL

ACCOUNT:			DATE:	SESSION:			TIME:	
PAIR:	START EMOJI:	ENTRY TIME FRAME:	TRADE TYPE:	RISK TO REWARD RATIO:	RISK % LEVEL (%/$1000)		BALANCE:	
ENTRY CONFIRMATIONS: 1. 2. 3.		ENTRY: 1. 2. 3.	STOP LOSS: 1. 2. 3.		TAKE PROFIT: 1. 2. 3.		TRADE GOAL:	
POWER POINTS: (WHAT WORKED) 1. 2. 3.			END EMOJI:	+, - PIP$/PROFIT$			ACTUAL LOSS/PROFITS	

ACCOUNT:			DATE:	SESSION:			TIME:	
PAIR:	START EMOJI:	ENTRY TIME FRAME:	TRADE TYPE:	RISK TO REWARD RATIO:	RISK % LEVEL (%/$1000)		BALANCE:	
ENTRY CONFIRMATIONS: 1. 2. 3.		ENTRY: 1. 2. 3.	STOP LOSS: 1. 2. 3.		TAKE PROFIT: 1. 2. 3.		TRADE GOAL:	
POWER POINTS: (WHAT WORKED) 1. 2. 3.			END EMOJI:	+, - PIP$/PROFIT$			ACTUAL LOSS/PROFITS	

ACCOUNT:			DATE:	SESSION:			TIME:	
PAIR:	START EMOJI:	ENTRY TIME FRAME:	TRADE TYPE:	RISK TO REWARD RATIO:	RISK % LEVEL (%/$1000)		BALANCE:	
ENTRY CONFIRMATIONS: 1. 2. 3.		ENTRY: 1. 2. 3.	STOP LOSS: 1. 2. 3.		TAKE PROFIT: 1. 2. 3.		TRADE GOAL:	
POWER POINTS: (WHAT WORKED) 1. 2. 3.			END EMOJI:	+, - PIP$/PROFIT$			ACTUAL LOSS/PROFITS	

TRADING JOURNAL

ACCOUNT:			DATE:	SESSION:		TIME:	
PAIR:	START EMOJI:	ENTRY TIME FRAME:	TRADE TYPE:	RISK TO REWARD RATIO:	RISK % LEVEL (%/$1000)	BALANCE:	
ENTRY CONFIRMATIONS: 1. 2. 3.	ENTRY: 1. 2. 3.		STOP LOSS: 1. 2. 3.		TAKE PROFIT: 1. 2. 3.	TRADE GOAL:	
POWER POINTS: (WHAT WORKED) 1. 2. 3.			END EMOJI:	+, - PIP$/PROFIT$		ACTUAL LOSS/PROFITS	

ACCOUNT:			DATE:	SESSION:		TIME:	
PAIR:	START EMOJI:	ENTRY TIME FRAME:	TRADE TYPE:	RISK TO REWARD RATIO:	RISK % LEVEL (%/$1000)	BALANCE:	
ENTRY CONFIRMATIONS: 1. 2. 3.	ENTRY: 1. 2. 3.		STOP LOSS: 1. 2. 3.		TAKE PROFIT: 1. 2. 3.	TRADE GOAL:	
POWER POINTS: (WHAT WORKED) 1. 2. 3.			END EMOJI:	+, - PIP$/PROFIT$		ACTUAL LOSS/PROFITS	

ACCOUNT:			DATE:	SESSION:		TIME:	
PAIR:	START EMOJI:	ENTRY TIME FRAME:	TRADE TYPE:	RISK TO REWARD RATIO:	RISK % LEVEL (%/$1000)	BALANCE:	
ENTRY CONFIRMATIONS: 1. 2. 3.	ENTRY: 1. 2. 3.		STOP LOSS: 1. 2. 3.		TAKE PROFIT: 1. 2. 3.	TRADE GOAL:	
POWER POINTS: (WHAT WORKED) 1. 2. 3.			END EMOJI:	+, - PIP$/PROFIT$		ACTUAL LOSS/PROFITS	

TRADING JOURNAL

ACCOUNT:			DATE:	SESSION:			TIME:	
PAIR:	START EMOJI:	ENTRY TIME FRAME:	TRADE TYPE:	RISK TO REWARD RATIO:	RISK % LEVEL (%/$1000)		BALANCE:	
ENTRY CONFIRMATIONS: 1. 2. 3.		ENTRY: 1. 2. 3.	STOP LOSS: 1. 2. 3.			TAKE PROFIT: 1. 2. 3.	TRADE GOAL:	
POWER POINTS: (WHAT WORKED) 1. 2. 3.			END EMOJI:	+, - PIP$/PROFIT$			ACTUAL LOSS/PROFITS	

ACCOUNT:			DATE:	SESSION:			TIME:	
PAIR:	START EMOJI:	ENTRY TIME FRAME:	TRADE TYPE:	RISK TO REWARD RATIO:	RISK % LEVEL (%/$1000)		BALANCE:	
ENTRY CONFIRMATIONS: 1. 2. 3.		ENTRY: 1. 2. 3.	STOP LOSS: 1. 2. 3.			TAKE PROFIT: 1. 2. 3.	TRADE GOAL:	
POWER POINTS: (WHAT WORKED) 1. 2. 3.			END EMOJI:	+, - PIP$/PROFIT$			ACTUAL LOSS/PROFITS	

ACCOUNT:			DATE:	SESSION:			TIME:	
PAIR:	START EMOJI:	ENTRY TIME FRAME:	TRADE TYPE:	RISK TO REWARD RATIO:	RISK % LEVEL (%/$1000)		BALANCE:	
ENTRY CONFIRMATIONS: 1. 2. 3.		ENTRY: 1. 2. 3.	STOP LOSS: 1. 2. 3.			TAKE PROFIT: 1. 2. 3.	TRADE GOAL:	
POWER POINTS: (WHAT WORKED) 1. 2. 3.			END EMOJI:	+, - PIP$/PROFIT$			ACTUAL LOSS/PROFITS	

TRADING JOURNAL

ACCOUNT:			DATE:	SESSION:			TIME:
PAIR:	START EMOJI:	ENTRY TIME FRAME:	TRADE TYPE:	RISK TO REWARD RATIO:	RISK % LEVEL (%/$1000)		BALANCE:
ENTRY CONFIRMATIONS: 1. 2. 3.		ENTRY: 1. 2. 3.	STOP LOSS: 1. 2. 3.		TAKE PROFIT: 1. 2. 3.		TRADE GOAL:
POWER POINTS: (WHAT WORKED) 1. 2. 3.			END EMOJI:	+, - PIP$/PROFIT$			ACTUAL LOSS/PROFITS

ACCOUNT:			DATE:	SESSION:			TIME:
PAIR:	START EMOJI:	ENTRY TIME FRAME:	TRADE TYPE:	RISK TO REWARD RATIO:	RISK % LEVEL (%/$1000)		BALANCE:
ENTRY CONFIRMATIONS: 1. 2. 3.		ENTRY: 1. 2. 3.	STOP LOSS: 1. 2. 3.		TAKE PROFIT: 1. 2. 3.		TRADE GOAL:
POWER POINTS: (WHAT WORKED) 1. 2. 3.			END EMOJI:	+, - PIP$/PROFIT$			ACTUAL LOSS/PROFITS

ACCOUNT:			DATE:	SESSION:			TIME:
PAIR:	START EMOJI:	ENTRY TIME FRAME:	TRADE TYPE:	RISK TO REWARD RATIO:	RISK % LEVEL (%/$1000)		BALANCE:
ENTRY CONFIRMATIONS: 1. 2. 3.		ENTRY: 1. 2. 3.	STOP LOSS: 1. 2. 3.		TAKE PROFIT: 1. 2. 3.		TRADE GOAL:
POWER POINTS: (WHAT WORKED) 1. 2. 3.			END EMOJI:	+, - PIP$/PROFIT$			ACTUAL LOSS/PROFITS

TRADING JOURNAL

ACCOUNT:			DATE:	SESSION:			TIME:	
PAIR:	START EMOJI:	ENTRY TIME FRAME:	TRADE TYPE:	RISK TO REWARD RATIO:	RISK % LEVEL (%/$1000)		BALANCE:	
ENTRY CONFIRMATIONS: 1. 2. 3.		ENTRY: 1. 2. 3.	STOP LOSS: 1. 2. 3.			TAKE PROFIT: 1. 2. 3.	TRADE GOAL:	
POWER POINTS: (WHAT WORKED) 1. 2. 3.			END EMOJI:	+, - PIP$/PROFIT$			ACTUAL LOSS/PROFITS	

ACCOUNT:			DATE:	SESSION:			TIME:	
PAIR:	START EMOJI:	ENTRY TIME FRAME:	TRADE TYPE:	RISK TO REWARD RATIO:	RISK % LEVEL (%/$1000)		BALANCE:	
ENTRY CONFIRMATIONS: 1. 2. 3.		ENTRY: 1. 2. 3.	STOP LOSS: 1. 2. 3.			TAKE PROFIT: 1. 2. 3.	TRADE GOAL:	
POWER POINTS: (WHAT WORKED) 1. 2. 3.			END EMOJI:	+, - PIP$/PROFIT$			ACTUAL LOSS/PROFITS	

ACCOUNT:			DATE:	SESSION:			TIME:	
PAIR:	START EMOJI:	ENTRY TIME FRAME:	TRADE TYPE:	RISK TO REWARD RATIO:	RISK % LEVEL (%/$1000)		BALANCE:	
ENTRY CONFIRMATIONS: 1. 2. 3.		ENTRY: 1. 2. 3.	STOP LOSS: 1. 2. 3.			TAKE PROFIT: 1. 2. 3.	TRADE GOAL:	
POWER POINTS: (WHAT WORKED) 1. 2. 3.			END EMOJI:	+, - PIP$/PROFIT$			ACTUAL LOSS/PROFITS	

TRADING JOURNAL

ACCOUNT:			DATE:	SESSION:			TIME:	
PAIR:	START EMOJI:	ENTRY TIME FRAME:	TRADE TYPE:	RISK TO REWARD RATIO:	RISK % LEVEL (%/$1000)		BALANCE:	
ENTRY CONFIRMATIONS: 1. 2. 3.		ENTRY: 1. 2. 3.	STOP LOSS: 1. 2. 3.			TAKE PROFIT: 1. 2. 3.	TRADE GOAL:	
POWER POINTS: (WHAT WORKED) 1. 2. 3.			END EMOJI:	+, - PIP$/PROFIT$			ACTUAL LOSS/PROFITS	

ACCOUNT:			DATE:	SESSION:			TIME:	
PAIR:	START EMOJI:	ENTRY TIME FRAME:	TRADE TYPE:	RISK TO REWARD RATIO:	RISK % LEVEL (%/$1000)		BALANCE:	
ENTRY CONFIRMATIONS: 1. 2. 3.		ENTRY: 1. 2. 3.	STOP LOSS: 1. 2. 3.			TAKE PROFIT: 1. 2. 3.	TRADE GOAL:	
POWER POINTS: (WHAT WORKED) 1. 2. 3.			END EMOJI:	+, - PIP$/PROFIT$			ACTUAL LOSS/PROFITS	

ACCOUNT:			DATE:	SESSION:			TIME:	
PAIR:	START EMOJI:	ENTRY TIME FRAME:	TRADE TYPE:	RISK TO REWARD RATIO:	RISK % LEVEL (%/$1000)		BALANCE:	
ENTRY CONFIRMATIONS: 1. 2. 3.		ENTRY: 1. 2. 3.	STOP LOSS: 1. 2. 3.			TAKE PROFIT: 1. 2. 3.	TRADE GOAL:	
POWER POINTS: (WHAT WORKED) 1. 2. 3.			END EMOJI:	+, - PIP$/PROFIT$			ACTUAL LOSS/PROFITS	

TRADING JOURNAL

ACCOUNT:			DATE:	SESSION:		TIME:	
PAIR:	START EMOJI:	ENTRY TIME FRAME:	TRADE TYPE:	RISK TO REWARD RATIO:	RISK % LEVEL (%/$1000)	BALANCE:	
ENTRY CONFIRMATIONS: 1. 2. 3.		ENTRY: 1. 2. 3.	STOP LOSS: 1. 2. 3.		TAKE PROFIT: 1. 2. 3.	TRADE GOAL:	
POWER POINTS: (WHAT WORKED) 1. 2. 3.			END EMOJI:	+, - PIP$/PROFIT$		ACTUAL LOSS/PROFITS	

ACCOUNT:			DATE:	SESSION:		TIME:	
PAIR:	START EMOJI:	ENTRY TIME FRAME:	TRADE TYPE:	RISK TO REWARD RATIO:	RISK % LEVEL (%/$1000)	BALANCE:	
ENTRY CONFIRMATIONS: 1. 2. 3.		ENTRY: 1. 2. 3.	STOP LOSS: 1. 2. 3.		TAKE PROFIT: 1. 2. 3.	TRADE GOAL:	
POWER POINTS: (WHAT WORKED) 1. 2. 3.			END EMOJI:	+, - PIP$/PROFIT$		ACTUAL LOSS/PROFITS	

ACCOUNT:			DATE:	SESSION:		TIME:	
PAIR:	START EMOJI:	ENTRY TIME FRAME:	TRADE TYPE:	RISK TO REWARD RATIO:	RISK % LEVEL (%/$1000)	BALANCE:	
ENTRY CONFIRMATIONS: 1. 2. 3.		ENTRY: 1. 2. 3.	STOP LOSS: 1. 2. 3.		TAKE PROFIT: 1. 2. 3.	TRADE GOAL:	
POWER POINTS: (WHAT WORKED) 1. 2. 3.			END EMOJI:	+, - PIP$/PROFIT$		ACTUAL LOSS/PROFITS	

TRADING JOURNAL

ACCOUNT:			DATE:	SESSION:		TIME:	
PAIR:	START EMOJI:	ENTRY TIME FRAME:	TRADE TYPE:	RISK TO REWARD RATIO:	RISK % LEVEL (%/$1000)	BALANCE:	
ENTRY CONFIRMATIONS: 1. 2. 3.		ENTRY: 1. 2. 3.	STOP LOSS: 1. 2. 3.		TAKE PROFIT: 1. 2. 3.	TRADE GOAL:	
POWER POINTS: (WHAT WORKED) 1. 2. 3.			END EMOJI:	+, - PIP$/PROFIT$		ACTUAL LOSS/PROFITS	

ACCOUNT:			DATE:	SESSION:		TIME:	
PAIR:	START EMOJI:	ENTRY TIME FRAME:	TRADE TYPE:	RISK TO REWARD RATIO:	RISK % LEVEL (%/$1000)	BALANCE:	
ENTRY CONFIRMATIONS: 1. 2. 3.		ENTRY: 1. 2. 3.	STOP LOSS: 1. 2. 3.		TAKE PROFIT: 1. 2. 3.	TRADE GOAL:	
POWER POINTS: (WHAT WORKED) 1. 2. 3.			END EMOJI:	+, - PIP$/PROFIT$		ACTUAL LOSS/PROFITS	

ACCOUNT:			DATE:	SESSION:		TIME:	
PAIR:	START EMOJI:	ENTRY TIME FRAME:	TRADE TYPE:	RISK TO REWARD RATIO:	RISK % LEVEL (%/$1000)	BALANCE:	
ENTRY CONFIRMATIONS: 1. 2. 3.		ENTRY: 1. 2. 3.	STOP LOSS: 1. 2. 3.		TAKE PROFIT: 1. 2. 3.	TRADE GOAL:	
POWER POINTS: (WHAT WORKED) 1. 2. 3.			END EMOJI:	+, - PIP$/PROFIT$		ACTUAL LOSS/PROFITS	

TRADING JOURNAL

ACCOUNT:			DATE:	SESSION:			TIME:	
PAIR:	START EMOJI:	ENTRY TIME FRAME:	TRADE TYPE:	RISK TO REWARD RATIO:	RISK % LEVEL (%/$1000)		BALANCE:	
ENTRY CONFIRMATIONS: 1. 2. 3.		ENTRY: 1. 2. 3.	STOP LOSS: 1. 2. 3.		TAKE PROFIT: 1. 2. 3.		TRADE GOAL:	
POWER POINTS: (WHAT WORKED) 1. 2. 3.			END EMOJI:	+, - PIP$/PROFIT$			ACTUAL LOSS/PROFITS	

ACCOUNT:			DATE:	SESSION:			TIME:	
PAIR:	START EMOJI:	ENTRY TIME FRAME:	TRADE TYPE:	RISK TO REWARD RATIO:	RISK % LEVEL (%/$1000)		BALANCE:	
ENTRY CONFIRMATIONS: 1. 2. 3.		ENTRY: 1. 2. 3.	STOP LOSS: 1. 2. 3.		TAKE PROFIT: 1. 2. 3.		TRADE GOAL:	
POWER POINTS: (WHAT WORKED) 1. 2. 3.			END EMOJI:	+, - PIP$/PROFIT$			ACTUAL LOSS/PROFITS	

ACCOUNT:			DATE:	SESSION:			TIME:	
PAIR:	START EMOJI:	ENTRY TIME FRAME:	TRADE TYPE:	RISK TO REWARD RATIO:	RISK % LEVEL (%/$1000)		BALANCE:	
ENTRY CONFIRMATIONS: 1. 2. 3.		ENTRY: 1. 2. 3.	STOP LOSS: 1. 2. 3.		TAKE PROFIT: 1. 2. 3.		TRADE GOAL:	
POWER POINTS: (WHAT WORKED) 1. 2. 3.			END EMOJI:	+, - PIP$/PROFIT$			ACTUAL LOSS/PROFITS	

TRADING JOURNAL

ACCOUNT:			DATE:	SESSION:			TIME:
PAIR:	START EMOJI:	ENTRY TIME FRAME:	TRADE TYPE:	RISK TO REWARD RATIO:	RISK % LEVEL (%/$1000)		BALANCE:
ENTRY CONFIRMATIONS: 1. 2. 3.		ENTRY: 1. 2. 3.	STOP LOSS: 1. 2. 3.		TAKE PROFIT: 1. 2. 3.		TRADE GOAL:
POWER POINTS: (WHAT WORKED) 1. 2. 3.			END EMOJI:	+, - PIP$/PROFIT$			ACTUAL LOSS/PROFITS

ACCOUNT:			DATE:	SESSION:			TIME:
PAIR:	START EMOJI:	ENTRY TIME FRAME:	TRADE TYPE:	RISK TO REWARD RATIO:	RISK % LEVEL (%/$1000)		BALANCE:
ENTRY CONFIRMATIONS: 1. 2. 3.		ENTRY: 1. 2. 3.	STOP LOSS: 1. 2. 3.		TAKE PROFIT: 1. 2. 3.		TRADE GOAL:
POWER POINTS: (WHAT WORKED) 1. 2. 3.			END EMOJI:	+, - PIP$/PROFIT$			ACTUAL LOSS/PROFITS

ACCOUNT:			DATE:	SESSION:			TIME:
PAIR:	START EMOJI:	ENTRY TIME FRAME:	TRADE TYPE:	RISK TO REWARD RATIO:	RISK % LEVEL (%/$1000)		BALANCE:
ENTRY CONFIRMATIONS: 1. 2. 3.		ENTRY: 1. 2. 3.	STOP LOSS: 1. 2. 3.		TAKE PROFIT: 1. 2. 3.		TRADE GOAL:
POWER POINTS: (WHAT WORKED) 1. 2. 3.			END EMOJI:	+, - PIP$/PROFIT$			ACTUAL LOSS/PROFITS

TRADING JOURNAL

ACCOUNT:			DATE:	SESSION:			TIME:	
PAIR:	START EMOJI:	ENTRY TIME FRAME:	TRADE TYPE:	RISK TO REWARD RATIO:		RISK % LEVEL (%/$1000)	BALANCE:	
ENTRY CONFIRMATIONS: 1. 2. 3.		ENTRY: 1. 2. 3.	STOP LOSS: 1. 2. 3.			TAKE PROFIT: 1. 2. 3.	TRADE GOAL:	
POWER POINTS: (WHAT WORKED) 1. 2. 3.			END EMOJI:	+, - PIP$/PROFIT$			ACTUAL LOSS/PROFITS	

ACCOUNT:			DATE:	SESSION:			TIME:	
PAIR:	START EMOJI:	ENTRY TIME FRAME:	TRADE TYPE:	RISK TO REWARD RATIO:		RISK % LEVEL (%/$1000)	BALANCE:	
ENTRY CONFIRMATIONS: 1. 2. 3.		ENTRY: 1. 2. 3.	STOP LOSS: 1. 2. 3.			TAKE PROFIT: 1. 2. 3.	TRADE GOAL:	
POWER POINTS: (WHAT WORKED) 1. 2. 3.			END EMOJI:	+, - PIP$/PROFIT$			ACTUAL LOSS/PROFITS	

ACCOUNT:			DATE:	SESSION:			TIME:	
PAIR:	START EMOJI:	ENTRY TIME FRAME:	TRADE TYPE:	RISK TO REWARD RATIO:		RISK % LEVEL (%/$1000)	BALANCE:	
ENTRY CONFIRMATIONS: 1. 2. 3.		ENTRY: 1. 2. 3.	STOP LOSS: 1. 2. 3.			TAKE PROFIT: 1. 2. 3.	TRADE GOAL:	
POWER POINTS: (WHAT WORKED) 1. 2. 3.			END EMOJI:	+, - PIP$/PROFIT$			ACTUAL LOSS/PROFITS	

TRADING JOURNAL

ACCOUNT:			DATE:	SESSION:			TIME:
PAIR:	START EMOJI:	ENTRY TIME FRAME:	TRADE TYPE:	RISK TO REWARD RATIO:	RISK % LEVEL (%/$1000)		BALANCE:
ENTRY CONFIRMATIONS: 1. 2. 3.		ENTRY: 1. 2. 3.	STOP LOSS: 1. 2. 3.		TAKE PROFIT: 1. 2. 3.		TRADE GOAL:
POWER POINTS: (WHAT WORKED) 1. 2. 3.			END EMOJI:	+, - PIP$/PROFIT$			ACTUAL LOSS/PROFITS

ACCOUNT:			DATE:	SESSION:			TIME:
PAIR:	START EMOJI:	ENTRY TIME FRAME:	TRADE TYPE:	RISK TO REWARD RATIO:	RISK % LEVEL (%/$1000)		BALANCE:
ENTRY CONFIRMATIONS: 1. 2. 3.		ENTRY: 1. 2. 3.	STOP LOSS: 1. 2. 3.		TAKE PROFIT: 1. 2. 3.		TRADE GOAL:
POWER POINTS: (WHAT WORKED) 1. 2. 3.			END EMOJI:	+, - PIP$/PROFIT$			ACTUAL LOSS/PROFITS

ACCOUNT:			DATE:	SESSION:			TIME:
PAIR:	START EMOJI:	ENTRY TIME FRAME:	TRADE TYPE:	RISK TO REWARD RATIO:	RISK % LEVEL (%/$1000)		BALANCE:
ENTRY CONFIRMATIONS: 1. 2. 3.		ENTRY: 1. 2. 3.	STOP LOSS: 1. 2. 3.		TAKE PROFIT: 1. 2. 3.		TRADE GOAL:
POWER POINTS: (WHAT WORKED) 1. 2. 3.			END EMOJI:	+, - PIP$/PROFIT$			ACTUAL LOSS/PROFITS

TRADING JOURNAL

ACCOUNT:			DATE:	SESSION:			TIME:	
PAIR:	START EMOJI:	ENTRY TIME FRAME:	TRADE TYPE:	RISK TO REWARD RATIO:	RISK % LEVEL (%/$1000)		BALANCE:	
ENTRY CONFIRMATIONS: 1. 2. 3.		ENTRY: 1. 2. 3.	STOP LOSS: 1. 2. 3.			TAKE PROFIT: 1. 2. 3.	TRADE GOAL:	
POWER POINTS: (WHAT WORKED) 1. 2. 3.			END EMOJI:	+, - PIP$/PROFIT$			ACTUAL LOSS/PROFITS	

ACCOUNT:			DATE:	SESSION:			TIME:	
PAIR:	START EMOJI:	ENTRY TIME FRAME:	TRADE TYPE:	RISK TO REWARD RATIO:	RISK % LEVEL (%/$1000)		BALANCE:	
ENTRY CONFIRMATIONS: 1. 2. 3.		ENTRY: 1. 2. 3.	STOP LOSS: 1. 2. 3.			TAKE PROFIT: 1. 2. 3.	TRADE GOAL:	
POWER POINTS: (WHAT WORKED) 1. 2. 3.			END EMOJI:	+, - PIP$/PROFIT$			ACTUAL LOSS/PROFITS	

ACCOUNT:			DATE:	SESSION:			TIME:	
PAIR:	START EMOJI:	ENTRY TIME FRAME:	TRADE TYPE:	RISK TO REWARD RATIO:	RISK % LEVEL (%/$1000)		BALANCE:	
ENTRY CONFIRMATIONS: 1. 2. 3.		ENTRY: 1. 2. 3.	STOP LOSS: 1. 2. 3.			TAKE PROFIT: 1. 2. 3.	TRADE GOAL:	
POWER POINTS: (WHAT WORKED) 1. 2. 3.			END EMOJI:	+, - PIP$/PROFIT$			ACTUAL LOSS/PROFITS	

TRADING JOURNAL

ACCOUNT:			DATE:	SESSION:			TIME:
PAIR:	START EMOJI:	ENTRY TIME FRAME:	TRADE TYPE:	RISK TO REWARD RATIO:	RISK % LEVEL (%/$1000)		BALANCE:
ENTRY CONFIRMATIONS: 1. 2. 3.		ENTRY: 1. 2. 3.	STOP LOSS: 1. 2. 3.			TAKE PROFIT: 1. 2. 3.	TRADE GOAL:
POWER POINTS: (WHAT WORKED) 1. 2. 3.			END EMOJI:	+, - PIP$/PROFIT$			ACTUAL LOSS/PROFITS

ACCOUNT:			DATE:	SESSION:			TIME:
PAIR:	START EMOJI:	ENTRY TIME FRAME:	TRADE TYPE:	RISK TO REWARD RATIO:	RISK % LEVEL (%/$1000)		BALANCE:
ENTRY CONFIRMATIONS: 1. 2. 3.		ENTRY: 1. 2. 3.	STOP LOSS: 1. 2. 3.			TAKE PROFIT: 1. 2. 3.	TRADE GOAL:
POWER POINTS: (WHAT WORKED) 1. 2. 3.			END EMOJI:	+, - PIP$/PROFIT$			ACTUAL LOSS/PROFITS

ACCOUNT:			DATE:	SESSION:			TIME:
PAIR:	START EMOJI:	ENTRY TIME FRAME:	TRADE TYPE:	RISK TO REWARD RATIO:	RISK % LEVEL (%/$1000)		BALANCE:
ENTRY CONFIRMATIONS: 1. 2. 3.		ENTRY: 1. 2. 3.	STOP LOSS: 1. 2. 3.			TAKE PROFIT: 1. 2. 3.	TRADE GOAL:
POWER POINTS: (WHAT WORKED) 1. 2. 3.			END EMOJI:	+, - PIP$/PROFIT$			ACTUAL LOSS/PROFITS

PART 2: AUTHENTIC TRADING (FOR REAL)

"Life is 10% what happens and 90% how I react to it."
~~Charles Swindoll

There is a good chance that your trading experience has already morphed into a real trading account, funded by you. There are most likely a number of trades you have placed with this account. A regular review of your overall performance may reveal additional clues and information to strengthen your trading performance.

As a checkup on your overall FOREX trading experience, the following questions may provide food for thought.

1. Profitable Trading Wisdom is mine because:

I Read:

_____

_____

I Listened to:

_____

_____

I Watched:

_____

_____

I learned:

_____

_____

Today, I will:

_____

_____

START...

_____

_____

CONTINUE...

_____

_____

STOP...

_____

_____

My Broker works because:

_____

_____

GRATITUDE POWER Notes:

_____

_____

_____

_____

_____

_____

_____

_____

_____

_____

_____

_____

"Not everything that can be counted counts, and not
everything that counts can be counted."
~~Albert Einstein

TRADING JOURNAL

ACCOUNT:			DATE:	SESSION:			TIME:	
PAIR:	START EMOJI:	ENTRY TIME FRAME:	TRADE TYPE:	RISK TO REWARD RATIO:	RISK % LEVEL (%/$1000)		BALANCE:	
ENTRY CONFIRMATIONS: 1. 2. 3.		ENTRY: 1. 2. 3.	STOP LOSS: 1. 2. 3.			TAKE PROFIT: 1. 2. 3.	TRADE GOAL:	
POWER POINTS: (WHAT WORKED) 1. 2. 3.			END EMOJI:	+, - PIP$/PROFIT$			ACTUAL LOSS/PROFITS	

ACCOUNT:			DATE:	SESSION:			TIME:	
PAIR:	START EMOJI:	ENTRY TIME FRAME:	TRADE TYPE:	RISK TO REWARD RATIO:	RISK % LEVEL (%/$1000)		BALANCE:	
ENTRY CONFIRMATIONS: 1. 2. 3.		ENTRY: 1. 2. 3.	STOP LOSS: 1. 2. 3.			TAKE PROFIT: 1. 2. 3.	TRADE GOAL:	
POWER POINTS: (WHAT WORKED) 1. 2. 3.			END EMOJI:	+, - PIP$/PROFIT$			ACTUAL LOSS/PROFITS	

ACCOUNT:			DATE:	SESSION:			TIME:	
PAIR:	START EMOJI:	ENTRY TIME FRAME:	TRADE TYPE:	RISK TO REWARD RATIO:	RISK % LEVEL (%/$1000)		BALANCE:	
ENTRY CONFIRMATIONS: 1. 2. 3.		ENTRY: 1. 2. 3.	STOP LOSS: 1. 2. 3.			TAKE PROFIT: 1. 2. 3.	TRADE GOAL:	
POWER POINTS: (WHAT WORKED) 1. 2. 3.			END EMOJI:	+, - PIP$/PROFIT$			ACTUAL LOSS/PROFITS	

TRADING JOURNAL

ACCOUNT:			DATE:	SESSION:			TIME:
PAIR:	START EMOJI:	ENTRY TIME FRAME:	TRADE TYPE:	RISK TO REWARD RATIO:	RISK % LEVEL (%/$1000)		BALANCE:
ENTRY CONFIRMATIONS: 1. 2. 3.		ENTRY: 1. 2. 3.	STOP LOSS: 1. 2. 3.		TAKE PROFIT: 1. 2. 3.		TRADE GOAL:
POWER POINTS: (WHAT WORKED) 1. 2. 3.			END EMOJI:	+, - PIP$/PROFIT$			ACTUAL LOSS/PROFITS

ACCOUNT:			DATE:	SESSION:			TIME:
PAIR:	START EMOJI:	ENTRY TIME FRAME:	TRADE TYPE:	RISK TO REWARD RATIO:	RISK % LEVEL (%/$1000)		BALANCE:
ENTRY CONFIRMATIONS: 1. 2. 3.		ENTRY: 1. 2. 3.	STOP LOSS: 1. 2. 3.		TAKE PROFIT: 1. 2. 3.		TRADE GOAL:
POWER POINTS: (WHAT WORKED) 1. 2. 3.			END EMOJI:	+, - PIP$/PROFIT$			ACTUAL LOSS/PROFITS

ACCOUNT:			DATE:	SESSION:			TIME:
PAIR:	START EMOJI:	ENTRY TIME FRAME:	TRADE TYPE:	RISK TO REWARD RATIO:	RISK % LEVEL (%/$1000)		BALANCE:
ENTRY CONFIRMATIONS: 1. 2. 3.		ENTRY: 1. 2. 3.	STOP LOSS: 1. 2. 3.		TAKE PROFIT: 1. 2. 3.		TRADE GOAL:
POWER POINTS: (WHAT WORKED) 1. 2. 3.			END EMOJI:	+, - PIP$/PROFIT$			ACTUAL LOSS/PROFITS

TRADING JOURNAL

ACCOUNT:			DATE:	SESSION:			TIME:
PAIR:	START EMOJI:	ENTRY TIME FRAME:	TRADE TYPE:	RISK TO REWARD RATIO:	RISK % LEVEL (%/$1000)		BALANCE:
ENTRY CONFIRMATIONS: 1. 2. 3.		ENTRY: 1. 2. 3.	STOP LOSS: 1. 2. 3.		TAKE PROFIT: 1. 2. 3.		TRADE GOAL:
POWER POINTS: (WHAT WORKED) 1. 2. 3.			END EMOJI:	+, - PIP$/PROFIT$			ACTUAL LOSS/PROFITS

ACCOUNT:			DATE:	SESSION:			TIME:
PAIR:	START EMOJI:	ENTRY TIME FRAME:	TRADE TYPE:	RISK TO REWARD RATIO:	RISK % LEVEL (%/$1000)		BALANCE:
ENTRY CONFIRMATIONS: 1. 2. 3.		ENTRY: 1. 2. 3.	STOP LOSS: 1. 2. 3.		TAKE PROFIT: 1. 2. 3.		TRADE GOAL:
POWER POINTS: (WHAT WORKED) 1. 2. 3.			END EMOJI:	+, - PIP$/PROFIT$			ACTUAL LOSS/PROFITS

ACCOUNT:			DATE:	SESSION:			TIME:
PAIR:	START EMOJI:	ENTRY TIME FRAME:	TRADE TYPE:	RISK TO REWARD RATIO:	RISK % LEVEL (%/$1000)		BALANCE:
ENTRY CONFIRMATIONS: 1. 2. 3.		ENTRY: 1. 2. 3.	STOP LOSS: 1. 2. 3.		TAKE PROFIT: 1. 2. 3.		TRADE GOAL:
POWER POINTS: (WHAT WORKED) 1. 2. 3.			END EMOJI:	+, - PIP$/PROFIT$			ACTUAL LOSS/PROFITS

TRADING JOURNAL

ACCOUNT:			DATE:	SESSION:		TIME:	
PAIR:	START EMOJI:	ENTRY TIME FRAME:	TRADE TYPE:	RISK TO REWARD RATIO:	RISK % LEVEL (%/$1000)	BALANCE:	
ENTRY CONFIRMATIONS: 1. 2. 3.		ENTRY: 1. 2. 3.	STOP LOSS: 1. 2. 3.		TAKE PROFIT: 1. 2. 3.	TRADE GOAL:	
POWER POINTS: (WHAT WORKED) 1. 2. 3.			END EMOJI:	+, - PIP$/PROFIT$		ACTUAL LOSS/PROFITS	

ACCOUNT:			DATE:	SESSION:		TIME:	
PAIR:	START EMOJI:	ENTRY TIME FRAME:	TRADE TYPE:	RISK TO REWARD RATIO:	RISK % LEVEL (%/$1000)	BALANCE:	
ENTRY CONFIRMATIONS: 1. 2. 3.		ENTRY: 1. 2. 3.	STOP LOSS: 1. 2. 3.		TAKE PROFIT: 1. 2. 3.	TRADE GOAL:	
POWER POINTS: (WHAT WORKED) 1. 2. 3.			END EMOJI:	+, - PIP$/PROFIT$		ACTUAL LOSS/PROFITS	

ACCOUNT:			DATE:	SESSION:		TIME:	
PAIR:	START EMOJI:	ENTRY TIME FRAME:	TRADE TYPE:	RISK TO REWARD RATIO:	RISK % LEVEL (%/$1000)	BALANCE:	
ENTRY CONFIRMATIONS: 1. 2. 3.		ENTRY: 1. 2. 3.	STOP LOSS: 1. 2. 3.		TAKE PROFIT: 1. 2. 3.	TRADE GOAL:	
POWER POINTS: (WHAT WORKED) 1. 2. 3.			END EMOJI:	+, - PIP$/PROFIT$		ACTUAL LOSS/PROFITS	

TRADING JOURNAL

ACCOUNT:			DATE:	SESSION:		TIME:	
PAIR:	START EMOJI:	ENTRY TIME FRAME:	TRADE TYPE:	RISK TO REWARD RATIO:	RISK % LEVEL (%/$1000)	BALANCE:	
ENTRY CONFIRMATIONS: 1. 2. 3.		ENTRY: 1. 2. 3.	STOP LOSS: 1. 2. 3.		TAKE PROFIT: 1. 2. 3.	TRADE GOAL:	
POWER POINTS: (WHAT WORKED) 1. 2. 3.			END EMOJI:	+, - PIP$/PROFIT$		ACTUAL LOSS/PROFITS	

ACCOUNT:			DATE:	SESSION:		TIME:	
PAIR:	START EMOJI:	ENTRY TIME FRAME:	TRADE TYPE:	RISK TO REWARD RATIO:	RISK % LEVEL (%/$1000)	BALANCE:	
ENTRY CONFIRMATIONS: 1. 2. 3.		ENTRY: 1. 2. 3.	STOP LOSS: 1. 2. 3.		TAKE PROFIT: 1. 2. 3.	TRADE GOAL:	
POWER POINTS: (WHAT WORKED) 1. 2. 3.			END EMOJI:	+, - PIP$/PROFIT$		ACTUAL LOSS/PROFITS	

ACCOUNT:			DATE:	SESSION:		TIME:	
PAIR:	START EMOJI:	ENTRY TIME FRAME:	TRADE TYPE:	RISK TO REWARD RATIO:	RISK % LEVEL (%/$1000)	BALANCE:	
ENTRY CONFIRMATIONS: 1. 2. 3.		ENTRY: 1. 2. 3.	STOP LOSS: 1. 2. 3.		TAKE PROFIT: 1. 2. 3.	TRADE GOAL:	
POWER POINTS: (WHAT WORKED) 1. 2. 3.			END EMOJI:	+, - PIP$/PROFIT$		ACTUAL LOSS/PROFITS	

TRADING JOURNAL

ACCOUNT:			DATE:	SESSION:		TIME:	
PAIR:	START EMOJI:	ENTRY TIME FRAME:	TRADE TYPE:	RISK TO REWARD RATIO:	RISK % LEVEL (%/$1000)	BALANCE:	
ENTRY CONFIRMATIONS: 1. 2. 3.		ENTRY: 1. 2. 3.	STOP LOSS: 1. 2. 3.		TAKE PROFIT: 1. 2. 3.	TRADE GOAL:	
POWER POINTS: (WHAT WORKED) 1. 2. 3.			END EMOJI:	+, - PIP$/PROFIT$		ACTUAL LOSS/PROFITS	

ACCOUNT:			DATE:	SESSION:		TIME:	
PAIR:	START EMOJI:	ENTRY TIME FRAME:	TRADE TYPE:	RISK TO REWARD RATIO:	RISK % LEVEL (%/$1000)	BALANCE:	
ENTRY CONFIRMATIONS: 1. 2. 3.		ENTRY: 1. 2. 3.	STOP LOSS: 1. 2. 3.		TAKE PROFIT: 1. 2. 3.	TRADE GOAL:	
POWER POINTS: (WHAT WORKED) 1. 2. 3.			END EMOJI:	+, - PIP$/PROFIT$		ACTUAL LOSS/PROFITS	

ACCOUNT:			DATE:	SESSION:		TIME:	
PAIR:	START EMOJI:	ENTRY TIME FRAME:	TRADE TYPE:	RISK TO REWARD RATIO:	RISK % LEVEL (%/$1000)	BALANCE:	
ENTRY CONFIRMATIONS: 1. 2. 3.		ENTRY: 1. 2. 3.	STOP LOSS: 1. 2. 3.		TAKE PROFIT: 1. 2. 3.	TRADE GOAL:	
POWER POINTS: (WHAT WORKED) 1. 2. 3.			END EMOJI:	+, - PIP$/PROFIT$		ACTUAL LOSS/PROFITS	

TRADING JOURNAL

ACCOUNT:			DATE:	SESSION:		TIME:	
PAIR:	START EMOJI:	ENTRY TIME FRAME:	TRADE TYPE:	RISK TO REWARD RATIO:	RISK % LEVEL (%/$1000)	BALANCE:	
ENTRY CONFIRMATIONS: 1. 2. 3.		ENTRY: 1. 2. 3.	STOP LOSS: 1. 2. 3.		TAKE PROFIT: 1. 2. 3.	TRADE GOAL:	
POWER POINTS: (WHAT WORKED) 1. 2. 3.			END EMOJI:	+, - PIP$/PROFIT$		ACTUAL LOSS/PROFITS	

ACCOUNT:			DATE:	SESSION:		TIME:	
PAIR:	START EMOJI:	ENTRY TIME FRAME:	TRADE TYPE:	RISK TO REWARD RATIO:	RISK % LEVEL (%/$1000)	BALANCE:	
ENTRY CONFIRMATIONS: 1. 2. 3.		ENTRY: 1. 2. 3.	STOP LOSS: 1. 2. 3.		TAKE PROFIT: 1. 2. 3.	TRADE GOAL:	
POWER POINTS: (WHAT WORKED) 1. 2. 3.			END EMOJI:	+, - PIP$/PROFIT$		ACTUAL LOSS/PROFITS	

ACCOUNT:			DATE:	SESSION:		TIME:	
PAIR:	START EMOJI:	ENTRY TIME FRAME:	TRADE TYPE:	RISK TO REWARD RATIO:	RISK % LEVEL (%/$1000)	BALANCE:	
ENTRY CONFIRMATIONS: 1. 2. 3.		ENTRY: 1. 2. 3.	STOP LOSS: 1. 2. 3.		TAKE PROFIT: 1. 2. 3.	TRADE GOAL:	
POWER POINTS: (WHAT WORKED) 1. 2. 3.			END EMOJI:	+, - PIP$/PROFIT$		ACTUAL LOSS/PROFITS	

TRADING JOURNAL

ACCOUNT:			DATE:	SESSION:			TIME:	
PAIR:	START EMOJI:	ENTRY TIME FRAME:	TRADE TYPE:	RISK TO REWARD RATIO:	RISK % LEVEL (%/$1000)		BALANCE:	
ENTRY CONFIRMATIONS: 1. 2. 3.		ENTRY: 1. 2. 3.	STOP LOSS: 1. 2. 3.			TAKE PROFIT: 1. 2. 3.	TRADE GOAL:	
POWER POINTS: (WHAT WORKED) 1. 2. 3.			END EMOJI:	+, - PIP$/PROFIT$			ACTUAL LOSS/PROFITS	

ACCOUNT:			DATE:	SESSION:			TIME:	
PAIR:	START EMOJI:	ENTRY TIME FRAME:	TRADE TYPE:	RISK TO REWARD RATIO:	RISK % LEVEL (%/$1000)		BALANCE:	
ENTRY CONFIRMATIONS: 1. 2. 3.		ENTRY: 1. 2. 3.	STOP LOSS: 1. 2. 3.			TAKE PROFIT: 1. 2. 3.	TRADE GOAL:	
POWER POINTS: (WHAT WORKED) 1. 2. 3.			END EMOJI:	+, - PIP$/PROFIT$			ACTUAL LOSS/PROFITS	

ACCOUNT:			DATE:	SESSION:			TIME:	
PAIR:	START EMOJI:	ENTRY TIME FRAME:	TRADE TYPE:	RISK TO REWARD RATIO:	RISK % LEVEL (%/$1000)		BALANCE:	
ENTRY CONFIRMATIONS: 1. 2. 3.		ENTRY: 1. 2. 3.	STOP LOSS: 1. 2. 3.			TAKE PROFIT: 1. 2. 3.	TRADE GOAL:	
POWER POINTS: (WHAT WORKED) 1. 2. 3.			END EMOJI:	+, - PIP$/PROFIT$			ACTUAL LOSS/PROFITS	

TRADING JOURNAL

ACCOUNT:			DATE:	SESSION:			TIME:	
PAIR:	START EMOJI:	ENTRY TIME FRAME:	TRADE TYPE:	RISK TO REWARD RATIO:		RISK % LEVEL (%/$1000)	BALANCE:	
ENTRY CONFIRMATIONS: 1. 2. 3.		ENTRY: 1. 2. 3.	STOP LOSS: 1. 2. 3.			TAKE PROFIT: 1. 2. 3.	TRADE GOAL:	
POWER POINTS: (WHAT WORKED) 1. 2. 3.			END EMOJI:	+, - PIP$/PROFIT$			ACTUAL LOSS/PROFITS	

ACCOUNT:			DATE:	SESSION:			TIME:	
PAIR:	START EMOJI:	ENTRY TIME FRAME:	TRADE TYPE:	RISK TO REWARD RATIO:		RISK % LEVEL (%/$1000)	BALANCE:	
ENTRY CONFIRMATIONS: 1. 2. 3.		ENTRY: 1. 2. 3.	STOP LOSS: 1. 2. 3.			TAKE PROFIT: 1. 2. 3.	TRADE GOAL:	
POWER POINTS: (WHAT WORKED) 1. 2. 3.			END EMOJI:	+, - PIP$/PROFIT$			ACTUAL LOSS/PROFITS	

ACCOUNT:			DATE:	SESSION:			TIME:	
PAIR:	START EMOJI:	ENTRY TIME FRAME:	TRADE TYPE:	RISK TO REWARD RATIO:		RISK % LEVEL (%/$1000)	BALANCE:	
ENTRY CONFIRMATIONS: 1. 2. 3.		ENTRY: 1. 2. 3.	STOP LOSS: 1. 2. 3.			TAKE PROFIT: 1. 2. 3.	TRADE GOAL:	
POWER POINTS: (WHAT WORKED) 1. 2. 3.			END EMOJI:	+, - PIP$/PROFIT$			ACTUAL LOSS/PROFITS	

TRADING JOURNAL

ACCOUNT:			DATE:	SESSION:			TIME:
PAIR:	START EMOJI:	ENTRY TIME FRAME:	TRADE TYPE:	RISK TO REWARD RATIO:	RISK % LEVEL (%/$1000)		BALANCE:
ENTRY CONFIRMATIONS: 1. 2. 3.		ENTRY: 1. 2. 3.	STOP LOSS: 1. 2. 3.		TAKE PROFIT: 1. 2. 3.		TRADE GOAL:
POWER POINTS: (WHAT WORKED) 1. 2. 3.			END EMOJI:	+, - PIP$/PROFIT$			ACTUAL LOSS/PROFITS

ACCOUNT:			DATE:	SESSION:			TIME:
PAIR:	START EMOJI:	ENTRY TIME FRAME:	TRADE TYPE:	RISK TO REWARD RATIO:	RISK % LEVEL (%/$1000)		BALANCE:
ENTRY CONFIRMATIONS: 1. 2. 3.		ENTRY: 1. 2. 3.	STOP LOSS: 1. 2. 3.		TAKE PROFIT: 1. 2. 3.		TRADE GOAL:
POWER POINTS: (WHAT WORKED) 1. 2. 3.			END EMOJI:	+, - PIP$/PROFIT$			ACTUAL LOSS/PROFITS

ACCOUNT:			DATE:	SESSION:			TIME:
PAIR:	START EMOJI:	ENTRY TIME FRAME:	TRADE TYPE:	RISK TO REWARD RATIO:	RISK % LEVEL (%/$1000)		BALANCE:
ENTRY CONFIRMATIONS: 1. 2. 3.		ENTRY: 1. 2. 3.	STOP LOSS: 1. 2. 3.		TAKE PROFIT: 1. 2. 3.		TRADE GOAL:
POWER POINTS: (WHAT WORKED) 1. 2. 3.			END EMOJI:	+, - PIP$/PROFIT$			ACTUAL LOSS/PROFITS

TRADING JOURNAL

ACCOUNT:			DATE:	SESSION:		TIME:	
PAIR:	START EMOJI:	ENTRY TIME FRAME:	TRADE TYPE:	RISK TO REWARD RATIO:	RISK % LEVEL (%/$1000)	BALANCE:	
ENTRY CONFIRMATIONS: 1. 2. 3.		ENTRY: 1. 2. 3.	STOP LOSS: 1. 2. 3.		TAKE PROFIT: 1. 2. 3.	TRADE GOAL:	
POWER POINTS: (WHAT WORKED) 1. 2. 3.			END EMOJI:	+, - PIP$/PROFIT$		ACTUAL LOSS/PROFITS	

ACCOUNT:			DATE:	SESSION:		TIME:	
PAIR:	START EMOJI:	ENTRY TIME FRAME:	TRADE TYPE:	RISK TO REWARD RATIO:	RISK % LEVEL (%/$1000)	BALANCE:	
ENTRY CONFIRMATIONS: 1. 2. 3.		ENTRY: 1. 2. 3.	STOP LOSS: 1. 2. 3.		TAKE PROFIT: 1. 2. 3.	TRADE GOAL:	
POWER POINTS: (WHAT WORKED) 1. 2. 3.			END EMOJI:	+, - PIP$/PROFIT$		ACTUAL LOSS/PROFITS	

ACCOUNT:			DATE:	SESSION:		TIME:	
PAIR:	START EMOJI:	ENTRY TIME FRAME:	TRADE TYPE:	RISK TO REWARD RATIO:	RISK % LEVEL (%/$1000)	BALANCE:	
ENTRY CONFIRMATIONS: 1. 2. 3.		ENTRY: 1. 2. 3.	STOP LOSS: 1. 2. 3.		TAKE PROFIT: 1. 2. 3.	TRADE GOAL:	
POWER POINTS: (WHAT WORKED) 1. 2. 3.			END EMOJI:	+, - PIP$/PROFIT$		ACTUAL LOSS/PROFITS	

TRADING JOURNAL

ACCOUNT:			DATE:	SESSION:			TIME:	
PAIR:	START EMOJI:	ENTRY TIME FRAME:	TRADE TYPE:	RISK TO REWARD RATIO:	RISK % LEVEL (%/$1000)		BALANCE:	
ENTRY CONFIRMATIONS: 1. 2. 3.		ENTRY: 1. 2. 3.	STOP LOSS: 1. 2. 3.			TAKE PROFIT: 1. 2. 3.	TRADE GOAL:	
POWER POINTS: (WHAT WORKED) 1. 2. 3.			END EMOJI:	+, - PIP$/PROFIT$			ACTUAL LOSS/PROFITS	

ACCOUNT:			DATE:	SESSION:			TIME:	
PAIR:	START EMOJI:	ENTRY TIME FRAME:	TRADE TYPE:	RISK TO REWARD RATIO:	RISK % LEVEL (%/$1000)		BALANCE:	
ENTRY CONFIRMATIONS: 1. 2. 3.		ENTRY: 1. 2. 3.	STOP LOSS: 1. 2. 3.			TAKE PROFIT: 1. 2. 3.	TRADE GOAL:	
POWER POINTS: (WHAT WORKED) 1. 2. 3.			END EMOJI:	+, - PIP$/PROFIT$			ACTUAL LOSS/PROFITS	

ACCOUNT:			DATE:	SESSION:			TIME:	
PAIR:	START EMOJI:	ENTRY TIME FRAME:	TRADE TYPE:	RISK TO REWARD RATIO:	RISK % LEVEL (%/$1000)		BALANCE:	
ENTRY CONFIRMATIONS: 1. 2. 3.		ENTRY: 1. 2. 3.	STOP LOSS: 1. 2. 3.			TAKE PROFIT: 1. 2. 3.	TRADE GOAL:	
POWER POINTS: (WHAT WORKED) 1. 2. 3.			END EMOJI:	+, - PIP$/PROFIT$			ACTUAL LOSS/PROFITS	

TRADING JOURNAL

ACCOUNT:			DATE:	SESSION:			TIME:
PAIR:	START EMOJI:	ENTRY TIME FRAME:	TRADE TYPE:	RISK TO REWARD RATIO:	RISK % LEVEL (%/$1000)		BALANCE:
ENTRY CONFIRMATIONS: 1. 2. 3.		ENTRY: 1. 2. 3.	STOP LOSS: 1. 2. 3.		TAKE PROFIT: 1. 2. 3.		TRADE GOAL:
POWER POINTS: (WHAT WORKED) 1. 2. 3.			END EMOJI:	+, - PIP$/PROFIT$			ACTUAL LOSS/PROFITS

ACCOUNT:			DATE:	SESSION:			TIME:
PAIR:	START EMOJI:	ENTRY TIME FRAME:	TRADE TYPE:	RISK TO REWARD RATIO:	RISK % LEVEL (%/$1000)		BALANCE:
ENTRY CONFIRMATIONS: 1. 2. 3.		ENTRY: 1. 2. 3.	STOP LOSS: 1. 2. 3.		TAKE PROFIT: 1. 2. 3.		TRADE GOAL:
POWER POINTS: (WHAT WORKED) 1. 2. 3.			END EMOJI:	+, - PIP$/PROFIT$			ACTUAL LOSS/PROFITS

ACCOUNT:			DATE:	SESSION:			TIME:
PAIR:	START EMOJI:	ENTRY TIME FRAME:	TRADE TYPE:	RISK TO REWARD RATIO:	RISK % LEVEL (%/$1000)		BALANCE:
ENTRY CONFIRMATIONS: 1. 2. 3.		ENTRY: 1. 2. 3.	STOP LOSS: 1. 2. 3.		TAKE PROFIT: 1. 2. 3.		TRADE GOAL:
POWER POINTS: (WHAT WORKED) 1. 2. 3.			END EMOJI:	+, - PIP$/PROFIT$			ACTUAL LOSS/PROFITS

TRADING JOURNAL

ACCOUNT:			DATE:	SESSION:		TIME:	
PAIR:	START EMOJI:	ENTRY TIME FRAME:	TRADE TYPE:	RISK TO REWARD RATIO:	RISK % LEVEL (%/$1000)	BALANCE:	
ENTRY CONFIRMATIONS: 1. 2. 3.		ENTRY: 1. 2. 3.	STOP LOSS: 1. 2. 3.		TAKE PROFIT: 1. 2. 3.	TRADE GOAL:	
POWER POINTS: (WHAT WORKED) 1. 2. 3.			END EMOJI:	+, - PIP$/PROFIT$		ACTUAL LOSS/PROFITS	

ACCOUNT:			DATE:	SESSION:		TIME:	
PAIR:	START EMOJI:	ENTRY TIME FRAME:	TRADE TYPE:	RISK TO REWARD RATIO:	RISK % LEVEL (%/$1000)	BALANCE:	
ENTRY CONFIRMATIONS: 1. 2. 3.		ENTRY: 1. 2. 3.	STOP LOSS: 1. 2. 3.		TAKE PROFIT: 1. 2. 3.	TRADE GOAL:	
POWER POINTS: (WHAT WORKED) 1. 2. 3.			END EMOJI:	+, - PIP$/PROFIT$		ACTUAL LOSS/PROFITS	

ACCOUNT:			DATE:	SESSION:		TIME:	
PAIR:	START EMOJI:	ENTRY TIME FRAME:	TRADE TYPE:	RISK TO REWARD RATIO:	RISK % LEVEL (%/$1000)	BALANCE:	
ENTRY CONFIRMATIONS: 1. 2. 3.		ENTRY: 1. 2. 3.	STOP LOSS: 1. 2. 3.		TAKE PROFIT: 1. 2. 3.	TRADE GOAL:	
POWER POINTS: (WHAT WORKED) 1. 2. 3.			END EMOJI:	+, - PIP$/PROFIT$		ACTUAL LOSS/PROFITS	

TRADING JOURNAL

ACCOUNT:			DATE:	SESSION:		TIME:	
PAIR:	START EMOJI:	ENTRY TIME FRAME:	TRADE TYPE:	RISK TO REWARD RATIO:	RISK % LEVEL (%/$1000)	BALANCE:	
ENTRY CONFIRMATIONS: 1. 2. 3.		ENTRY: 1. 2. 3.	STOP LOSS: 1. 2. 3.		TAKE PROFIT: 1. 2. 3.	TRADE GOAL:	
POWER POINTS: (WHAT WORKED) 1. 2. 3.			END EMOJI:	+, - PIP$/PROFIT$		ACTUAL LOSS/PROFITS	

ACCOUNT:			DATE:	SESSION:		TIME:	
PAIR:	START EMOJI:	ENTRY TIME FRAME:	TRADE TYPE:	RISK TO REWARD RATIO:	RISK % LEVEL (%/$1000)	BALANCE:	
ENTRY CONFIRMATIONS: 1. 2. 3.		ENTRY: 1. 2. 3.	STOP LOSS: 1. 2. 3.		TAKE PROFIT: 1. 2. 3.	TRADE GOAL:	
POWER POINTS: (WHAT WORKED) 1. 2. 3.			END EMOJI:	+, - PIP$/PROFIT$		ACTUAL LOSS/PROFITS	

ACCOUNT:			DATE:	SESSION:		TIME:	
PAIR:	START EMOJI:	ENTRY TIME FRAME:	TRADE TYPE:	RISK TO REWARD RATIO:	RISK % LEVEL (%/$1000)	BALANCE:	
ENTRY CONFIRMATIONS: 1. 2. 3.		ENTRY: 1. 2. 3.	STOP LOSS: 1. 2. 3.		TAKE PROFIT: 1. 2. 3.	TRADE GOAL:	
POWER POINTS: (WHAT WORKED) 1. 2. 3.			END EMOJI:	+, - PIP$/PROFIT$		ACTUAL LOSS/PROFITS	

TRADING JOURNAL

ACCOUNT:			DATE:	SESSION:		TIME:	
PAIR:	START EMOJI:	ENTRY TIME FRAME:	TRADE TYPE:	RISK TO REWARD RATIO:	RISK % LEVEL (%/$1000)	BALANCE:	
ENTRY CONFIRMATIONS: 1. 2. 3.		ENTRY: 1. 2. 3.	STOP LOSS: 1. 2. 3.		TAKE PROFIT: 1. 2. 3.	TRADE GOAL:	
POWER POINTS: (WHAT WORKED) 1. 2. 3.			END EMOJI:	+, - PIP$/PROFIT$		ACTUAL LOSS/PROFITS	

ACCOUNT:			DATE:	SESSION:		TIME:	
PAIR:	START EMOJI:	ENTRY TIME FRAME:	TRADE TYPE:	RISK TO REWARD RATIO:	RISK % LEVEL (%/$1000)	BALANCE:	
ENTRY CONFIRMATIONS: 1. 2. 3.		ENTRY: 1. 2. 3.	STOP LOSS: 1. 2. 3.		TAKE PROFIT: 1. 2. 3.	TRADE GOAL:	
POWER POINTS: (WHAT WORKED) 1. 2. 3.			END EMOJI:	+, - PIP$/PROFIT$		ACTUAL LOSS/PROFITS	

ACCOUNT:			DATE:	SESSION:		TIME:	
PAIR:	START EMOJI:	ENTRY TIME FRAME:	TRADE TYPE:	RISK TO REWARD RATIO:	RISK % LEVEL (%/$1000)	BALANCE:	
ENTRY CONFIRMATIONS: 1. 2. 3.		ENTRY: 1. 2. 3.	STOP LOSS: 1. 2. 3.		TAKE PROFIT: 1. 2. 3.	TRADE GOAL:	
POWER POINTS: (WHAT WORKED) 1. 2. 3.			END EMOJI:	+, - PIP$/PROFIT$		ACTUAL LOSS/PROFITS	

TRADING JOURNAL

ACCOUNT:			DATE:	SESSION:			TIME:	
PAIR:	START EMOJI:	ENTRY TIME FRAME:	TRADE TYPE:	RISK TO REWARD RATIO:		RISK % LEVEL (%/$1000)	BALANCE:	
ENTRY CONFIRMATIONS: 1. 2. 3.		ENTRY: 1. 2. 3.	STOP LOSS: 1. 2. 3.			TAKE PROFIT: 1. 2. 3.	TRADE GOAL:	
POWER POINTS: (WHAT WORKED) 1. 2. 3.			END EMOJI:	+, - PIP$/PROFIT$			ACTUAL LOSS/PROFITS	

ACCOUNT:			DATE:	SESSION:			TIME:	
PAIR:	START EMOJI:	ENTRY TIME FRAME:	TRADE TYPE:	RISK TO REWARD RATIO:		RISK % LEVEL (%/$1000)	BALANCE:	
ENTRY CONFIRMATIONS: 1. 2. 3.		ENTRY: 1. 2. 3.	STOP LOSS: 1. 2. 3.			TAKE PROFIT: 1. 2. 3.	TRADE GOAL:	
POWER POINTS: (WHAT WORKED) 1. 2. 3.			END EMOJI:	+, - PIP$/PROFIT$			ACTUAL LOSS/PROFITS	

ACCOUNT:			DATE:	SESSION:			TIME:	
PAIR:	START EMOJI:	ENTRY TIME FRAME:	TRADE TYPE:	RISK TO REWARD RATIO:		RISK % LEVEL (%/$1000)	BALANCE:	
ENTRY CONFIRMATIONS: 1. 2. 3.		ENTRY: 1. 2. 3.	STOP LOSS: 1. 2. 3.			TAKE PROFIT: 1. 2. 3.	TRADE GOAL:	
POWER POINTS: (WHAT WORKED) 1. 2. 3.			END EMOJI:	+, - PIP$/PROFIT$			ACTUAL LOSS/PROFITS	

TRADING JOURNAL

ACCOUNT:			DATE:	SESSION:			TIME:	
PAIR:	START EMOJI:	ENTRY TIME FRAME:	TRADE TYPE:	RISK TO REWARD RATIO:	RISK % LEVEL (%/$1000)		BALANCE:	
ENTRY CONFIRMATIONS: 1. 2. 3.		ENTRY: 1. 2. 3.	STOP LOSS: 1. 2. 3.			TAKE PROFIT: 1. 2. 3.	TRADE GOAL:	
POWER POINTS: (WHAT WORKED) 1. 2. 3.			END EMOJI:	+, - PIP$/PROFIT$			ACTUAL LOSS/PROFITS	

ACCOUNT:			DATE:	SESSION:			TIME:	
PAIR:	START EMOJI:	ENTRY TIME FRAME:	TRADE TYPE:	RISK TO REWARD RATIO:	RISK % LEVEL (%/$1000)		BALANCE:	
ENTRY CONFIRMATIONS: 1. 2. 3.		ENTRY: 1. 2. 3.	STOP LOSS: 1. 2. 3.			TAKE PROFIT: 1. 2. 3.	TRADE GOAL:	
POWER POINTS: (WHAT WORKED) 1. 2. 3.			END EMOJI:	+, - PIP$/PROFIT$			ACTUAL LOSS/PROFITS	

ACCOUNT:			DATE:	SESSION:			TIME:	
PAIR:	START EMOJI:	ENTRY TIME FRAME:	TRADE TYPE:	RISK TO REWARD RATIO:	RISK % LEVEL (%/$1000)		BALANCE:	
ENTRY CONFIRMATIONS: 1. 2. 3.		ENTRY: 1. 2. 3.	STOP LOSS: 1. 2. 3.			TAKE PROFIT: 1. 2. 3.	TRADE GOAL:	
POWER POINTS: (WHAT WORKED) 1. 2. 3.			END EMOJI:	+, - PIP$/PROFIT$			ACTUAL LOSS/PROFITS	

TRADING JOURNAL

ACCOUNT:			DATE:	SESSION:			TIME:	
PAIR:	START EMOJI:	ENTRY TIME FRAME:	TRADE TYPE:	RISK TO REWARD RATIO:		RISK % LEVEL (%/$1000)	BALANCE:	
ENTRY CONFIRMATIONS: 1. 2. 3.		ENTRY: 1. 2. 3.	STOP LOSS: 1. 2. 3.			TAKE PROFIT: 1. 2. 3.	TRADE GOAL:	
POWER POINTS: (WHAT WORKED) 1. 2. 3.			END EMOJI:	+, - PIP$/PROFIT$			ACTUAL LOSS/PROFITS	

ACCOUNT:			DATE:	SESSION:			TIME:	
PAIR:	START EMOJI:	ENTRY TIME FRAME:	TRADE TYPE:	RISK TO REWARD RATIO:		RISK % LEVEL (%/$1000)	BALANCE:	
ENTRY CONFIRMATIONS: 1. 2. 3.		ENTRY: 1. 2. 3.	STOP LOSS: 1. 2. 3.			TAKE PROFIT: 1. 2. 3.	TRADE GOAL:	
POWER POINTS: (WHAT WORKED) 1. 2. 3.			END EMOJI:	+, - PIP$/PROFIT$			ACTUAL LOSS/PROFITS	

ACCOUNT:			DATE:	SESSION:			TIME:	
PAIR:	START EMOJI:	ENTRY TIME FRAME:	TRADE TYPE:	RISK TO REWARD RATIO:		RISK % LEVEL (%/$1000)	BALANCE:	
ENTRY CONFIRMATIONS: 1. 2. 3.		ENTRY: 1. 2. 3.	STOP LOSS: 1. 2. 3.			TAKE PROFIT: 1. 2. 3.	TRADE GOAL:	
POWER POINTS: (WHAT WORKED) 1. 2. 3.			END EMOJI:	+, - PIP$/PROFIT$			ACTUAL LOSS/PROFITS	

TRADING JOURNAL

ACCOUNT:			DATE:	SESSION:			TIME:
PAIR:	START EMOJI:	ENTRY TIME FRAME:	TRADE TYPE:	RISK TO REWARD RATIO:	RISK % LEVEL (%/$1000)		BALANCE:
ENTRY CONFIRMATIONS: 1. 2. 3.		ENTRY: 1. 2. 3.	STOP LOSS: 1. 2. 3.			TAKE PROFIT: 1. 2. 3.	TRADE GOAL:
POWER POINTS: (WHAT WORKED) 1. 2. 3.			END EMOJI:	+, - PIP$/PROFIT$			ACTUAL LOSS/PROFITS

ACCOUNT:			DATE:	SESSION:			TIME:
PAIR:	START EMOJI:	ENTRY TIME FRAME:	TRADE TYPE:	RISK TO REWARD RATIO:	RISK % LEVEL (%/$1000)		BALANCE:
ENTRY CONFIRMATIONS: 1. 2. 3.		ENTRY: 1. 2. 3.	STOP LOSS: 1. 2. 3.			TAKE PROFIT: 1. 2. 3.	TRADE GOAL:
POWER POINTS: (WHAT WORKED) 1. 2. 3.			END EMOJI:	+, - PIP$/PROFIT$			ACTUAL LOSS/PROFITS

ACCOUNT:			DATE:	SESSION:			TIME:
PAIR:	START EMOJI:	ENTRY TIME FRAME:	TRADE TYPE:	RISK TO REWARD RATIO:	RISK % LEVEL (%/$1000)		BALANCE:
ENTRY CONFIRMATIONS: 1. 2. 3.		ENTRY: 1. 2. 3.	STOP LOSS: 1. 2. 3.			TAKE PROFIT: 1. 2. 3.	TRADE GOAL:
POWER POINTS: (WHAT WORKED) 1. 2. 3.			END EMOJI:	+, - PIP$/PROFIT$			ACTUAL LOSS/PROFITS

TRADING JOURNAL

ACCOUNT:			DATE:	SESSION:			TIME:	
PAIR:	START EMOJI:	ENTRY TIME FRAME:	TRADE TYPE:	RISK TO REWARD RATIO:	RISK % LEVEL (%/$1000)		BALANCE:	
ENTRY CONFIRMATIONS: 1. 2. 3.		ENTRY: 1. 2. 3.	STOP LOSS: 1. 2. 3.			TAKE PROFIT: 1. 2. 3.	TRADE GOAL:	
POWER POINTS: (WHAT WORKED) 1. 2. 3.			END EMOJI:	+, - PIP$/PROFIT$			ACTUAL LOSS/PROFITS	

ACCOUNT:			DATE:	SESSION:			TIME:	
PAIR:	START EMOJI:	ENTRY TIME FRAME:	TRADE TYPE:	RISK TO REWARD RATIO:	RISK % LEVEL (%/$1000)		BALANCE:	
ENTRY CONFIRMATIONS: 1. 2. 3.		ENTRY: 1. 2. 3.	STOP LOSS: 1. 2. 3.			TAKE PROFIT: 1. 2. 3.	TRADE GOAL:	
POWER POINTS: (WHAT WORKED) 1. 2. 3.			END EMOJI:	+, - PIP$/PROFIT$			ACTUAL LOSS/PROFITS	

ACCOUNT:			DATE:	SESSION:			TIME:	
PAIR:	START EMOJI:	ENTRY TIME FRAME:	TRADE TYPE:	RISK TO REWARD RATIO:	RISK % LEVEL (%/$1000)		BALANCE:	
ENTRY CONFIRMATIONS: 1. 2. 3.		ENTRY: 1. 2. 3.	STOP LOSS: 1. 2. 3.			TAKE PROFIT: 1. 2. 3.	TRADE GOAL:	
POWER POINTS: (WHAT WORKED) 1. 2. 3.			END EMOJI:	+, - PIP$/PROFIT$			ACTUAL LOSS/PROFITS	

TRADING JOURNAL

ACCOUNT:			DATE:	SESSION:			TIME:
PAIR:	START EMOJI:	ENTRY TIME FRAME:	TRADE TYPE:	RISK TO REWARD RATIO:	RISK % LEVEL (%/$1000)		BALANCE:
ENTRY CONFIRMATIONS: 1. 2. 3.		ENTRY: 1. 2. 3.	STOP LOSS: 1. 2. 3.		TAKE PROFIT: 1. 2. 3.		TRADE GOAL:
POWER POINTS: (WHAT WORKED) 1. 2. 3.			END EMOJI:	+, - PIP$/PROFIT$		ACTUAL LOSS/PROFITS	

ACCOUNT:			DATE:	SESSION:			TIME:
PAIR:	START EMOJI:	ENTRY TIME FRAME:	TRADE TYPE:	RISK TO REWARD RATIO:	RISK % LEVEL (%/$1000)		BALANCE:
ENTRY CONFIRMATIONS: 1. 2. 3.		ENTRY: 1. 2. 3.	STOP LOSS: 1. 2. 3.		TAKE PROFIT: 1. 2. 3.		TRADE GOAL:
POWER POINTS: (WHAT WORKED) 1. 2. 3.			END EMOJI:	+, - PIP$/PROFIT$		ACTUAL LOSS/PROFITS	

ACCOUNT:			DATE:	SESSION:			TIME:
PAIR:	START EMOJI:	ENTRY TIME FRAME:	TRADE TYPE:	RISK TO REWARD RATIO:	RISK % LEVEL (%/$1000)		BALANCE:
ENTRY CONFIRMATIONS: 1. 2. 3.		ENTRY: 1. 2. 3.	STOP LOSS: 1. 2. 3.		TAKE PROFIT: 1. 2. 3.		TRADE GOAL:
POWER POINTS: (WHAT WORKED) 1. 2. 3.			END EMOJI:	+, - PIP$/PROFIT$		ACTUAL LOSS/PROFITS	

TRADING JOURNAL

ACCOUNT:			DATE:	SESSION:		TIME:	
PAIR:	START EMOJI:	ENTRY TIME FRAME:	TRADE TYPE:	RISK TO REWARD RATIO:	RISK % LEVEL (%/$1000)	BALANCE:	
ENTRY CONFIRMATIONS: 1. 2. 3.		ENTRY: 1. 2. 3.	STOP LOSS: 1. 2. 3.		TAKE PROFIT: 1. 2. 3.	TRADE GOAL:	
POWER POINTS: (WHAT WORKED) 1. 2. 3.			END EMOJI:	+, - PIP$/PROFIT$		ACTUAL LOSS/PROFITS	

ACCOUNT:			DATE:	SESSION:		TIME:	
PAIR:	START EMOJI:	ENTRY TIME FRAME:	TRADE TYPE:	RISK TO REWARD RATIO:	RISK % LEVEL (%/$1000)	BALANCE:	
ENTRY CONFIRMATIONS: 1. 2. 3.		ENTRY: 1. 2. 3.	STOP LOSS: 1. 2. 3.		TAKE PROFIT: 1. 2. 3.	TRADE GOAL:	
POWER POINTS: (WHAT WORKED) 1. 2. 3.			END EMOJI:	+, - PIP$/PROFIT$		ACTUAL LOSS/PROFITS	

ACCOUNT:			DATE:	SESSION:		TIME:	
PAIR:	START EMOJI:	ENTRY TIME FRAME:	TRADE TYPE:	RISK TO REWARD RATIO:	RISK % LEVEL (%/$1000)	BALANCE:	
ENTRY CONFIRMATIONS: 1. 2. 3.		ENTRY: 1. 2. 3.	STOP LOSS: 1. 2. 3.		TAKE PROFIT: 1. 2. 3.	TRADE GOAL:	
POWER POINTS: (WHAT WORKED) 1. 2. 3.			END EMOJI:	+, - PIP$/PROFIT$		ACTUAL LOSS/PROFITS	

TRADING JOURNAL

ACCOUNT:			DATE:	SESSION:			TIME:	
PAIR:	START EMOJI:	ENTRY TIME FRAME:	TRADE TYPE:	RISK TO REWARD RATIO:	RISK % LEVEL (%/$1000)		BALANCE:	
ENTRY CONFIRMATIONS: 1. 2. 3.		ENTRY: 1. 2. 3.	STOP LOSS: 1. 2. 3.			TAKE PROFIT: 1. 2. 3.	TRADE GOAL:	
POWER POINTS: (WHAT WORKED) 1. 2. 3.			END EMOJI:	+, - PIP$/PROFIT$			ACTUAL LOSS/PROFITS	

ACCOUNT:			DATE:	SESSION:			TIME:	
PAIR:	START EMOJI:	ENTRY TIME FRAME:	TRADE TYPE:	RISK TO REWARD RATIO:	RISK % LEVEL (%/$1000)		BALANCE:	
ENTRY CONFIRMATIONS: 1. 2. 3.		ENTRY: 1. 2. 3.	STOP LOSS: 1. 2. 3.			TAKE PROFIT: 1. 2. 3.	TRADE GOAL:	
POWER POINTS: (WHAT WORKED) 1. 2. 3.			END EMOJI:	+, - PIP$/PROFIT$			ACTUAL LOSS/PROFITS	

ACCOUNT:			DATE:	SESSION:			TIME:	
PAIR:	START EMOJI:	ENTRY TIME FRAME:	TRADE TYPE:	RISK TO REWARD RATIO:	RISK % LEVEL (%/$1000)		BALANCE:	
ENTRY CONFIRMATIONS: 1. 2. 3.		ENTRY: 1. 2. 3.	STOP LOSS: 1. 2. 3.			TAKE PROFIT: 1. 2. 3.	TRADE GOAL:	
POWER POINTS: (WHAT WORKED) 1. 2. 3.			END EMOJI:	+, - PIP$/PROFIT$			ACTUAL LOSS/PROFITS	

TRADING JOURNAL

ACCOUNT:			DATE:	SESSION:			TIME:	
PAIR:	START EMOJI:	ENTRY TIME FRAME:	TRADE TYPE:	RISK TO REWARD RATIO:	RISK % LEVEL (%/$1000)		BALANCE:	
ENTRY CONFIRMATIONS: 1. 2. 3.		ENTRY: 1. 2. 3.	STOP LOSS: 1. 2. 3.			TAKE PROFIT: 1. 2. 3.	TRADE GOAL:	
POWER POINTS: (WHAT WORKED) 1. 2. 3.			END EMOJI:	+, - PIP$/PROFIT$			ACTUAL LOSS/PROFITS	

ACCOUNT:			DATE:	SESSION:			TIME:	
PAIR:	START EMOJI:	ENTRY TIME FRAME:	TRADE TYPE:	RISK TO REWARD RATIO:	RISK % LEVEL (%/$1000)		BALANCE:	
ENTRY CONFIRMATIONS: 1. 2. 3.		ENTRY: 1. 2. 3.	STOP LOSS: 1. 2. 3.			TAKE PROFIT: 1. 2. 3.	TRADE GOAL:	
POWER POINTS: (WHAT WORKED) 1. 2. 3.			END EMOJI:	+, - PIP$/PROFIT$			ACTUAL LOSS/PROFITS	

ACCOUNT:			DATE:	SESSION:			TIME:	
PAIR:	START EMOJI:	ENTRY TIME FRAME:	TRADE TYPE:	RISK TO REWARD RATIO:	RISK % LEVEL (%/$1000)		BALANCE:	
ENTRY CONFIRMATIONS: 1. 2. 3.		ENTRY: 1. 2. 3.	STOP LOSS: 1. 2. 3.			TAKE PROFIT: 1. 2. 3.	TRADE GOAL:	
POWER POINTS: (WHAT WORKED) 1. 2. 3.			END EMOJI:	+, - PIP$/PROFIT$			ACTUAL LOSS/PROFITS	

TRADING JOURNAL

ACCOUNT:			DATE:	SESSION:		TIME:	
PAIR:	START EMOJI:	ENTRY TIME FRAME:	TRADE TYPE:	RISK TO REWARD RATIO:	RISK % LEVEL (%/$1000)	BALANCE:	
ENTRY CONFIRMATIONS: 1. 2. 3.		ENTRY: 1. 2. 3.	STOP LOSS: 1. 2. 3.		TAKE PROFIT: 1. 2. 3.	TRADE GOAL:	
POWER POINTS: (WHAT WORKED) 1. 2. 3.			END EMOJI:	+, - PIP$/PROFIT$		ACTUAL LOSS/PROFITS	

ACCOUNT:			DATE:	SESSION:		TIME:	
PAIR:	START EMOJI:	ENTRY TIME FRAME:	TRADE TYPE:	RISK TO REWARD RATIO:	RISK % LEVEL (%/$1000)	BALANCE:	
ENTRY CONFIRMATIONS: 1. 2. 3.		ENTRY: 1. 2. 3.	STOP LOSS: 1. 2. 3.		TAKE PROFIT: 1. 2. 3.	TRADE GOAL:	
POWER POINTS: (WHAT WORKED) 1. 2. 3.			END EMOJI:	+, - PIP$/PROFIT$		ACTUAL LOSS/PROFITS	

ACCOUNT:			DATE:	SESSION:		TIME:	
PAIR:	START EMOJI:	ENTRY TIME FRAME:	TRADE TYPE:	RISK TO REWARD RATIO:	RISK % LEVEL (%/$1000)	BALANCE:	
ENTRY CONFIRMATIONS: 1. 2. 3.		ENTRY: 1. 2. 3.	STOP LOSS: 1. 2. 3.		TAKE PROFIT: 1. 2. 3.	TRADE GOAL:	
POWER POINTS: (WHAT WORKED) 1. 2. 3.			END EMOJI:	+, - PIP$/PROFIT$		ACTUAL LOSS/PROFITS	

TRADING JOURNAL

ACCOUNT:			DATE:	SESSION:			TIME:	
PAIR:	START EMOJI:	ENTRY TIME FRAME:	TRADE TYPE:	RISK TO REWARD RATIO:	RISK % LEVEL (%/$1000)		BALANCE:	
ENTRY CONFIRMATIONS: 1. 2. 3.		ENTRY: 1. 2. 3.	STOP LOSS: 1. 2. 3.			TAKE PROFIT: 1. 2. 3.	TRADE GOAL:	
POWER POINTS: (WHAT WORKED) 1. 2. 3.			END EMOJI:	+, - PIP$/PROFIT$			ACTUAL LOSS/PROFITS	

ACCOUNT:			DATE:	SESSION:			TIME:	
PAIR:	START EMOJI:	ENTRY TIME FRAME:	TRADE TYPE:	RISK TO REWARD RATIO:	RISK % LEVEL (%/$1000)		BALANCE:	
ENTRY CONFIRMATIONS: 1. 2. 3.		ENTRY: 1. 2. 3.	STOP LOSS: 1. 2. 3.			TAKE PROFIT: 1. 2. 3.	TRADE GOAL:	
POWER POINTS: (WHAT WORKED) 1. 2. 3.			END EMOJI:	+, - PIP$/PROFIT$			ACTUAL LOSS/PROFITS	

ACCOUNT:			DATE:	SESSION:			TIME:	
PAIR:	START EMOJI:	ENTRY TIME FRAME:	TRADE TYPE:	RISK TO REWARD RATIO:	RISK % LEVEL (%/$1000)		BALANCE:	
ENTRY CONFIRMATIONS: 1. 2. 3.		ENTRY: 1. 2. 3.	STOP LOSS: 1. 2. 3.			TAKE PROFIT: 1. 2. 3.	TRADE GOAL:	
POWER POINTS: (WHAT WORKED) 1. 2. 3.			END EMOJI:	+, - PIP$/PROFIT$			ACTUAL LOSS/PROFITS	

TRADING JOURNAL

ACCOUNT:			DATE:	SESSION:		TIME:
PAIR:	START EMOJI:	ENTRY TIME FRAME:	TRADE TYPE:	RISK TO REWARD RATIO:	RISK % LEVEL (%/$1000)	BALANCE:
ENTRY CONFIRMATIONS: 1. 2. 3.		ENTRY: 1. 2. 3.	STOP LOSS: 1. 2. 3.		TAKE PROFIT: 1. 2. 3.	TRADE GOAL:
POWER POINTS: (WHAT WORKED) 1. 2. 3.			END EMOJI:	+, - PIP$/PROFIT$		ACTUAL LOSS/PROFITS

ACCOUNT:			DATE:	SESSION:		TIME:
PAIR:	START EMOJI:	ENTRY TIME FRAME:	TRADE TYPE:	RISK TO REWARD RATIO:	RISK % LEVEL (%/$1000)	BALANCE:
ENTRY CONFIRMATIONS: 1. 2. 3.		ENTRY: 1. 2. 3.	STOP LOSS: 1. 2. 3.		TAKE PROFIT: 1. 2. 3.	TRADE GOAL:
POWER POINTS: (WHAT WORKED) 1. 2. 3.			END EMOJI:	+, - PIP$/PROFIT$		ACTUAL LOSS/PROFITS

ACCOUNT:			DATE:	SESSION:		TIME:
PAIR:	START EMOJI:	ENTRY TIME FRAME:	TRADE TYPE:	RISK TO REWARD RATIO:	RISK % LEVEL (%/$1000)	BALANCE:
ENTRY CONFIRMATIONS: 1. 2. 3.		ENTRY: 1. 2. 3.	STOP LOSS: 1. 2. 3.		TAKE PROFIT: 1. 2. 3.	TRADE GOAL:
POWER POINTS: (WHAT WORKED) 1. 2. 3.			END EMOJI:	+, - PIP$/PROFIT$		ACTUAL LOSS/PROFITS

TRADING JOURNAL

ACCOUNT:			DATE:	SESSION:			TIME:	
PAIR:	START EMOJI:	ENTRY TIME FRAME:	TRADE TYPE:	RISK TO REWARD RATIO:	RISK % LEVEL (%/$1000)		BALANCE:	
ENTRY CONFIRMATIONS: 1. 2. 3.		ENTRY: 1. 2. 3.	STOP LOSS: 1. 2. 3.			TAKE PROFIT: 1. 2. 3.	TRADE GOAL:	
POWER POINTS: (WHAT WORKED) 1. 2. 3.			END EMOJI:	+, - PIP$/PROFIT$			ACTUAL LOSS/PROFITS	

ACCOUNT:			DATE:	SESSION:			TIME:	
PAIR:	START EMOJI:	ENTRY TIME FRAME:	TRADE TYPE:	RISK TO REWARD RATIO:	RISK % LEVEL (%/$1000)		BALANCE:	
ENTRY CONFIRMATIONS: 1. 2. 3.		ENTRY: 1. 2. 3.	STOP LOSS: 1. 2. 3.			TAKE PROFIT: 1. 2. 3.	TRADE GOAL:	
POWER POINTS: (WHAT WORKED) 1. 2. 3.			END EMOJI:	+, - PIP$/PROFIT$			ACTUAL LOSS/PROFITS	

ACCOUNT:			DATE:	SESSION:			TIME:	
PAIR:	START EMOJI:	ENTRY TIME FRAME:	TRADE TYPE:	RISK TO REWARD RATIO:	RISK % LEVEL (%/$1000)		BALANCE:	
ENTRY CONFIRMATIONS: 1. 2. 3.		ENTRY: 1. 2. 3.	STOP LOSS: 1. 2. 3.			TAKE PROFIT: 1. 2. 3.	TRADE GOAL:	
POWER POINTS: (WHAT WORKED) 1. 2. 3.			END EMOJI:	+, - PIP$/PROFIT$			ACTUAL LOSS/PROFITS	

TRADING JOURNAL

ACCOUNT:			DATE:	SESSION:		TIME:	
PAIR:	START EMOJI:	ENTRY TIME FRAME:	TRADE TYPE:	RISK TO REWARD RATIO:	RISK % LEVEL (%/$1000)	BALANCE:	
ENTRY CONFIRMATIONS: 1. 2. 3.		ENTRY: 1. 2. 3.	STOP LOSS: 1. 2. 3.		TAKE PROFIT: 1. 2. 3.	TRADE GOAL:	
POWER POINTS: (WHAT WORKED) 1. 2. 3.			END EMOJI:	+, - PIP$/PROFIT$		ACTUAL LOSS/PROFITS	

ACCOUNT:			DATE:	SESSION:		TIME:	
PAIR:	START EMOJI:	ENTRY TIME FRAME:	TRADE TYPE:	RISK TO REWARD RATIO:	RISK % LEVEL (%/$1000)	BALANCE:	
ENTRY CONFIRMATIONS: 1. 2. 3.		ENTRY: 1. 2. 3.	STOP LOSS: 1. 2. 3.		TAKE PROFIT: 1. 2. 3.	TRADE GOAL:	
POWER POINTS: (WHAT WORKED) 1. 2. 3.			END EMOJI:	+, - PIP$/PROFIT$		ACTUAL LOSS/PROFITS	

ACCOUNT:			DATE:	SESSION:		TIME:	
PAIR:	START EMOJI:	ENTRY TIME FRAME:	TRADE TYPE:	RISK TO REWARD RATIO:	RISK % LEVEL (%/$1000)	BALANCE:	
ENTRY CONFIRMATIONS: 1. 2. 3.		ENTRY: 1. 2. 3.	STOP LOSS: 1. 2. 3.		TAKE PROFIT: 1. 2. 3.	TRADE GOAL:	
POWER POINTS: (WHAT WORKED) 1. 2. 3.			END EMOJI:	+, - PIP$/PROFIT$		ACTUAL LOSS/PROFITS	

TRADING JOURNAL

ACCOUNT:			DATE:	SESSION:		TIME:	
PAIR:	START EMOJI:	ENTRY TIME FRAME:	TRADE TYPE:	RISK TO REWARD RATIO:	RISK % LEVEL (%/$1000)	BALANCE:	
ENTRY CONFIRMATIONS: 1. 2. 3.		ENTRY: 1. 2. 3.	STOP LOSS: 1. 2. 3.		TAKE PROFIT: 1. 2. 3.	TRADE GOAL:	
POWER POINTS: (WHAT WORKED) 1. 2. 3.			END EMOJI:	+, - PIP$/PROFIT$		ACTUAL LOSS/PROFITS	

ACCOUNT:			DATE:	SESSION:		TIME:	
PAIR:	START EMOJI:	ENTRY TIME FRAME:	TRADE TYPE:	RISK TO REWARD RATIO:	RISK % LEVEL (%/$1000)	BALANCE:	
ENTRY CONFIRMATIONS: 1. 2. 3.		ENTRY: 1. 2. 3.	STOP LOSS: 1. 2. 3.		TAKE PROFIT: 1. 2. 3.	TRADE GOAL:	
POWER POINTS: (WHAT WORKED) 1. 2. 3.			END EMOJI:	+, - PIP$/PROFIT$		ACTUAL LOSS/PROFITS	

ACCOUNT:			DATE:	SESSION:		TIME:	
PAIR:	START EMOJI:	ENTRY TIME FRAME:	TRADE TYPE:	RISK TO REWARD RATIO:	RISK % LEVEL (%/$1000)	BALANCE:	
ENTRY CONFIRMATIONS: 1. 2. 3.		ENTRY: 1. 2. 3.	STOP LOSS: 1. 2. 3.		TAKE PROFIT: 1. 2. 3.	TRADE GOAL:	
POWER POINTS: (WHAT WORKED) 1. 2. 3.			END EMOJI:	+, - PIP$/PROFIT$		ACTUAL LOSS/PROFITS	

TRADING JOURNAL

ACCOUNT:			DATE:	SESSION:		TIME:	
PAIR:	START EMOJI:	ENTRY TIME FRAME:	TRADE TYPE:	RISK TO REWARD RATIO:	RISK % LEVEL (%/$1000)	BALANCE:	
ENTRY CONFIRMATIONS: 1. 2. 3.		ENTRY: 1. 2. 3.	STOP LOSS: 1. 2. 3.		TAKE PROFIT: 1. 2. 3.	TRADE GOAL:	
POWER POINTS: (WHAT WORKED) 1. 2. 3.			END EMOJI:	+, - PIP$/PROFIT$		ACTUAL LOSS/PROFITS	

ACCOUNT:			DATE:	SESSION:		TIME:	
PAIR:	START EMOJI:	ENTRY TIME FRAME:	TRADE TYPE:	RISK TO REWARD RATIO:	RISK % LEVEL (%/$1000)	BALANCE:	
ENTRY CONFIRMATIONS: 1. 2. 3.		ENTRY: 1. 2. 3.	STOP LOSS: 1. 2. 3.		TAKE PROFIT: 1. 2. 3.	TRADE GOAL:	
POWER POINTS: (WHAT WORKED) 1. 2. 3.			END EMOJI:	+, - PIP$/PROFIT$		ACTUAL LOSS/PROFITS	

ACCOUNT:			DATE:	SESSION:		TIME:	
PAIR:	START EMOJI:	ENTRY TIME FRAME:	TRADE TYPE:	RISK TO REWARD RATIO:	RISK % LEVEL (%/$1000)	BALANCE:	
ENTRY CONFIRMATIONS: 1. 2. 3.		ENTRY: 1. 2. 3.	STOP LOSS: 1. 2. 3.		TAKE PROFIT: 1. 2. 3.	TRADE GOAL:	
POWER POINTS: (WHAT WORKED) 1. 2. 3.			END EMOJI:	+, - PIP$/PROFIT$		ACTUAL LOSS/PROFITS	

TRADING JOURNAL

ACCOUNT:			DATE:	SESSION:			TIME:	
PAIR:	START EMOJI:	ENTRY TIME FRAME:	TRADE TYPE:	RISK TO REWARD RATIO:		RISK % LEVEL (%/$1000)	BALANCE:	
ENTRY CONFIRMATIONS: 1. 2. 3.		ENTRY: 1. 2. 3.	STOP LOSS: 1. 2. 3.			TAKE PROFIT: 1. 2. 3.	TRADE GOAL:	
POWER POINTS: (WHAT WORKED) 1. 2. 3.			END EMOJI:	+, - PIP$/PROFIT$			ACTUAL LOSS/PROFITS	

ACCOUNT:			DATE:	SESSION:			TIME:	
PAIR:	START EMOJI:	ENTRY TIME FRAME:	TRADE TYPE:	RISK TO REWARD RATIO:		RISK % LEVEL (%/$1000)	BALANCE:	
ENTRY CONFIRMATIONS: 1. 2. 3.		ENTRY: 1. 2. 3.	STOP LOSS: 1. 2. 3.			TAKE PROFIT: 1. 2. 3.	TRADE GOAL:	
POWER POINTS: (WHAT WORKED) 1. 2. 3.			END EMOJI:	+, - PIP$/PROFIT$			ACTUAL LOSS/PROFITS	

ACCOUNT:			DATE:	SESSION:			TIME:	
PAIR:	START EMOJI:	ENTRY TIME FRAME:	TRADE TYPE:	RISK TO REWARD RATIO:		RISK % LEVEL (%/$1000)	BALANCE:	
ENTRY CONFIRMATIONS: 1. 2. 3.		ENTRY: 1. 2. 3.	STOP LOSS: 1. 2. 3.			TAKE PROFIT: 1. 2. 3.	TRADE GOAL:	
POWER POINTS: (WHAT WORKED) 1. 2. 3.			END EMOJI:	+, - PIP$/PROFIT$			ACTUAL LOSS/PROFITS	

TRADING JOURNAL

ACCOUNT:			DATE:	SESSION:			TIME:
PAIR:	START EMOJI:	ENTRY TIME FRAME:	TRADE TYPE:	RISK TO REWARD RATIO:	RISK % LEVEL (%/$1000)		BALANCE:
ENTRY CONFIRMATIONS: 1. 2. 3.		ENTRY: 1. 2. 3.	STOP LOSS: 1. 2. 3.		TAKE PROFIT: 1. 2. 3.		TRADE GOAL:
POWER POINTS: (WHAT WORKED) 1. 2. 3.			END EMOJI:	+, - PIP$/PROFIT$			ACTUAL LOSS/PROFITS

ACCOUNT:			DATE:	SESSION:			TIME:
PAIR:	START EMOJI:	ENTRY TIME FRAME:	TRADE TYPE:	RISK TO REWARD RATIO:	RISK % LEVEL (%/$1000)		BALANCE:
ENTRY CONFIRMATIONS: 1. 2. 3.		ENTRY: 1. 2. 3.	STOP LOSS: 1. 2. 3.		TAKE PROFIT: 1. 2. 3.		TRADE GOAL:
POWER POINTS: (WHAT WORKED) 1. 2. 3.			END EMOJI:	+, - PIP$/PROFIT$			ACTUAL LOSS/PROFITS

ACCOUNT:			DATE:	SESSION:			TIME:
PAIR:	START EMOJI:	ENTRY TIME FRAME:	TRADE TYPE:	RISK TO REWARD RATIO:	RISK % LEVEL (%/$1000)		BALANCE:
ENTRY CONFIRMATIONS: 1. 2. 3.		ENTRY: 1. 2. 3.	STOP LOSS: 1. 2. 3.		TAKE PROFIT: 1. 2. 3.		TRADE GOAL:
POWER POINTS: (WHAT WORKED) 1. 2. 3.			END EMOJI:	+, - PIP$/PROFIT$			ACTUAL LOSS/PROFITS

TRADING JOURNAL

ACCOUNT:			DATE:	SESSION:			TIME:
PAIR:	START EMOJI:	ENTRY TIME FRAME:	TRADE TYPE:	RISK TO REWARD RATIO:	RISK % LEVEL (%/$1000)		BALANCE:
ENTRY CONFIRMATIONS: 1. 2. 3.		ENTRY: 1. 2. 3.	STOP LOSS: 1. 2. 3.		TAKE PROFIT: 1. 2. 3.		TRADE GOAL:
POWER POINTS: (WHAT WORKED) 1. 2. 3.			END EMOJI:	+, - PIP$/PROFIT$			ACTUAL LOSS/PROFITS

ACCOUNT:			DATE:	SESSION:			TIME:
PAIR:	START EMOJI:	ENTRY TIME FRAME:	TRADE TYPE:	RISK TO REWARD RATIO:	RISK % LEVEL (%/$1000)		BALANCE:
ENTRY CONFIRMATIONS: 1. 2. 3.		ENTRY: 1. 2. 3.	STOP LOSS: 1. 2. 3.		TAKE PROFIT: 1. 2. 3.		TRADE GOAL:
POWER POINTS: (WHAT WORKED) 1. 2. 3.			END EMOJI:	+, - PIP$/PROFIT$			ACTUAL LOSS/PROFITS

ACCOUNT:			DATE:	SESSION:			TIME:
PAIR:	START EMOJI:	ENTRY TIME FRAME:	TRADE TYPE:	RISK TO REWARD RATIO:	RISK % LEVEL (%/$1000)		BALANCE:
ENTRY CONFIRMATIONS: 1. 2. 3.		ENTRY: 1. 2. 3.	STOP LOSS: 1. 2. 3.		TAKE PROFIT: 1. 2. 3.		TRADE GOAL:
POWER POINTS: (WHAT WORKED) 1. 2. 3.			END EMOJI:	+, - PIP$/PROFIT$			ACTUAL LOSS/PROFITS

TRADING JOURNAL

ACCOUNT:			DATE:	SESSION:			TIME:
PAIR:	START EMOJI:	ENTRY TIME FRAME:	TRADE TYPE:	RISK TO REWARD RATIO:	RISK % LEVEL (%/$1000)		BALANCE:
ENTRY CONFIRMATIONS: 1. 2. 3.		ENTRY: 1. 2. 3.	STOP LOSS: 1. 2. 3.		TAKE PROFIT: 1. 2. 3.		TRADE GOAL:
POWER POINTS: (WHAT WORKED) 1. 2. 3.			END EMOJI:	+, - PIP$/PROFIT$		ACTUAL LOSS/PROFITS	

ACCOUNT:			DATE:	SESSION:			TIME:
PAIR:	START EMOJI:	ENTRY TIME FRAME:	TRADE TYPE:	RISK TO REWARD RATIO:	RISK % LEVEL (%/$1000)		BALANCE:
ENTRY CONFIRMATIONS: 1. 2. 3.		ENTRY: 1. 2. 3.	STOP LOSS: 1. 2. 3.		TAKE PROFIT: 1. 2. 3.		TRADE GOAL:
POWER POINTS: (WHAT WORKED) 1. 2. 3.			END EMOJI:	+, - PIP$/PROFIT$		ACTUAL LOSS/PROFITS	

ACCOUNT:			DATE:	SESSION:			TIME:
PAIR:	START EMOJI:	ENTRY TIME FRAME:	TRADE TYPE:	RISK TO REWARD RATIO:	RISK % LEVEL (%/$1000)		BALANCE:
ENTRY CONFIRMATIONS: 1. 2. 3.		ENTRY: 1. 2. 3.	STOP LOSS: 1. 2. 3.		TAKE PROFIT: 1. 2. 3.		TRADE GOAL:
POWER POINTS: (WHAT WORKED) 1. 2. 3.			END EMOJI:	+, - PIP$/PROFIT$		ACTUAL LOSS/PROFITS	

TRADING JOURNAL

ACCOUNT:			DATE:	SESSION:			TIME:
PAIR:	START EMOJI:	ENTRY TIME FRAME:	TRADE TYPE:	RISK TO REWARD RATIO:	RISK % LEVEL (%/$1000)		BALANCE:
ENTRY CONFIRMATIONS: 1. 2. 3.		ENTRY: 1. 2. 3.	STOP LOSS: 1. 2. 3.		TAKE PROFIT: 1. 2. 3.		TRADE GOAL:
POWER POINTS: (WHAT WORKED) 1. 2. 3.			END EMOJI:	+, - PIP$/PROFIT$			ACTUAL LOSS/PROFITS

ACCOUNT:			DATE:	SESSION:			TIME:
PAIR:	START EMOJI:	ENTRY TIME FRAME:	TRADE TYPE:	RISK TO REWARD RATIO:	RISK % LEVEL (%/$1000)		BALANCE:
ENTRY CONFIRMATIONS: 1. 2. 3.		ENTRY: 1. 2. 3.	STOP LOSS: 1. 2. 3.		TAKE PROFIT: 1. 2. 3.		TRADE GOAL:
POWER POINTS: (WHAT WORKED) 1. 2. 3.			END EMOJI:	+, - PIP$/PROFIT$			ACTUAL LOSS/PROFITS

ACCOUNT:			DATE:	SESSION:			TIME:
PAIR:	START EMOJI:	ENTRY TIME FRAME:	TRADE TYPE:	RISK TO REWARD RATIO:	RISK % LEVEL (%/$1000)		BALANCE:
ENTRY CONFIRMATIONS: 1. 2. 3.		ENTRY: 1. 2. 3.	STOP LOSS: 1. 2. 3.		TAKE PROFIT: 1. 2. 3.		TRADE GOAL:
POWER POINTS: (WHAT WORKED) 1. 2. 3.			END EMOJI:	+, - PIP$/PROFIT$			ACTUAL LOSS/PROFITS

TRADING JOURNAL

ACCOUNT:			DATE:	SESSION:			TIME:	
PAIR:	START EMOJI:	ENTRY TIME FRAME:	TRADE TYPE:	RISK TO REWARD RATIO:	RISK % LEVEL (%/\$1000)		BALANCE:	
ENTRY CONFIRMATIONS: 1. 2. 3.		ENTRY: 1. 2. 3.	STOP LOSS: 1. 2. 3.			TAKE PROFIT: 1. 2. 3.	TRADE GOAL:	
POWER POINTS: (WHAT WORKED) 1. 2. 3.			END EMOJI:	+, - PIP\$/PROFIT\$			ACTUAL LOSS/PROFITS	

ACCOUNT:			DATE:	SESSION:			TIME:	
PAIR:	START EMOJI:	ENTRY TIME FRAME:	TRADE TYPE:	RISK TO REWARD RATIO:	RISK % LEVEL (%/\$1000)		BALANCE:	
ENTRY CONFIRMATIONS: 1. 2. 3.		ENTRY: 1. 2. 3.	STOP LOSS: 1. 2. 3.			TAKE PROFIT: 1. 2. 3.	TRADE GOAL:	
POWER POINTS: (WHAT WORKED) 1. 2. 3.			END EMOJI:	+, - PIP\$/PROFIT\$			ACTUAL LOSS/PROFITS	

ACCOUNT:			DATE:	SESSION:			TIME:	
PAIR:	START EMOJI:	ENTRY TIME FRAME:	TRADE TYPE:	RISK TO REWARD RATIO:	RISK % LEVEL (%/\$1000)		BALANCE:	
ENTRY CONFIRMATIONS: 1. 2. 3.		ENTRY: 1. 2. 3.	STOP LOSS: 1. 2. 3.			TAKE PROFIT: 1. 2. 3.	TRADE GOAL:	
POWER POINTS: (WHAT WORKED) 1. 2. 3.			END EMOJI:	+, - PIP\$/PROFIT\$			ACTUAL LOSS/PROFITS	

TRADING JOURNAL

ACCOUNT:			DATE:	SESSION:		TIME:	
PAIR:	START EMOJI:	ENTRY TIME FRAME:	TRADE TYPE:	RISK TO REWARD RATIO:	RISK % LEVEL (%/$1000)	BALANCE:	
ENTRY CONFIRMATIONS: 1. 2. 3.		ENTRY: 1. 2. 3.	STOP LOSS: 1. 2. 3.		TAKE PROFIT: 1. 2. 3.	TRADE GOAL:	
POWER POINTS: (WHAT WORKED) 1. 2. 3.			END EMOJI:	+, - PIP$/PROFIT$		ACTUAL LOSS/PROFITS	

ACCOUNT:			DATE:	SESSION:		TIME:	
PAIR:	START EMOJI:	ENTRY TIME FRAME:	TRADE TYPE:	RISK TO REWARD RATIO:	RISK % LEVEL (%/$1000)	BALANCE:	
ENTRY CONFIRMATIONS: 1. 2. 3.		ENTRY: 1. 2. 3.	STOP LOSS: 1. 2. 3.		TAKE PROFIT: 1. 2. 3.	TRADE GOAL:	
POWER POINTS: (WHAT WORKED) 1. 2. 3.			END EMOJI:	+, - PIP$/PROFIT$		ACTUAL LOSS/PROFITS	

ACCOUNT:			DATE:	SESSION:		TIME:	
PAIR:	START EMOJI:	ENTRY TIME FRAME:	TRADE TYPE:	RISK TO REWARD RATIO:	RISK % LEVEL (%/$1000)	BALANCE:	
ENTRY CONFIRMATIONS: 1. 2. 3.		ENTRY: 1. 2. 3.	STOP LOSS: 1. 2. 3.		TAKE PROFIT: 1. 2. 3.	TRADE GOAL:	
POWER POINTS: (WHAT WORKED) 1. 2. 3.			END EMOJI:	+, - PIP$/PROFIT$		ACTUAL LOSS/PROFITS	

TRADING JOURNAL

ACCOUNT:			DATE:	SESSION:			TIME:
PAIR:	START EMOJI:	ENTRY TIME FRAME:	TRADE TYPE:	RISK TO REWARD RATIO:	RISK % LEVEL (%/$1000)		BALANCE:
ENTRY CONFIRMATIONS: 1. 2. 3.		ENTRY: 1. 2. 3.	STOP LOSS: 1. 2. 3.		TAKE PROFIT: 1. 2. 3.		TRADE GOAL:
POWER POINTS: (WHAT WORKED) 1. 2. 3.			END EMOJI:	+, - PIP$/PROFIT$			ACTUAL LOSS/PROFITS

ACCOUNT:			DATE:	SESSION:			TIME:
PAIR:	START EMOJI:	ENTRY TIME FRAME:	TRADE TYPE:	RISK TO REWARD RATIO:	RISK % LEVEL (%/$1000)		BALANCE:
ENTRY CONFIRMATIONS: 1. 2. 3.		ENTRY: 1. 2. 3.	STOP LOSS: 1. 2. 3.		TAKE PROFIT: 1. 2. 3.		TRADE GOAL:
POWER POINTS: (WHAT WORKED) 1. 2. 3.			END EMOJI:	+, - PIP$/PROFIT$			ACTUAL LOSS/PROFITS

ACCOUNT:			DATE:	SESSION:			TIME:
PAIR:	START EMOJI:	ENTRY TIME FRAME:	TRADE TYPE:	RISK TO REWARD RATIO:	RISK % LEVEL (%/$1000)		BALANCE:
ENTRY CONFIRMATIONS: 1. 2. 3.		ENTRY: 1. 2. 3.	STOP LOSS: 1. 2. 3.		TAKE PROFIT: 1. 2. 3.		TRADE GOAL:
POWER POINTS: (WHAT WORKED) 1. 2. 3.			END EMOJI:	+, - PIP$/PROFIT$			ACTUAL LOSS/PROFITS

TRADING JOURNAL

ACCOUNT:			DATE:	SESSION:			TIME:
PAIR:	START EMOJI:	ENTRY TIME FRAME:	TRADE TYPE:	RISK TO REWARD RATIO:	RISK % LEVEL (%/$1000)		BALANCE:
ENTRY CONFIRMATIONS: 1. 2. 3.		ENTRY: 1. 2. 3.	STOP LOSS: 1. 2. 3.		TAKE PROFIT: 1. 2. 3.		TRADE GOAL:
POWER POINTS: (WHAT WORKED) 1. 2. 3.			END EMOJI:	+, - PIP$/PROFIT$			ACTUAL LOSS/PROFITS

ACCOUNT:			DATE:	SESSION:			TIME:
PAIR:	START EMOJI:	ENTRY TIME FRAME:	TRADE TYPE:	RISK TO REWARD RATIO:	RISK % LEVEL (%/$1000)		BALANCE:
ENTRY CONFIRMATIONS: 1. 2. 3.		ENTRY: 1. 2. 3.	STOP LOSS: 1. 2. 3.		TAKE PROFIT: 1. 2. 3.		TRADE GOAL:
POWER POINTS: (WHAT WORKED) 1. 2. 3.			END EMOJI:	+, - PIP$/PROFIT$			ACTUAL LOSS/PROFITS

ACCOUNT:			DATE:	SESSION:			TIME:
PAIR:	START EMOJI:	ENTRY TIME FRAME:	TRADE TYPE:	RISK TO REWARD RATIO:	RISK % LEVEL (%/$1000)		BALANCE:
ENTRY CONFIRMATIONS: 1. 2. 3.		ENTRY: 1. 2. 3.	STOP LOSS: 1. 2. 3.		TAKE PROFIT: 1. 2. 3.		TRADE GOAL:
POWER POINTS: (WHAT WORKED) 1. 2. 3.			END EMOJI:	+, - PIP$/PROFIT$			ACTUAL LOSS/PROFITS

TRADING JOURNAL

ACCOUNT:			DATE:	SESSION:		TIME:	
PAIR:	START EMOJI:	ENTRY TIME FRAME:	TRADE TYPE:	RISK TO REWARD RATIO:	RISK % LEVEL (%/$1000)	BALANCE:	
ENTRY CONFIRMATIONS: 1. 2. 3.		ENTRY: 1. 2. 3.	STOP LOSS: 1. 2. 3.		TAKE PROFIT: 1. 2. 3.	TRADE GOAL:	
POWER POINTS: (WHAT WORKED) 1. 2. 3.			END EMOJI:	+, - PIP$/PROFIT$		ACTUAL LOSS/PROFITS	

ACCOUNT:			DATE:	SESSION:		TIME:	
PAIR:	START EMOJI:	ENTRY TIME FRAME:	TRADE TYPE:	RISK TO REWARD RATIO:	RISK % LEVEL (%/$1000)	BALANCE:	
ENTRY CONFIRMATIONS: 1. 2. 3.		ENTRY: 1. 2. 3.	STOP LOSS: 1. 2. 3.		TAKE PROFIT: 1. 2. 3.	TRADE GOAL:	
POWER POINTS: (WHAT WORKED) 1. 2. 3.			END EMOJI:	+, - PIP$/PROFIT$		ACTUAL LOSS/PROFITS	

ACCOUNT:			DATE:	SESSION:		TIME:	
PAIR:	START EMOJI:	ENTRY TIME FRAME:	TRADE TYPE:	RISK TO REWARD RATIO:	RISK % LEVEL (%/$1000)	BALANCE:	
ENTRY CONFIRMATIONS: 1. 2. 3.		ENTRY: 1. 2. 3.	STOP LOSS: 1. 2. 3.		TAKE PROFIT: 1. 2. 3.	TRADE GOAL:	
POWER POINTS: (WHAT WORKED) 1. 2. 3.			END EMOJI:	+, - PIP$/PROFIT$		ACTUAL LOSS/PROFITS	

TRADING JOURNAL

ACCOUNT:			DATE:	SESSION:			TIME:
PAIR:	START EMOJI:	ENTRY TIME FRAME:	TRADE TYPE:	RISK TO REWARD RATIO:	RISK % LEVEL (%/$1000)		BALANCE:
ENTRY CONFIRMATIONS: 1. 2. 3.		ENTRY: 1. 2. 3.	STOP LOSS: 1. 2. 3.		TAKE PROFIT: 1. 2. 3.		TRADE GOAL:
POWER POINTS: (WHAT WORKED) 1. 2. 3.			END EMOJI:	+, - PIP$/PROFIT$			ACTUAL LOSS/PROFITS

ACCOUNT:			DATE:	SESSION:			TIME:
PAIR:	START EMOJI:	ENTRY TIME FRAME:	TRADE TYPE:	RISK TO REWARD RATIO:	RISK % LEVEL (%/$1000)		BALANCE:
ENTRY CONFIRMATIONS: 1. 2. 3.		ENTRY: 1. 2. 3.	STOP LOSS: 1. 2. 3.		TAKE PROFIT: 1. 2. 3.		TRADE GOAL:
POWER POINTS: (WHAT WORKED) 1. 2. 3.			END EMOJI:	+, - PIP$/PROFIT$			ACTUAL LOSS/PROFITS

ACCOUNT:			DATE:	SESSION:			TIME:
PAIR:	START EMOJI:	ENTRY TIME FRAME:	TRADE TYPE:	RISK TO REWARD RATIO:	RISK % LEVEL (%/$1000)		BALANCE:
ENTRY CONFIRMATIONS: 1. 2. 3.		ENTRY: 1. 2. 3.	STOP LOSS: 1. 2. 3.		TAKE PROFIT: 1. 2. 3.		TRADE GOAL:
POWER POINTS: (WHAT WORKED) 1. 2. 3.			END EMOJI:	+, - PIP$/PROFIT$			ACTUAL LOSS/PROFITS

TRADING JOURNAL

ACCOUNT:				DATE:	SESSION:		TIME:
PAIR:	START EMOJI:	ENTRY TIME FRAME:	TRADE TYPE:	RISK TO REWARD RATIO:	RISK % LEVEL (%/$1000)		BALANCE:
ENTRY CONFIRMATIONS: 1. 2. 3.		ENTRY: 1. 2. 3.	STOP LOSS: 1. 2. 3.		TAKE PROFIT: 1. 2. 3.		TRADE GOAL:
POWER POINTS: (WHAT WORKED) 1. 2. 3.			END EMOJI:	+, - PIP$/PROFIT$		ACTUAL LOSS/PROFITS	

ACCOUNT:				DATE:	SESSION:		TIME:
PAIR:	START EMOJI:	ENTRY TIME FRAME:	TRADE TYPE:	RISK TO REWARD RATIO:	RISK % LEVEL (%/$1000)		BALANCE:
ENTRY CONFIRMATIONS: 1. 2. 3.		ENTRY: 1. 2. 3.	STOP LOSS: 1. 2. 3.		TAKE PROFIT: 1. 2. 3.		TRADE GOAL:
POWER POINTS: (WHAT WORKED) 1. 2. 3.			END EMOJI:	+, - PIP$/PROFIT$		ACTUAL LOSS/PROFITS	

ACCOUNT:				DATE:	SESSION:		TIME:
PAIR:	START EMOJI:	ENTRY TIME FRAME:	TRADE TYPE:	RISK TO REWARD RATIO:	RISK % LEVEL (%/$1000)		BALANCE:
ENTRY CONFIRMATIONS: 1. 2. 3.		ENTRY: 1. 2. 3.	STOP LOSS: 1. 2. 3.		TAKE PROFIT: 1. 2. 3.		TRADE GOAL:
POWER POINTS: (WHAT WORKED) 1. 2. 3.			END EMOJI:	+, - PIP$/PROFIT$		ACTUAL LOSS/PROFITS	

TRADING JOURNAL

ACCOUNT:			DATE:	SESSION:			TIME:	
PAIR:	START EMOJI:	ENTRY TIME FRAME:	TRADE TYPE:	RISK TO REWARD RATIO:	RISK % LEVEL (%/$1000)		BALANCE:	
ENTRY CONFIRMATIONS: 1. 2. 3.		ENTRY: 1. 2. 3.	STOP LOSS: 1. 2. 3.		TAKE PROFIT: 1. 2. 3.		TRADE GOAL:	
POWER POINTS: (WHAT WORKED) 1. 2. 3.			END EMOJI:	+, - PIP$/PROFIT$			ACTUAL LOSS/PROFITS	

ACCOUNT:			DATE:	SESSION:			TIME:	
PAIR:	START EMOJI:	ENTRY TIME FRAME:	TRADE TYPE:	RISK TO REWARD RATIO:	RISK % LEVEL (%/$1000)		BALANCE:	
ENTRY CONFIRMATIONS: 1. 2. 3.		ENTRY: 1. 2. 3.	STOP LOSS: 1. 2. 3.		TAKE PROFIT: 1. 2. 3.		TRADE GOAL:	
POWER POINTS: (WHAT WORKED) 1. 2. 3.			END EMOJI:	+, - PIP$/PROFIT$			ACTUAL LOSS/PROFITS	

ACCOUNT:			DATE:	SESSION:			TIME:	
PAIR:	START EMOJI:	ENTRY TIME FRAME:	TRADE TYPE:	RISK TO REWARD RATIO:	RISK % LEVEL (%/$1000)		BALANCE:	
ENTRY CONFIRMATIONS: 1. 2. 3.		ENTRY: 1. 2. 3.	STOP LOSS: 1. 2. 3.		TAKE PROFIT: 1. 2. 3.		TRADE GOAL:	
POWER POINTS: (WHAT WORKED) 1. 2. 3.			END EMOJI:	+, - PIP$/PROFIT$			ACTUAL LOSS/PROFITS	

TRADING JOURNAL

ACCOUNT:			DATE:	SESSION:		TIME:	
PAIR:	START EMOJI:	ENTRY TIME FRAME:	TRADE TYPE:	RISK TO REWARD RATIO:	RISK % LEVEL (%/$1000)	BALANCE:	
ENTRY CONFIRMATIONS: 1. 2. 3.		ENTRY: 1. 2. 3.	STOP LOSS: 1. 2. 3.		TAKE PROFIT: 1. 2. 3.	TRADE GOAL:	
POWER POINTS: (WHAT WORKED) 1. 2. 3.			END EMOJI:	+, - PIP$/PROFIT$		ACTUAL LOSS/PROFITS	

ACCOUNT:			DATE:	SESSION:		TIME:	
PAIR:	START EMOJI:	ENTRY TIME FRAME:	TRADE TYPE:	RISK TO REWARD RATIO:	RISK % LEVEL (%/$1000)	BALANCE:	
ENTRY CONFIRMATIONS: 1. 2. 3.		ENTRY: 1. 2. 3.	STOP LOSS: 1. 2. 3.		TAKE PROFIT: 1. 2. 3.	TRADE GOAL:	
POWER POINTS: (WHAT WORKED) 1. 2. 3.			END EMOJI:	+, - PIP$/PROFIT$		ACTUAL LOSS/PROFITS	

ACCOUNT:			DATE:	SESSION:		TIME:	
PAIR:	START EMOJI:	ENTRY TIME FRAME:	TRADE TYPE:	RISK TO REWARD RATIO:	RISK % LEVEL (%/$1000)	BALANCE:	
ENTRY CONFIRMATIONS: 1. 2. 3.		ENTRY: 1. 2. 3.	STOP LOSS: 1. 2. 3.		TAKE PROFIT: 1. 2. 3.	TRADE GOAL:	
POWER POINTS: (WHAT WORKED) 1. 2. 3.			END EMOJI:	+, - PIP$/PROFIT$		ACTUAL LOSS/PROFITS	

TRADING JOURNAL

ACCOUNT:			DATE:	SESSION:			TIME:	
PAIR:	START EMOJI:	ENTRY TIME FRAME:	TRADE TYPE:	RISK TO REWARD RATIO:	RISK % LEVEL (%/$1000)		BALANCE:	
ENTRY CONFIRMATIONS: 1. 2. 3.		ENTRY: 1. 2. 3.	STOP LOSS: 1. 2. 3.			TAKE PROFIT: 1. 2. 3.	TRADE GOAL:	
POWER POINTS: (WHAT WORKED) 1. 2. 3.			END EMOJI:	+, - PIP$/PROFIT$			ACTUAL LOSS/PROFITS	

ACCOUNT:			DATE:	SESSION:			TIME:	
PAIR:	START EMOJI:	ENTRY TIME FRAME:	TRADE TYPE:	RISK TO REWARD RATIO:	RISK % LEVEL (%/$1000)		BALANCE:	
ENTRY CONFIRMATIONS: 1. 2. 3.		ENTRY: 1. 2. 3.	STOP LOSS: 1. 2. 3.			TAKE PROFIT: 1. 2. 3.	TRADE GOAL:	
POWER POINTS: (WHAT WORKED) 1. 2. 3.			END EMOJI:	+, - PIP$/PROFIT$			ACTUAL LOSS/PROFITS	

ACCOUNT:			DATE:	SESSION:			TIME:	
PAIR:	START EMOJI:	ENTRY TIME FRAME:	TRADE TYPE:	RISK TO REWARD RATIO:	RISK % LEVEL (%/$1000)		BALANCE:	
ENTRY CONFIRMATIONS: 1. 2. 3.		ENTRY: 1. 2. 3.	STOP LOSS: 1. 2. 3.			TAKE PROFIT: 1. 2. 3.	TRADE GOAL:	
POWER POINTS: (WHAT WORKED) 1. 2. 3.			END EMOJI:	+, - PIP$/PROFIT$			ACTUAL LOSS/PROFITS	

TRADING JOURNAL

ACCOUNT:			DATE:	SESSION:			TIME:
PAIR:	START EMOJI:	ENTRY TIME FRAME:	TRADE TYPE:	RISK TO REWARD RATIO:	RISK % LEVEL (%/$1000)		BALANCE:
ENTRY CONFIRMATIONS: 1. 2. 3.		ENTRY: 1. 2. 3.	STOP LOSS: 1. 2. 3.		TAKE PROFIT: 1. 2. 3.		TRADE GOAL:
POWER POINTS: (WHAT WORKED) 1. 2. 3.			END EMOJI:	+, - PIP$/PROFIT$			ACTUAL LOSS/PROFITS

ACCOUNT:			DATE:	SESSION:			TIME:
PAIR:	START EMOJI:	ENTRY TIME FRAME:	TRADE TYPE:	RISK TO REWARD RATIO:	RISK % LEVEL (%/$1000)		BALANCE:
ENTRY CONFIRMATIONS: 1. 2. 3.		ENTRY: 1. 2. 3.	STOP LOSS: 1. 2. 3.		TAKE PROFIT: 1. 2. 3.		TRADE GOAL:
POWER POINTS: (WHAT WORKED) 1. 2. 3.			END EMOJI:	+, - PIP$/PROFIT$			ACTUAL LOSS/PROFITS

ACCOUNT:			DATE:	SESSION:			TIME:
PAIR:	START EMOJI:	ENTRY TIME FRAME:	TRADE TYPE:	RISK TO REWARD RATIO:	RISK % LEVEL (%/$1000)		BALANCE:
ENTRY CONFIRMATIONS: 1. 2. 3.		ENTRY: 1. 2. 3.	STOP LOSS: 1. 2. 3.		TAKE PROFIT: 1. 2. 3.		TRADE GOAL:
POWER POINTS: (WHAT WORKED) 1. 2. 3.			END EMOJI:	+, - PIP$/PROFIT$			ACTUAL LOSS/PROFITS

TRADING JOURNAL

ACCOUNT:			DATE:	SESSION:			TIME:	
PAIR:	START EMOJI:	ENTRY TIME FRAME:	TRADE TYPE:	RISK TO REWARD RATIO:	RISK % LEVEL (%/$1000)		BALANCE:	
ENTRY CONFIRMATIONS: 1. 2. 3.		ENTRY: 1. 2. 3.	STOP LOSS: 1. 2. 3.			TAKE PROFIT: 1. 2. 3.	TRADE GOAL:	
POWER POINTS: (WHAT WORKED) 1. 2. 3.			END EMOJI:	+, - PIP$/PROFIT$			ACTUAL LOSS/PROFITS	

ACCOUNT:			DATE:	SESSION:			TIME:	
PAIR:	START EMOJI:	ENTRY TIME FRAME:	TRADE TYPE:	RISK TO REWARD RATIO:	RISK % LEVEL (%/$1000)		BALANCE:	
ENTRY CONFIRMATIONS: 1. 2. 3.		ENTRY: 1. 2. 3.	STOP LOSS: 1. 2. 3.			TAKE PROFIT: 1. 2. 3.	TRADE GOAL:	
POWER POINTS: (WHAT WORKED) 1. 2. 3.			END EMOJI:	+, - PIP$/PROFIT$			ACTUAL LOSS/PROFITS	

ACCOUNT:			DATE:	SESSION:			TIME:	
PAIR:	START EMOJI:	ENTRY TIME FRAME:	TRADE TYPE:	RISK TO REWARD RATIO:	RISK % LEVEL (%/$1000)		BALANCE:	
ENTRY CONFIRMATIONS: 1. 2. 3.		ENTRY: 1. 2. 3.	STOP LOSS: 1. 2. 3.			TAKE PROFIT: 1. 2. 3.	TRADE GOAL:	
POWER POINTS: (WHAT WORKED) 1. 2. 3.			END EMOJI:	+, - PIP$/PROFIT$			ACTUAL LOSS/PROFITS	

TRADING JOURNAL

ACCOUNT:			DATE:	SESSION:			TIME:
PAIR:	START EMOJI:	ENTRY TIME FRAME:	TRADE TYPE:	RISK TO REWARD RATIO:	RISK % LEVEL (%/\$1000)		BALANCE:
ENTRY CONFIRMATIONS: 1. 2. 3.		ENTRY: 1. 2. 3.	STOP LOSS: 1. 2. 3.		TAKE PROFIT: 1. 2. 3.		TRADE GOAL:
POWER POINTS: (WHAT WORKED) 1. 2. 3.			END EMOJI:	+, - PIP\$/PROFIT\$			ACTUAL LOSS/PROFITS

ACCOUNT:			DATE:	SESSION:			TIME:
PAIR:	START EMOJI:	ENTRY TIME FRAME:	TRADE TYPE:	RISK TO REWARD RATIO:	RISK % LEVEL (%/\$1000)		BALANCE:
ENTRY CONFIRMATIONS: 1. 2. 3.		ENTRY: 1. 2. 3.	STOP LOSS: 1. 2. 3.		TAKE PROFIT: 1. 2. 3.		TRADE GOAL:
POWER POINTS: (WHAT WORKED) 1. 2. 3.			END EMOJI:	+, - PIP\$/PROFIT\$			ACTUAL LOSS/PROFITS

ACCOUNT:			DATE:	SESSION:			TIME:
PAIR:	START EMOJI:	ENTRY TIME FRAME:	TRADE TYPE:	RISK TO REWARD RATIO:	RISK % LEVEL (%/\$1000)		BALANCE:
ENTRY CONFIRMATIONS: 1. 2. 3.		ENTRY: 1. 2. 3.	STOP LOSS: 1. 2. 3.		TAKE PROFIT: 1. 2. 3.		TRADE GOAL:
POWER POINTS: (WHAT WORKED) 1. 2. 3.			END EMOJI:	+, - PIP\$/PROFIT\$			ACTUAL LOSS/PROFITS

TRADING JOURNAL

ACCOUNT:			DATE:	SESSION:		TIME:	
PAIR:	START EMOJI:	ENTRY TIME FRAME:	TRADE TYPE:	RISK TO REWARD RATIO:	RISK % LEVEL (%/$1000)	BALANCE:	
ENTRY CONFIRMATIONS: 1. 2. 3.		ENTRY: 1. 2. 3.	STOP LOSS: 1. 2. 3.		TAKE PROFIT: 1. 2. 3.	TRADE GOAL:	
POWER POINTS: (WHAT WORKED) 1. 2. 3.			END EMOJI:	+, - PIP$/PROFIT$		ACTUAL LOSS/PROFITS	

ACCOUNT:			DATE:	SESSION:		TIME:	
PAIR:	START EMOJI:	ENTRY TIME FRAME:	TRADE TYPE:	RISK TO REWARD RATIO:	RISK % LEVEL (%/$1000)	BALANCE:	
ENTRY CONFIRMATIONS: 1. 2. 3.		ENTRY: 1. 2. 3.	STOP LOSS: 1. 2. 3.		TAKE PROFIT: 1. 2. 3.	TRADE GOAL:	
POWER POINTS: (WHAT WORKED) 1. 2. 3.			END EMOJI:	+, - PIP$/PROFIT$		ACTUAL LOSS/PROFITS	

ACCOUNT:			DATE:	SESSION:		TIME:	
PAIR:	START EMOJI:	ENTRY TIME FRAME:	TRADE TYPE:	RISK TO REWARD RATIO:	RISK % LEVEL (%/$1000)	BALANCE:	
ENTRY CONFIRMATIONS: 1. 2. 3.		ENTRY: 1. 2. 3.	STOP LOSS: 1. 2. 3.		TAKE PROFIT: 1. 2. 3.	TRADE GOAL:	
POWER POINTS: (WHAT WORKED) 1. 2. 3.			END EMOJI:	+, - PIP$/PROFIT$		ACTUAL LOSS/PROFITS	

TRADING JOURNAL

ACCOUNT:			DATE:	SESSION:			TIME:
PAIR:	START EMOJI:	ENTRY TIME FRAME:	TRADE TYPE:	RISK TO REWARD RATIO:	RISK % LEVEL (%/$1000)		BALANCE:
ENTRY CONFIRMATIONS: 1. 2. 3.		ENTRY: 1. 2. 3.	STOP LOSS: 1. 2. 3.		TAKE PROFIT: 1. 2. 3.		TRADE GOAL:
POWER POINTS: (WHAT WORKED) 1. 2. 3.			END EMOJI:	+, - PIP$/PROFIT$			ACTUAL LOSS/PROFITS

ACCOUNT:			DATE:	SESSION:			TIME:
PAIR:	START EMOJI:	ENTRY TIME FRAME:	TRADE TYPE:	RISK TO REWARD RATIO:	RISK % LEVEL (%/$1000)		BALANCE:
ENTRY CONFIRMATIONS: 1. 2. 3.		ENTRY: 1. 2. 3.	STOP LOSS: 1. 2. 3.		TAKE PROFIT: 1. 2. 3.		TRADE GOAL:
POWER POINTS: (WHAT WORKED) 1. 2. 3.			END EMOJI:	+, - PIP$/PROFIT$			ACTUAL LOSS/PROFITS

ACCOUNT:			DATE:	SESSION:			TIME:
PAIR:	START EMOJI:	ENTRY TIME FRAME:	TRADE TYPE:	RISK TO REWARD RATIO:	RISK % LEVEL (%/$1000)		BALANCE:
ENTRY CONFIRMATIONS: 1. 2. 3.		ENTRY: 1. 2. 3.	STOP LOSS: 1. 2. 3.		TAKE PROFIT: 1. 2. 3.		TRADE GOAL:
POWER POINTS: (WHAT WORKED) 1. 2. 3.			END EMOJI:	+, - PIP$/PROFIT$			ACTUAL LOSS/PROFITS

TRADING JOURNAL

ACCOUNT:			DATE:	SESSION:		TIME:	
PAIR:	START EMOJI:	ENTRY TIME FRAME:	TRADE TYPE:	RISK TO REWARD RATIO:	RISK % LEVEL (%/$1000)	BALANCE:	
ENTRY CONFIRMATIONS: 1. 2. 3.		ENTRY: 1. 2. 3.	STOP LOSS: 1. 2. 3.		TAKE PROFIT: 1. 2. 3.	TRADE GOAL:	
POWER POINTS: (WHAT WORKED) 1. 2. 3.			END EMOJI:	+, - PIP$/PROFIT$		ACTUAL LOSS/PROFITS	

ACCOUNT:			DATE:	SESSION:		TIME:	
PAIR:	START EMOJI:	ENTRY TIME FRAME:	TRADE TYPE:	RISK TO REWARD RATIO:	RISK % LEVEL (%/$1000)	BALANCE:	
ENTRY CONFIRMATIONS: 1. 2. 3.		ENTRY: 1. 2. 3.	STOP LOSS: 1. 2. 3.		TAKE PROFIT: 1. 2. 3.	TRADE GOAL:	
POWER POINTS: (WHAT WORKED) 1. 2. 3.			END EMOJI:	+, - PIP$/PROFIT$		ACTUAL LOSS/PROFITS	

ACCOUNT:			DATE:	SESSION:		TIME:	
PAIR:	START EMOJI:	ENTRY TIME FRAME:	TRADE TYPE:	RISK TO REWARD RATIO:	RISK % LEVEL (%/$1000)	BALANCE:	
ENTRY CONFIRMATIONS: 1. 2. 3.		ENTRY: 1. 2. 3.	STOP LOSS: 1. 2. 3.		TAKE PROFIT: 1. 2. 3.	TRADE GOAL:	
POWER POINTS: (WHAT WORKED) 1. 2. 3.			END EMOJI:	+, - PIP$/PROFIT$		ACTUAL LOSS/PROFITS	

TRADING JOURNAL

ACCOUNT:			DATE:	SESSION:			TIME:
PAIR:	START EMOJI:	ENTRY TIME FRAME:	TRADE TYPE:	RISK TO REWARD RATIO:	RISK % LEVEL (%/$1000)		BALANCE:
ENTRY CONFIRMATIONS: 1. 2. 3.		ENTRY: 1. 2. 3.	STOP LOSS: 1. 2. 3.		TAKE PROFIT: 1. 2. 3.		TRADE GOAL:
POWER POINTS: (WHAT WORKED) 1. 2. 3.			END EMOJI:	+, - PIP$/PROFIT$			ACTUAL LOSS/PROFITS

ACCOUNT:			DATE:	SESSION:			TIME:
PAIR:	START EMOJI:	ENTRY TIME FRAME:	TRADE TYPE:	RISK TO REWARD RATIO:	RISK % LEVEL (%/$1000)		BALANCE:
ENTRY CONFIRMATIONS: 1. 2. 3.		ENTRY: 1. 2. 3.	STOP LOSS: 1. 2. 3.		TAKE PROFIT: 1. 2. 3.		TRADE GOAL:
POWER POINTS: (WHAT WORKED) 1. 2. 3.			END EMOJI:	+, - PIP$/PROFIT$			ACTUAL LOSS/PROFITS

ACCOUNT:			DATE:	SESSION:			TIME:
PAIR:	START EMOJI:	ENTRY TIME FRAME:	TRADE TYPE:	RISK TO REWARD RATIO:	RISK % LEVEL (%/$1000)		BALANCE:
ENTRY CONFIRMATIONS: 1. 2. 3.		ENTRY: 1. 2. 3.	STOP LOSS: 1. 2. 3.		TAKE PROFIT: 1. 2. 3.		TRADE GOAL:
POWER POINTS: (WHAT WORKED) 1. 2. 3.			END EMOJI:	+, - PIP$/PROFIT$			ACTUAL LOSS/PROFITS

TRADING JOURNAL

ACCOUNT:			DATE:	SESSION:			TIME:
PAIR:	START EMOJI:	ENTRY TIME FRAME:	TRADE TYPE:	RISK TO REWARD RATIO:	RISK % LEVEL (%/$1000)		BALANCE:
ENTRY CONFIRMATIONS: 1. 2. 3.		ENTRY: 1. 2. 3.	STOP LOSS: 1. 2. 3.		TAKE PROFIT: 1. 2. 3.		TRADE GOAL:
POWER POINTS: (WHAT WORKED) 1. 2. 3.			END EMOJI:	+, - PIP$/PROFIT$		ACTUAL LOSS/PROFITS	

ACCOUNT:			DATE:	SESSION:			TIME:
PAIR:	START EMOJI:	ENTRY TIME FRAME:	TRADE TYPE:	RISK TO REWARD RATIO:	RISK % LEVEL (%/$1000)		BALANCE:
ENTRY CONFIRMATIONS: 1. 2. 3.		ENTRY: 1. 2. 3.	STOP LOSS: 1. 2. 3.		TAKE PROFIT: 1. 2. 3.		TRADE GOAL:
POWER POINTS: (WHAT WORKED) 1. 2. 3.			END EMOJI:	+, - PIP$/PROFIT$		ACTUAL LOSS/PROFITS	

ACCOUNT:			DATE:	SESSION:			TIME:
PAIR:	START EMOJI:	ENTRY TIME FRAME:	TRADE TYPE:	RISK TO REWARD RATIO:	RISK % LEVEL (%/$1000)		BALANCE:
ENTRY CONFIRMATIONS: 1. 2. 3.		ENTRY: 1. 2. 3.	STOP LOSS: 1. 2. 3.		TAKE PROFIT: 1. 2. 3.		TRADE GOAL:
POWER POINTS: (WHAT WORKED) 1. 2. 3.			END EMOJI:	+, - PIP$/PROFIT$		ACTUAL LOSS/PROFITS	

TRADING JOURNAL

ACCOUNT:			DATE:	SESSION:		TIME:	
PAIR:	START EMOJI:	ENTRY TIME FRAME:	TRADE TYPE:	RISK TO REWARD RATIO:	RISK % LEVEL (%/$1000)	BALANCE:	
ENTRY CONFIRMATIONS: 1. 2. 3.		ENTRY: 1. 2. 3.	STOP LOSS: 1. 2. 3.		TAKE PROFIT: 1. 2. 3.	TRADE GOAL:	
POWER POINTS: (WHAT WORKED) 1. 2. 3.			END EMOJI:	+, - PIP$/PROFIT$		ACTUAL LOSS/PROFITS	

ACCOUNT:			DATE:	SESSION:		TIME:	
PAIR:	START EMOJI:	ENTRY TIME FRAME:	TRADE TYPE:	RISK TO REWARD RATIO:	RISK % LEVEL (%/$1000)	BALANCE:	
ENTRY CONFIRMATIONS: 1. 2. 3.		ENTRY: 1. 2. 3.	STOP LOSS: 1. 2. 3.		TAKE PROFIT: 1. 2. 3.	TRADE GOAL:	
POWER POINTS: (WHAT WORKED) 1. 2. 3.			END EMOJI:	+, - PIP$/PROFIT$		ACTUAL LOSS/PROFITS	

ACCOUNT:			DATE:	SESSION:		TIME:	
PAIR:	START EMOJI:	ENTRY TIME FRAME:	TRADE TYPE:	RISK TO REWARD RATIO:	RISK % LEVEL (%/$1000)	BALANCE:	
ENTRY CONFIRMATIONS: 1. 2. 3.		ENTRY: 1. 2. 3.	STOP LOSS: 1. 2. 3.		TAKE PROFIT: 1. 2. 3.	TRADE GOAL:	
POWER POINTS: (WHAT WORKED) 1. 2. 3.			END EMOJI:	+, - PIP$/PROFIT$		ACTUAL LOSS/PROFITS	

TRADING JOURNAL

ACCOUNT:			DATE:	SESSION:			TIME:
PAIR:	START EMOJI:	ENTRY TIME FRAME:	TRADE TYPE:	RISK TO REWARD RATIO:	RISK % LEVEL (%/$1000)		BALANCE:
ENTRY CONFIRMATIONS: 1. 2. 3.		ENTRY: 1. 2. 3.	STOP LOSS: 1. 2. 3.		TAKE PROFIT: 1. 2. 3.		TRADE GOAL:
POWER POINTS: (WHAT WORKED) 1. 2. 3.			END EMOJI:	+, - PIP$/PROFIT$			ACTUAL LOSS/PROFITS

ACCOUNT:			DATE:	SESSION:			TIME:
PAIR:	START EMOJI:	ENTRY TIME FRAME:	TRADE TYPE:	RISK TO REWARD RATIO:	RISK % LEVEL (%/$1000)		BALANCE:
ENTRY CONFIRMATIONS: 1. 2. 3.		ENTRY: 1. 2. 3.	STOP LOSS: 1. 2. 3.		TAKE PROFIT: 1. 2. 3.		TRADE GOAL:
POWER POINTS: (WHAT WORKED) 1. 2. 3.			END EMOJI:	+, - PIP$/PROFIT$			ACTUAL LOSS/PROFITS

ACCOUNT:			DATE:	SESSION:			TIME:
PAIR:	START EMOJI:	ENTRY TIME FRAME:	TRADE TYPE:	RISK TO REWARD RATIO:	RISK % LEVEL (%/$1000)		BALANCE:
ENTRY CONFIRMATIONS: 1. 2. 3.		ENTRY: 1. 2. 3.	STOP LOSS: 1. 2. 3.		TAKE PROFIT: 1. 2. 3.		TRADE GOAL:
POWER POINTS: (WHAT WORKED) 1. 2. 3.			END EMOJI:	+, - PIP$/PROFIT$			ACTUAL LOSS/PROFITS

TRADING JOURNAL

ACCOUNT:			DATE:	SESSION:			TIME:
PAIR:	START EMOJI:	ENTRY TIME FRAME:	TRADE TYPE:	RISK TO REWARD RATIO:	RISK % LEVEL (%/$1000)		BALANCE:
ENTRY CONFIRMATIONS: 1. 2. 3.		ENTRY: 1. 2. 3.	STOP LOSS: 1. 2. 3.		TAKE PROFIT: 1. 2. 3.		TRADE GOAL:
POWER POINTS: (WHAT WORKED) 1. 2. 3.			END EMOJI:	+, - PIP$/PROFIT$			ACTUAL LOSS/PROFITS

ACCOUNT:			DATE:	SESSION:			TIME:
PAIR:	START EMOJI:	ENTRY TIME FRAME:	TRADE TYPE:	RISK TO REWARD RATIO:	RISK % LEVEL (%/$1000)		BALANCE:
ENTRY CONFIRMATIONS: 1. 2. 3.		ENTRY: 1. 2. 3.	STOP LOSS: 1. 2. 3.		TAKE PROFIT: 1. 2. 3.		TRADE GOAL:
POWER POINTS: (WHAT WORKED) 1. 2. 3.			END EMOJI:	+, - PIP$/PROFIT$			ACTUAL LOSS/PROFITS

ACCOUNT:			DATE:	SESSION:			TIME:
PAIR:	START EMOJI:	ENTRY TIME FRAME:	TRADE TYPE:	RISK TO REWARD RATIO:	RISK % LEVEL (%/$1000)		BALANCE:
ENTRY CONFIRMATIONS: 1. 2. 3.		ENTRY: 1. 2. 3.	STOP LOSS: 1. 2. 3.		TAKE PROFIT: 1. 2. 3.		TRADE GOAL:
POWER POINTS: (WHAT WORKED) 1. 2. 3.			END EMOJI:	+, - PIP$/PROFIT$			ACTUAL LOSS/PROFITS

TRADING JOURNAL

ACCOUNT:			DATE:	SESSION:			TIME:	
PAIR:	START EMOJI:	ENTRY TIME FRAME:	TRADE TYPE:	RISK TO REWARD RATIO:	RISK % LEVEL (%/$1000)		BALANCE:	
ENTRY CONFIRMATIONS: 1. 2. 3.		ENTRY: 1. 2. 3.	STOP LOSS: 1. 2. 3.			TAKE PROFIT: 1. 2. 3.	TRADE GOAL:	
POWER POINTS: (WHAT WORKED) 1. 2. 3.			END EMOJI:	+, - PIP$/PROFIT$			ACTUAL LOSS/PROFITS	

ACCOUNT:			DATE:	SESSION:			TIME:	
PAIR:	START EMOJI:	ENTRY TIME FRAME:	TRADE TYPE:	RISK TO REWARD RATIO:	RISK % LEVEL (%/$1000)		BALANCE:	
ENTRY CONFIRMATIONS: 1. 2. 3.		ENTRY: 1. 2. 3.	STOP LOSS: 1. 2. 3.			TAKE PROFIT: 1. 2. 3.	TRADE GOAL:	
POWER POINTS: (WHAT WORKED) 1. 2. 3.			END EMOJI:	+, - PIP$/PROFIT$			ACTUAL LOSS/PROFITS	

ACCOUNT:			DATE:	SESSION:			TIME:	
PAIR:	START EMOJI:	ENTRY TIME FRAME:	TRADE TYPE:	RISK TO REWARD RATIO:	RISK % LEVEL (%/$1000)		BALANCE:	
ENTRY CONFIRMATIONS: 1. 2. 3.		ENTRY: 1. 2. 3.	STOP LOSS: 1. 2. 3.			TAKE PROFIT: 1. 2. 3.	TRADE GOAL:	
POWER POINTS: (WHAT WORKED) 1. 2. 3.			END EMOJI:	+, - PIP$/PROFIT$			ACTUAL LOSS/PROFITS	

TRADING JOURNAL

ACCOUNT:			DATE:	SESSION:		TIME:	
PAIR:	START EMOJI:	ENTRY TIME FRAME:	TRADE TYPE:	RISK TO REWARD RATIO:	RISK % LEVEL (%/$1000)	BALANCE:	
ENTRY CONFIRMATIONS: 1. 2. 3.		ENTRY: 1. 2. 3.	STOP LOSS: 1. 2. 3.		TAKE PROFIT: 1. 2. 3.	TRADE GOAL:	
POWER POINTS: (WHAT WORKED) 1. 2. 3.			END EMOJI:	+, - PIP$/PROFIT$		ACTUAL LOSS/PROFITS	

ACCOUNT:			DATE:	SESSION:		TIME:	
PAIR:	START EMOJI:	ENTRY TIME FRAME:	TRADE TYPE:	RISK TO REWARD RATIO:	RISK % LEVEL (%/$1000)	BALANCE:	
ENTRY CONFIRMATIONS: 1. 2. 3.		ENTRY: 1. 2. 3.	STOP LOSS: 1. 2. 3.		TAKE PROFIT: 1. 2. 3.	TRADE GOAL:	
POWER POINTS: (WHAT WORKED) 1. 2. 3.			END EMOJI:	+, - PIP$/PROFIT$		ACTUAL LOSS/PROFITS	

ACCOUNT:			DATE:	SESSION:		TIME:	
PAIR:	START EMOJI:	ENTRY TIME FRAME:	TRADE TYPE:	RISK TO REWARD RATIO:	RISK % LEVEL (%/$1000)	BALANCE:	
ENTRY CONFIRMATIONS: 1. 2. 3.		ENTRY: 1. 2. 3.	STOP LOSS: 1. 2. 3.		TAKE PROFIT: 1. 2. 3.	TRADE GOAL:	
POWER POINTS: (WHAT WORKED) 1. 2. 3.			END EMOJI:	+, - PIP$/PROFIT$		ACTUAL LOSS/PROFITS	

TRADING JOURNAL

ACCOUNT:			DATE:	SESSION:			TIME:	
PAIR:	START EMOJI:	ENTRY TIME FRAME:	TRADE TYPE:	RISK TO REWARD RATIO:	RISK % LEVEL (%/$1000)		BALANCE:	
ENTRY CONFIRMATIONS: 1. 2. 3.		ENTRY: 1. 2. 3.	STOP LOSS: 1. 2. 3.		TAKE PROFIT: 1. 2. 3.		TRADE GOAL:	
POWER POINTS: (WHAT WORKED) 1. 2. 3.			END EMOJI:	+, - PIP$/PROFIT$			ACTUAL LOSS/PROFITS	

ACCOUNT:			DATE:	SESSION:			TIME:	
PAIR:	START EMOJI:	ENTRY TIME FRAME:	TRADE TYPE:	RISK TO REWARD RATIO:	RISK % LEVEL (%/$1000)		BALANCE:	
ENTRY CONFIRMATIONS: 1. 2. 3.		ENTRY: 1. 2. 3.	STOP LOSS: 1. 2. 3.		TAKE PROFIT: 1. 2. 3.		TRADE GOAL:	
POWER POINTS: (WHAT WORKED) 1. 2. 3.			END EMOJI:	+, - PIP$/PROFIT$			ACTUAL LOSS/PROFITS	

ACCOUNT:			DATE:	SESSION:			TIME:	
PAIR:	START EMOJI:	ENTRY TIME FRAME:	TRADE TYPE:	RISK TO REWARD RATIO:	RISK % LEVEL (%/$1000)		BALANCE:	
ENTRY CONFIRMATIONS: 1. 2. 3.		ENTRY: 1. 2. 3.	STOP LOSS: 1. 2. 3.		TAKE PROFIT: 1. 2. 3.		TRADE GOAL:	
POWER POINTS: (WHAT WORKED) 1. 2. 3.			END EMOJI:	+, - PIP$/PROFIT$			ACTUAL LOSS/PROFITS	

TRADING JOURNAL

ACCOUNT:			DATE:	SESSION:			TIME:
PAIR:	START EMOJI:	ENTRY TIME FRAME:	TRADE TYPE:	RISK TO REWARD RATIO:	RISK % LEVEL (%/$1000)		BALANCE:
ENTRY CONFIRMATIONS: 1. 2. 3.		ENTRY: 1. 2. 3.	STOP LOSS: 1. 2. 3.		TAKE PROFIT: 1. 2. 3.		TRADE GOAL:
POWER POINTS: (WHAT WORKED) 1. 2. 3.			END EMOJI:	+, - PIP$/PROFIT$			ACTUAL LOSS/PROFITS

ACCOUNT:			DATE:	SESSION:			TIME:
PAIR:	START EMOJI:	ENTRY TIME FRAME:	TRADE TYPE:	RISK TO REWARD RATIO:	RISK % LEVEL (%/$1000)		BALANCE:
ENTRY CONFIRMATIONS: 1. 2. 3.		ENTRY: 1. 2. 3.	STOP LOSS: 1. 2. 3.		TAKE PROFIT: 1. 2. 3.		TRADE GOAL:
POWER POINTS: (WHAT WORKED) 1. 2. 3.			END EMOJI:	+, - PIP$/PROFIT$			ACTUAL LOSS/PROFITS

ACCOUNT:			DATE:	SESSION:			TIME:
PAIR:	START EMOJI:	ENTRY TIME FRAME:	TRADE TYPE:	RISK TO REWARD RATIO:	RISK % LEVEL (%/$1000)		BALANCE:
ENTRY CONFIRMATIONS: 1. 2. 3.		ENTRY: 1. 2. 3.	STOP LOSS: 1. 2. 3.		TAKE PROFIT: 1. 2. 3.		TRADE GOAL:
POWER POINTS: (WHAT WORKED) 1. 2. 3.			END EMOJI:	+, - PIP$/PROFIT$			ACTUAL LOSS/PROFITS

TRADING JOURNAL

ACCOUNT:			DATE:	SESSION:			TIME:	
PAIR:	START EMOJI:	ENTRY TIME FRAME:	TRADE TYPE:	RISK TO REWARD RATIO:	RISK % LEVEL (%/$1000)		BALANCE:	
ENTRY CONFIRMATIONS: 1. 2. 3.		ENTRY: 1. 2. 3.	STOP LOSS: 1. 2. 3.		TAKE PROFIT: 1. 2. 3.		TRADE GOAL:	
POWER POINTS: (WHAT WORKED) 1. 2. 3.			END EMOJI:	+, - PIP$/PROFIT$			ACTUAL LOSS/PROFITS	

ACCOUNT:			DATE:	SESSION:			TIME:	
PAIR:	START EMOJI:	ENTRY TIME FRAME:	TRADE TYPE:	RISK TO REWARD RATIO:	RISK % LEVEL (%/$1000)		BALANCE:	
ENTRY CONFIRMATIONS: 1. 2. 3.		ENTRY: 1. 2. 3.	STOP LOSS: 1. 2. 3.		TAKE PROFIT: 1. 2. 3.		TRADE GOAL:	
POWER POINTS: (WHAT WORKED) 1. 2. 3.			END EMOJI:	+, - PIP$/PROFIT$			ACTUAL LOSS/PROFITS	

ACCOUNT:			DATE:	SESSION:			TIME:	
PAIR:	START EMOJI:	ENTRY TIME FRAME:	TRADE TYPE:	RISK TO REWARD RATIO:	RISK % LEVEL (%/$1000)		BALANCE:	
ENTRY CONFIRMATIONS: 1. 2. 3.		ENTRY: 1. 2. 3.	STOP LOSS: 1. 2. 3.		TAKE PROFIT: 1. 2. 3.		TRADE GOAL:	
POWER POINTS: (WHAT WORKED) 1. 2. 3.			END EMOJI:	+, - PIP$/PROFIT$			ACTUAL LOSS/PROFITS	

TRADING JOURNAL

ACCOUNT:			DATE:	SESSION:			TIME:	
PAIR:	START EMOJI:	ENTRY TIME FRAME:	TRADE TYPE:	RISK TO REWARD RATIO:	RISK % LEVEL (%/$1000)		BALANCE:	
ENTRY CONFIRMATIONS: 1. 2. 3.		ENTRY: 1. 2. 3.	STOP LOSS: 1. 2. 3.		TAKE PROFIT: 1. 2. 3.		TRADE GOAL:	
POWER POINTS: (WHAT WORKED) 1. 2. 3.			END EMOJI:	+, - PIP$/PROFIT$			ACTUAL LOSS/PROFITS	

ACCOUNT:			DATE:	SESSION:			TIME:	
PAIR:	START EMOJI:	ENTRY TIME FRAME:	TRADE TYPE:	RISK TO REWARD RATIO:	RISK % LEVEL (%/$1000)		BALANCE:	
ENTRY CONFIRMATIONS: 1. 2. 3.		ENTRY: 1. 2. 3.	STOP LOSS: 1. 2. 3.		TAKE PROFIT: 1. 2. 3.		TRADE GOAL:	
POWER POINTS: (WHAT WORKED) 1. 2. 3.			END EMOJI:	+, - PIP$/PROFIT$			ACTUAL LOSS/PROFITS	

ACCOUNT:			DATE:	SESSION:			TIME:	
PAIR:	START EMOJI:	ENTRY TIME FRAME:	TRADE TYPE:	RISK TO REWARD RATIO:	RISK % LEVEL (%/$1000)		BALANCE:	
ENTRY CONFIRMATIONS: 1. 2. 3.		ENTRY: 1. 2. 3.	STOP LOSS: 1. 2. 3.		TAKE PROFIT: 1. 2. 3.		TRADE GOAL:	
POWER POINTS: (WHAT WORKED) 1. 2. 3.			END EMOJI:	+, - PIP$/PROFIT$			ACTUAL LOSS/PROFITS	

TRADING JOURNAL

ACCOUNT:			DATE:	SESSION:			TIME:
PAIR:	START EMOJI:	ENTRY TIME FRAME:	TRADE TYPE:	RISK TO REWARD RATIO:	RISK % LEVEL (%/$1000)		BALANCE:
ENTRY CONFIRMATIONS: 1. 2. 3.		ENTRY: 1. 2. 3.	STOP LOSS: 1. 2. 3.		TAKE PROFIT: 1. 2. 3.		TRADE GOAL:
POWER POINTS: (WHAT WORKED) 1. 2. 3.			END EMOJI:	+, - PIP$/PROFIT$		ACTUAL LOSS/PROFITS	

ACCOUNT:			DATE:	SESSION:			TIME:
PAIR:	START EMOJI:	ENTRY TIME FRAME:	TRADE TYPE:	RISK TO REWARD RATIO:	RISK % LEVEL (%/$1000)		BALANCE:
ENTRY CONFIRMATIONS: 1. 2. 3.		ENTRY: 1. 2. 3.	STOP LOSS: 1. 2. 3.		TAKE PROFIT: 1. 2. 3.		TRADE GOAL:
POWER POINTS: (WHAT WORKED) 1. 2. 3.			END EMOJI:	+, - PIP$/PROFIT$		ACTUAL LOSS/PROFITS	

ACCOUNT:			DATE:	SESSION:			TIME:
PAIR:	START EMOJI:	ENTRY TIME FRAME:	TRADE TYPE:	RISK TO REWARD RATIO:	RISK % LEVEL (%/$1000)		BALANCE:
ENTRY CONFIRMATIONS: 1. 2. 3.		ENTRY: 1. 2. 3.	STOP LOSS: 1. 2. 3.		TAKE PROFIT: 1. 2. 3.		TRADE GOAL:
POWER POINTS: (WHAT WORKED) 1. 2. 3.			END EMOJI:	+, - PIP$/PROFIT$		ACTUAL LOSS/PROFITS	

TRADING JOURNAL

ACCOUNT:			DATE:	SESSION:			TIME:
PAIR:	START EMOJI:	ENTRY TIME FRAME:	TRADE TYPE:	RISK TO REWARD RATIO:	RISK % LEVEL (%/$1000)		BALANCE:
ENTRY CONFIRMATIONS: 1. 2. 3.		ENTRY: 1. 2. 3.	STOP LOSS: 1. 2. 3.		TAKE PROFIT: 1. 2. 3.		TRADE GOAL:
POWER POINTS: (WHAT WORKED) 1. 2. 3.			END EMOJI:	+, - PIP$/PROFIT$			ACTUAL LOSS/PROFITS

ACCOUNT:			DATE:	SESSION:			TIME:
PAIR:	START EMOJI:	ENTRY TIME FRAME:	TRADE TYPE:	RISK TO REWARD RATIO:	RISK % LEVEL (%/$1000)		BALANCE:
ENTRY CONFIRMATIONS: 1. 2. 3.		ENTRY: 1. 2. 3.	STOP LOSS: 1. 2. 3.		TAKE PROFIT: 1. 2. 3.		TRADE GOAL:
POWER POINTS: (WHAT WORKED) 1. 2. 3.			END EMOJI:	+, - PIP$/PROFIT$			ACTUAL LOSS/PROFITS

ACCOUNT:			DATE:	SESSION:			TIME:
PAIR:	START EMOJI:	ENTRY TIME FRAME:	TRADE TYPE:	RISK TO REWARD RATIO:	RISK % LEVEL (%/$1000)		BALANCE:
ENTRY CONFIRMATIONS: 1. 2. 3.		ENTRY: 1. 2. 3.	STOP LOSS: 1. 2. 3.		TAKE PROFIT: 1. 2. 3.		TRADE GOAL:
POWER POINTS: (WHAT WORKED) 1. 2. 3.			END EMOJI:	+, - PIP$/PROFIT$			ACTUAL LOSS/PROFITS

TRADING JOURNAL

ACCOUNT:			DATE:	SESSION:			TIME:
PAIR:	START EMOJI:	ENTRY TIME FRAME:	TRADE TYPE:	RISK TO REWARD RATIO:	RISK % LEVEL (%/$1000)		BALANCE:
ENTRY CONFIRMATIONS: 1. 2. 3.		ENTRY: 1. 2. 3.	STOP LOSS: 1. 2. 3.		TAKE PROFIT: 1. 2. 3.		TRADE GOAL:
POWER POINTS: (WHAT WORKED) 1. 2. 3.			END EMOJI:	+, - PIP$/PROFIT$			ACTUAL LOSS/PROFITS

ACCOUNT:			DATE:	SESSION:			TIME:
PAIR:	START EMOJI:	ENTRY TIME FRAME:	TRADE TYPE:	RISK TO REWARD RATIO:	RISK % LEVEL (%/$1000)		BALANCE:
ENTRY CONFIRMATIONS: 1. 2. 3.		ENTRY: 1. 2. 3.	STOP LOSS: 1. 2. 3.		TAKE PROFIT: 1. 2. 3.		TRADE GOAL:
POWER POINTS: (WHAT WORKED) 1. 2. 3.			END EMOJI:	+, - PIP$/PROFIT$			ACTUAL LOSS/PROFITS

ACCOUNT:			DATE:	SESSION:			TIME:
PAIR:	START EMOJI:	ENTRY TIME FRAME:	TRADE TYPE:	RISK TO REWARD RATIO:	RISK % LEVEL (%/$1000)		BALANCE:
ENTRY CONFIRMATIONS: 1. 2. 3.		ENTRY: 1. 2. 3.	STOP LOSS: 1. 2. 3.		TAKE PROFIT: 1. 2. 3.		TRADE GOAL:
POWER POINTS: (WHAT WORKED) 1. 2. 3.			END EMOJI:	+, - PIP$/PROFIT$			ACTUAL LOSS/PROFITS

TRADING JOURNAL

ACCOUNT:			DATE:	SESSION:		TIME:	
PAIR:	START EMOJI:	ENTRY TIME FRAME:	TRADE TYPE:	RISK TO REWARD RATIO:	RISK % LEVEL (%/$1000)	BALANCE:	
ENTRY CONFIRMATIONS: 1. 2. 3.		ENTRY: 1. 2. 3.	STOP LOSS: 1. 2. 3.		TAKE PROFIT: 1. 2. 3.	TRADE GOAL:	
POWER POINTS: (WHAT WORKED) 1. 2. 3.			END EMOJI:	+, - PIP$/PROFIT$		ACTUAL LOSS/PROFITS	

ACCOUNT:			DATE:	SESSION:		TIME:	
PAIR:	START EMOJI:	ENTRY TIME FRAME:	TRADE TYPE:	RISK TO REWARD RATIO:	RISK % LEVEL (%/$1000)	BALANCE:	
ENTRY CONFIRMATIONS: 1. 2. 3.		ENTRY: 1. 2. 3.	STOP LOSS: 1. 2. 3.		TAKE PROFIT: 1. 2. 3.	TRADE GOAL:	
POWER POINTS: (WHAT WORKED) 1. 2. 3.			END EMOJI:	+, - PIP$/PROFIT$		ACTUAL LOSS/PROFITS	

ACCOUNT:			DATE:	SESSION:		TIME:	
PAIR:	START EMOJI:	ENTRY TIME FRAME:	TRADE TYPE:	RISK TO REWARD RATIO:	RISK % LEVEL (%/$1000)	BALANCE:	
ENTRY CONFIRMATIONS: 1. 2. 3.		ENTRY: 1. 2. 3.	STOP LOSS: 1. 2. 3.		TAKE PROFIT: 1. 2. 3.	TRADE GOAL:	
POWER POINTS: (WHAT WORKED) 1. 2. 3.			END EMOJI:	+, - PIP$/PROFIT$		ACTUAL LOSS/PROFITS	

TRADING JOURNAL

ACCOUNT:			DATE:	SESSION:			TIME:	
PAIR:	START EMOJI:	ENTRY TIME FRAME:	TRADE TYPE:	RISK TO REWARD RATIO:		RISK % LEVEL (%/$1000)	BALANCE:	
ENTRY CONFIRMATIONS: 1. 2. 3.		ENTRY: 1. 2. 3.	STOP LOSS: 1. 2. 3.			TAKE PROFIT: 1. 2. 3.	TRADE GOAL:	
POWER POINTS: (WHAT WORKED) 1. 2. 3.			END EMOJI:	+, - PIP$/PROFIT$			ACTUAL LOSS/PROFITS	

ACCOUNT:			DATE:	SESSION:			TIME:	
PAIR:	START EMOJI:	ENTRY TIME FRAME:	TRADE TYPE:	RISK TO REWARD RATIO:		RISK % LEVEL (%/$1000)	BALANCE:	
ENTRY CONFIRMATIONS: 1. 2. 3.		ENTRY: 1. 2. 3.	STOP LOSS: 1. 2. 3.			TAKE PROFIT: 1. 2. 3.	TRADE GOAL:	
POWER POINTS: (WHAT WORKED) 1. 2. 3.			END EMOJI:	+, - PIP$/PROFIT$			ACTUAL LOSS/PROFITS	

ACCOUNT:			DATE:	SESSION:			TIME:	
PAIR:	START EMOJI:	ENTRY TIME FRAME:	TRADE TYPE:	RISK TO REWARD RATIO:		RISK % LEVEL (%/$1000)	BALANCE:	
ENTRY CONFIRMATIONS: 1. 2. 3.		ENTRY: 1. 2. 3.	STOP LOSS: 1. 2. 3.			TAKE PROFIT: 1. 2. 3.	TRADE GOAL:	
POWER POINTS: (WHAT WORKED) 1. 2. 3.			END EMOJI:	+, - PIP$/PROFIT$			ACTUAL LOSS/PROFITS	

TRADING JOURNAL

ACCOUNT:			DATE:	SESSION:		TIME:	
PAIR:	START EMOJI:	ENTRY TIME FRAME:	TRADE TYPE:	RISK TO REWARD RATIO:	RISK % LEVEL (%/$1000)	BALANCE:	
ENTRY CONFIRMATIONS: 1. 2. 3.		ENTRY: 1. 2. 3.	STOP LOSS: 1. 2. 3.		TAKE PROFIT: 1. 2. 3.	TRADE GOAL:	
POWER POINTS: (WHAT WORKED) 1. 2. 3.			END EMOJI:	+, - PIP$/PROFIT$		ACTUAL LOSS/PROFITS	

ACCOUNT:			DATE:	SESSION:		TIME:	
PAIR:	START EMOJI:	ENTRY TIME FRAME:	TRADE TYPE:	RISK TO REWARD RATIO:	RISK % LEVEL (%/$1000)	BALANCE:	
ENTRY CONFIRMATIONS: 1. 2. 3.		ENTRY: 1. 2. 3.	STOP LOSS: 1. 2. 3.		TAKE PROFIT: 1. 2. 3.	TRADE GOAL:	
POWER POINTS: (WHAT WORKED) 1. 2. 3.			END EMOJI:	+, - PIP$/PROFIT$		ACTUAL LOSS/PROFITS	

ACCOUNT:			DATE:	SESSION:		TIME:	
PAIR:	START EMOJI:	ENTRY TIME FRAME:	TRADE TYPE:	RISK TO REWARD RATIO:	RISK % LEVEL (%/$1000)	BALANCE:	
ENTRY CONFIRMATIONS: 1. 2. 3.		ENTRY: 1. 2. 3.	STOP LOSS: 1. 2. 3.		TAKE PROFIT: 1. 2. 3.	TRADE GOAL:	
POWER POINTS: (WHAT WORKED) 1. 2. 3.			END EMOJI:	+, - PIP$/PROFIT$		ACTUAL LOSS/PROFITS	

TRADING JOURNAL

ACCOUNT:			DATE:	SESSION:			TIME:	
PAIR:	START EMOJI:	ENTRY TIME FRAME:	TRADE TYPE:	RISK TO REWARD RATIO:	RISK % LEVEL (%/$1000)		BALANCE:	
ENTRY CONFIRMATIONS: 1. 2. 3.		ENTRY: 1. 2. 3.	STOP LOSS: 1. 2. 3.			TAKE PROFIT: 1. 2. 3.	TRADE GOAL:	
POWER POINTS: (WHAT WORKED) 1. 2. 3.			END EMOJI:	+, - PIP$/PROFIT$			ACTUAL LOSS/PROFITS	

ACCOUNT:			DATE:	SESSION:			TIME:	
PAIR:	START EMOJI:	ENTRY TIME FRAME:	TRADE TYPE:	RISK TO REWARD RATIO:	RISK % LEVEL (%/$1000)		BALANCE:	
ENTRY CONFIRMATIONS: 1. 2. 3.		ENTRY: 1. 2. 3.	STOP LOSS: 1. 2. 3.			TAKE PROFIT: 1. 2. 3.	TRADE GOAL:	
POWER POINTS: (WHAT WORKED) 1. 2. 3.			END EMOJI:	+, - PIP$/PROFIT$			ACTUAL LOSS/PROFITS	

ACCOUNT:			DATE:	SESSION:			TIME:	
PAIR:	START EMOJI:	ENTRY TIME FRAME:	TRADE TYPE:	RISK TO REWARD RATIO:	RISK % LEVEL (%/$1000)		BALANCE:	
ENTRY CONFIRMATIONS: 1. 2. 3.		ENTRY: 1. 2. 3.	STOP LOSS: 1. 2. 3.			TAKE PROFIT: 1. 2. 3.	TRADE GOAL:	
POWER POINTS: (WHAT WORKED) 1. 2. 3.			END EMOJI:	+, - PIP$/PROFIT$			ACTUAL LOSS/PROFITS	

TRADING JOURNAL

ACCOUNT:			DATE:	SESSION:		TIME:	
PAIR:	START EMOJI:	ENTRY TIME FRAME:	TRADE TYPE:	RISK TO REWARD RATIO:	RISK % LEVEL (%/$1000)	BALANCE:	
ENTRY CONFIRMATIONS: 1. 2. 3.	ENTRY: 1. 2. 3.		STOP LOSS: 1. 2. 3.		TAKE PROFIT: 1. 2. 3.	TRADE GOAL:	
POWER POINTS: (WHAT WORKED) 1. 2. 3.			END EMOJI:	+, - PIP$/PROFIT$		ACTUAL LOSS/PROFITS	

ACCOUNT:			DATE:	SESSION:		TIME:	
PAIR:	START EMOJI:	ENTRY TIME FRAME:	TRADE TYPE:	RISK TO REWARD RATIO:	RISK % LEVEL (%/$1000)	BALANCE:	
ENTRY CONFIRMATIONS: 1. 2. 3.	ENTRY: 1. 2. 3.		STOP LOSS: 1. 2. 3.		TAKE PROFIT: 1. 2. 3.	TRADE GOAL:	
POWER POINTS: (WHAT WORKED) 1. 2. 3.			END EMOJI:	+, - PIP$/PROFIT$		ACTUAL LOSS/PROFITS	

ACCOUNT:			DATE:	SESSION:		TIME:	
PAIR:	START EMOJI:	ENTRY TIME FRAME:	TRADE TYPE:	RISK TO REWARD RATIO:	RISK % LEVEL (%/$1000)	BALANCE:	
ENTRY CONFIRMATIONS: 1. 2. 3.	ENTRY: 1. 2. 3.		STOP LOSS: 1. 2. 3.		TAKE PROFIT: 1. 2. 3.	TRADE GOAL:	
POWER POINTS: (WHAT WORKED) 1. 2. 3.			END EMOJI:	+, - PIP$/PROFIT$		ACTUAL LOSS/PROFITS	

TRADING JOURNAL

ACCOUNT:			DATE:	SESSION:		TIME:	
PAIR:	START EMOJI:	ENTRY TIME FRAME:	TRADE TYPE:	RISK TO REWARD RATIO:	RISK % LEVEL (%/$1000)	BALANCE:	
ENTRY CONFIRMATIONS: 1. 2. 3.		ENTRY: 1. 2. 3.	STOP LOSS: 1. 2. 3.		TAKE PROFIT: 1. 2. 3.	TRADE GOAL:	
POWER POINTS: (WHAT WORKED) 1. 2. 3.			END EMOJI:	+, - PIP$/PROFIT$		ACTUAL LOSS/PROFITS	

ACCOUNT:			DATE:	SESSION:		TIME:	
PAIR:	START EMOJI:	ENTRY TIME FRAME:	TRADE TYPE:	RISK TO REWARD RATIO:	RISK % LEVEL (%/$1000)	BALANCE:	
ENTRY CONFIRMATIONS: 1. 2. 3.		ENTRY: 1. 2. 3.	STOP LOSS: 1. 2. 3.		TAKE PROFIT: 1. 2. 3.	TRADE GOAL:	
POWER POINTS: (WHAT WORKED) 1. 2. 3.			END EMOJI:	+, - PIP$/PROFIT$		ACTUAL LOSS/PROFITS	

ACCOUNT:			DATE:	SESSION:		TIME:	
PAIR:	START EMOJI:	ENTRY TIME FRAME:	TRADE TYPE:	RISK TO REWARD RATIO:	RISK % LEVEL (%/$1000)	BALANCE:	
ENTRY CONFIRMATIONS: 1. 2. 3.		ENTRY: 1. 2. 3.	STOP LOSS: 1. 2. 3.		TAKE PROFIT: 1. 2. 3.	TRADE GOAL:	
POWER POINTS: (WHAT WORKED) 1. 2. 3.			END EMOJI:	+, - PIP$/PROFIT$		ACTUAL LOSS/PROFITS	

TRADING JOURNAL

ACCOUNT:			DATE:	SESSION:		TIME:	
PAIR:	START EMOJI:	ENTRY TIME FRAME:	TRADE TYPE:	RISK TO REWARD RATIO:	RISK % LEVEL (%/$1000)	BALANCE:	
ENTRY CONFIRMATIONS: 1. 2. 3.		ENTRY: 1. 2. 3.	STOP LOSS: 1. 2. 3.		TAKE PROFIT: 1. 2. 3.	TRADE GOAL:	
POWER POINTS: (WHAT WORKED) 1. 2. 3.			END EMOJI:	+, - PIP$/PROFIT$		ACTUAL LOSS/PROFITS	

ACCOUNT:			DATE:	SESSION:		TIME:	
PAIR:	START EMOJI:	ENTRY TIME FRAME:	TRADE TYPE:	RISK TO REWARD RATIO:	RISK % LEVEL (%/$1000)	BALANCE:	
ENTRY CONFIRMATIONS: 1. 2. 3.		ENTRY: 1. 2. 3.	STOP LOSS: 1. 2. 3.		TAKE PROFIT: 1. 2. 3.	TRADE GOAL:	
POWER POINTS: (WHAT WORKED) 1. 2. 3.			END EMOJI:	+, - PIP$/PROFIT$		ACTUAL LOSS/PROFITS	

ACCOUNT:			DATE:	SESSION:		TIME:	
PAIR:	START EMOJI:	ENTRY TIME FRAME:	TRADE TYPE:	RISK TO REWARD RATIO:	RISK % LEVEL (%/$1000)	BALANCE:	
ENTRY CONFIRMATIONS: 1. 2. 3.		ENTRY: 1. 2. 3.	STOP LOSS: 1. 2. 3.		TAKE PROFIT: 1. 2. 3.	TRADE GOAL:	
POWER POINTS: (WHAT WORKED) 1. 2. 3.			END EMOJI:	+, - PIP$/PROFIT$		ACTUAL LOSS/PROFITS	

TRADING JOURNAL

ACCOUNT:			DATE:	SESSION:			TIME:	
PAIR:	START EMOJI:	ENTRY TIME FRAME:	TRADE TYPE:	RISK TO REWARD RATIO:	RISK % LEVEL (%/$1000)		BALANCE:	
ENTRY CONFIRMATIONS: 1. 2. 3.		ENTRY: 1. 2. 3.	STOP LOSS: 1. 2. 3.		TAKE PROFIT: 1. 2. 3.		TRADE GOAL:	
POWER POINTS: (WHAT WORKED) 1. 2. 3.			END EMOJI:	+, - PIP$/PROFIT$			ACTUAL LOSS/PROFITS	

ACCOUNT:			DATE:	SESSION:			TIME:	
PAIR:	START EMOJI:	ENTRY TIME FRAME:	TRADE TYPE:	RISK TO REWARD RATIO:	RISK % LEVEL (%/$1000)		BALANCE:	
ENTRY CONFIRMATIONS: 1. 2. 3.		ENTRY: 1. 2. 3.	STOP LOSS: 1. 2. 3.		TAKE PROFIT: 1. 2. 3.		TRADE GOAL:	
POWER POINTS: (WHAT WORKED) 1. 2. 3.			END EMOJI:	+, - PIP$/PROFIT$			ACTUAL LOSS/PROFITS	

ACCOUNT:			DATE:	SESSION:			TIME:	
PAIR:	START EMOJI:	ENTRY TIME FRAME:	TRADE TYPE:	RISK TO REWARD RATIO:	RISK % LEVEL (%/$1000)		BALANCE:	
ENTRY CONFIRMATIONS: 1. 2. 3.		ENTRY: 1. 2. 3.	STOP LOSS: 1. 2. 3.		TAKE PROFIT: 1. 2. 3.		TRADE GOAL:	
POWER POINTS: (WHAT WORKED) 1. 2. 3.			END EMOJI:	+, - PIP$/PROFIT$			ACTUAL LOSS/PROFITS	

TRADING JOURNAL

ACCOUNT:			DATE:	SESSION:			TIME:
PAIR:	START EMOJI:	ENTRY TIME FRAME:	TRADE TYPE:	RISK TO REWARD RATIO:	RISK % LEVEL (%/$1000)		BALANCE:
ENTRY CONFIRMATIONS: 1. 2. 3.		ENTRY: 1. 2. 3.	STOP LOSS: 1. 2. 3.		TAKE PROFIT: 1. 2. 3.		TRADE GOAL:
POWER POINTS: (WHAT WORKED) 1. 2. 3.			END EMOJI:	+, - PIP$/PROFIT$			ACTUAL LOSS/PROFITS

ACCOUNT:			DATE:	SESSION:			TIME:
PAIR:	START EMOJI:	ENTRY TIME FRAME:	TRADE TYPE:	RISK TO REWARD RATIO:	RISK % LEVEL (%/$1000)		BALANCE:
ENTRY CONFIRMATIONS: 1. 2. 3.		ENTRY: 1. 2. 3.	STOP LOSS: 1. 2. 3.		TAKE PROFIT: 1. 2. 3.		TRADE GOAL:
POWER POINTS: (WHAT WORKED) 1. 2. 3.			END EMOJI:	+, - PIP$/PROFIT$			ACTUAL LOSS/PROFITS

ACCOUNT:			DATE:	SESSION:			TIME:
PAIR:	START EMOJI:	ENTRY TIME FRAME:	TRADE TYPE:	RISK TO REWARD RATIO:	RISK % LEVEL (%/$1000)		BALANCE:
ENTRY CONFIRMATIONS: 1. 2. 3.		ENTRY: 1. 2. 3.	STOP LOSS: 1. 2. 3.		TAKE PROFIT: 1. 2. 3.		TRADE GOAL:
POWER POINTS: (WHAT WORKED) 1. 2. 3.			END EMOJI:	+, - PIP$/PROFIT$			ACTUAL LOSS/PROFITS

TRADING JOURNAL

ACCOUNT:			DATE:	SESSION:			TIME:	
PAIR:	START EMOJI:	ENTRY TIME FRAME:	TRADE TYPE:	RISK TO REWARD RATIO:	RISK % LEVEL (%/$1000)		BALANCE:	
ENTRY CONFIRMATIONS: 1. 2. 3.		ENTRY: 1. 2. 3.	STOP LOSS: 1. 2. 3.			TAKE PROFIT: 1. 2. 3.	TRADE GOAL:	
POWER POINTS: (WHAT WORKED) 1. 2. 3.			END EMOJI:	+, - PIP$/PROFIT$			ACTUAL LOSS/PROFITS	

ACCOUNT:			DATE:	SESSION:			TIME:	
PAIR:	START EMOJI:	ENTRY TIME FRAME:	TRADE TYPE:	RISK TO REWARD RATIO:	RISK % LEVEL (%/$1000)		BALANCE:	
ENTRY CONFIRMATIONS: 1. 2. 3.		ENTRY: 1. 2. 3.	STOP LOSS: 1. 2. 3.			TAKE PROFIT: 1. 2. 3.	TRADE GOAL:	
POWER POINTS: (WHAT WORKED) 1. 2. 3.			END EMOJI:	+, - PIP$/PROFIT$			ACTUAL LOSS/PROFITS	

ACCOUNT:			DATE:	SESSION:			TIME:	
PAIR:	START EMOJI:	ENTRY TIME FRAME:	TRADE TYPE:	RISK TO REWARD RATIO:	RISK % LEVEL (%/$1000)		BALANCE:	
ENTRY CONFIRMATIONS: 1. 2. 3.		ENTRY: 1. 2. 3.	STOP LOSS: 1. 2. 3.			TAKE PROFIT: 1. 2. 3.	TRADE GOAL:	
POWER POINTS: (WHAT WORKED) 1. 2. 3.			END EMOJI:	+, - PIP$/PROFIT$			ACTUAL LOSS/PROFITS	

TRADING JOURNAL

ACCOUNT:			DATE:	SESSION:			TIME:	
PAIR:	START EMOJI:	ENTRY TIME FRAME:	TRADE TYPE:	RISK TO REWARD RATIO:	RISK % LEVEL (%/$1000)		BALANCE:	
ENTRY CONFIRMATIONS: 1. 2. 3.		ENTRY: 1. 2. 3.	STOP LOSS: 1. 2. 3.			TAKE PROFIT: 1. 2. 3.	TRADE GOAL:	
POWER POINTS: (WHAT WORKED) 1. 2. 3.			END EMOJI:	+, - PIP$/PROFIT$			ACTUAL LOSS/PROFITS	

ACCOUNT:			DATE:	SESSION:			TIME:	
PAIR:	START EMOJI:	ENTRY TIME FRAME:	TRADE TYPE:	RISK TO REWARD RATIO:	RISK % LEVEL (%/$1000)		BALANCE:	
ENTRY CONFIRMATIONS: 1. 2. 3.		ENTRY: 1. 2. 3.	STOP LOSS: 1. 2. 3.			TAKE PROFIT: 1. 2. 3.	TRADE GOAL:	
POWER POINTS: (WHAT WORKED) 1. 2. 3.			END EMOJI:	+, - PIP$/PROFIT$			ACTUAL LOSS/PROFITS	

ACCOUNT:			DATE:	SESSION:			TIME:	
PAIR:	START EMOJI:	ENTRY TIME FRAME:	TRADE TYPE:	RISK TO REWARD RATIO:	RISK % LEVEL (%/$1000)		BALANCE:	
ENTRY CONFIRMATIONS: 1. 2. 3.		ENTRY: 1. 2. 3.	STOP LOSS: 1. 2. 3.			TAKE PROFIT: 1. 2. 3.	TRADE GOAL:	
POWER POINTS: (WHAT WORKED) 1. 2. 3.			END EMOJI:	+, - PIP$/PROFIT$			ACTUAL LOSS/PROFITS	

TRADING JOURNAL

ACCOUNT:			DATE:	SESSION:		TIME:	
PAIR:	START EMOJI:	ENTRY TIME FRAME:	TRADE TYPE:	RISK TO REWARD RATIO:	RISK % LEVEL (%/$1000)	BALANCE:	
ENTRY CONFIRMATIONS: 1. 2. 3.		ENTRY: 1. 2. 3.	STOP LOSS: 1. 2. 3.		TAKE PROFIT: 1. 2. 3.	TRADE GOAL:	
POWER POINTS: (WHAT WORKED) 1. 2. 3.			END EMOJI:	+, - PIP$/PROFIT$		ACTUAL LOSS/PROFITS	

ACCOUNT:			DATE:	SESSION:		TIME:	
PAIR:	START EMOJI:	ENTRY TIME FRAME:	TRADE TYPE:	RISK TO REWARD RATIO:	RISK % LEVEL (%/$1000)	BALANCE:	
ENTRY CONFIRMATIONS: 1. 2. 3.		ENTRY: 1. 2. 3.	STOP LOSS: 1. 2. 3.		TAKE PROFIT: 1. 2. 3.	TRADE GOAL:	
POWER POINTS: (WHAT WORKED) 1. 2. 3.			END EMOJI:	+, - PIP$/PROFIT$		ACTUAL LOSS/PROFITS	

ACCOUNT:			DATE:	SESSION:		TIME:	
PAIR:	START EMOJI:	ENTRY TIME FRAME:	TRADE TYPE:	RISK TO REWARD RATIO:	RISK % LEVEL (%/$1000)	BALANCE:	
ENTRY CONFIRMATIONS: 1. 2. 3.		ENTRY: 1. 2. 3.	STOP LOSS: 1. 2. 3.		TAKE PROFIT: 1. 2. 3.	TRADE GOAL:	
POWER POINTS: (WHAT WORKED) 1. 2. 3.			END EMOJI:	+, - PIP$/PROFIT$		ACTUAL LOSS/PROFITS	

TRADING JOURNAL

ACCOUNT:			DATE:	SESSION:			TIME:	
PAIR:	START EMOJI:	ENTRY TIME FRAME:	TRADE TYPE:	RISK TO REWARD RATIO:	RISK % LEVEL (%/$1000)		BALANCE:	
ENTRY CONFIRMATIONS: 1. 2. 3.		ENTRY: 1. 2. 3.	STOP LOSS: 1. 2. 3.			TAKE PROFIT: 1. 2. 3.	TRADE GOAL:	
POWER POINTS: (WHAT WORKED) 1. 2. 3.			END EMOJI:	+, - PIP$/PROFIT$			ACTUAL LOSS/PROFITS	

ACCOUNT:			DATE:	SESSION:			TIME:	
PAIR:	START EMOJI:	ENTRY TIME FRAME:	TRADE TYPE:	RISK TO REWARD RATIO:	RISK % LEVEL (%/$1000)		BALANCE:	
ENTRY CONFIRMATIONS: 1. 2. 3.		ENTRY: 1. 2. 3.	STOP LOSS: 1. 2. 3.			TAKE PROFIT: 1. 2. 3.	TRADE GOAL:	
POWER POINTS: (WHAT WORKED) 1. 2. 3.			END EMOJI:	+, - PIP$/PROFIT$			ACTUAL LOSS/PROFITS	

ACCOUNT:			DATE:	SESSION:			TIME:	
PAIR:	START EMOJI:	ENTRY TIME FRAME:	TRADE TYPE:	RISK TO REWARD RATIO:	RISK % LEVEL (%/$1000)		BALANCE:	
ENTRY CONFIRMATIONS: 1. 2. 3.		ENTRY: 1. 2. 3.	STOP LOSS: 1. 2. 3.			TAKE PROFIT: 1. 2. 3.	TRADE GOAL:	
POWER POINTS: (WHAT WORKED) 1. 2. 3.			END EMOJI:	+, - PIP$/PROFIT$			ACTUAL LOSS/PROFITS	

TRADING JOURNAL

ACCOUNT:			DATE:	SESSION:		TIME:	
PAIR:	START EMOJI:	ENTRY TIME FRAME:	TRADE TYPE:	RISK TO REWARD RATIO:	RISK % LEVEL (%/$1000)	BALANCE:	
ENTRY CONFIRMATIONS: 1. 2. 3.		ENTRY: 1. 2. 3.	STOP LOSS: 1. 2. 3.		TAKE PROFIT: 1. 2. 3.	TRADE GOAL:	
POWER POINTS: (WHAT WORKED) 1. 2. 3.			END EMOJI:	+, - PIP$/PROFIT$		ACTUAL LOSS/PROFITS	

ACCOUNT:			DATE:	SESSION:		TIME:	
PAIR:	START EMOJI:	ENTRY TIME FRAME:	TRADE TYPE:	RISK TO REWARD RATIO:	RISK % LEVEL (%/$1000)	BALANCE:	
ENTRY CONFIRMATIONS: 1. 2. 3.		ENTRY: 1. 2. 3.	STOP LOSS: 1. 2. 3.		TAKE PROFIT: 1. 2. 3.	TRADE GOAL:	
POWER POINTS: (WHAT WORKED) 1. 2. 3.			END EMOJI:	+, - PIP$/PROFIT$		ACTUAL LOSS/PROFITS	

ACCOUNT:			DATE:	SESSION:		TIME:	
PAIR:	START EMOJI:	ENTRY TIME FRAME:	TRADE TYPE:	RISK TO REWARD RATIO:	RISK % LEVEL (%/$1000)	BALANCE:	
ENTRY CONFIRMATIONS: 1. 2. 3.		ENTRY: 1. 2. 3.	STOP LOSS: 1. 2. 3.		TAKE PROFIT: 1. 2. 3.	TRADE GOAL:	
POWER POINTS: (WHAT WORKED) 1. 2. 3.			END EMOJI:	+, - PIP$/PROFIT$		ACTUAL LOSS/PROFITS	

TRADING JOURNAL

ACCOUNT:			DATE:	SESSION:		TIME:	
PAIR:	START EMOJI:	ENTRY TIME FRAME:	TRADE TYPE:	RISK TO REWARD RATIO:	RISK % LEVEL (%/$1000)	BALANCE:	
ENTRY CONFIRMATIONS: 1. 2. 3.		ENTRY: 1. 2. 3.	STOP LOSS: 1. 2. 3.		TAKE PROFIT: 1. 2. 3.	TRADE GOAL:	
POWER POINTS: (WHAT WORKED) 1. 2. 3.			END EMOJI:	+, - PIP$/PROFIT$		ACTUAL LOSS/PROFITS	

ACCOUNT:			DATE:	SESSION:		TIME:	
PAIR:	START EMOJI:	ENTRY TIME FRAME:	TRADE TYPE:	RISK TO REWARD RATIO:	RISK % LEVEL (%/$1000)	BALANCE:	
ENTRY CONFIRMATIONS: 1. 2. 3.		ENTRY: 1. 2. 3.	STOP LOSS: 1. 2. 3.		TAKE PROFIT: 1. 2. 3.	TRADE GOAL:	
POWER POINTS: (WHAT WORKED) 1. 2. 3.			END EMOJI:	+, - PIP$/PROFIT$		ACTUAL LOSS/PROFITS	

ACCOUNT:			DATE:	SESSION:		TIME:	
PAIR:	START EMOJI:	ENTRY TIME FRAME:	TRADE TYPE:	RISK TO REWARD RATIO:	RISK % LEVEL (%/$1000)	BALANCE:	
ENTRY CONFIRMATIONS: 1. 2. 3.		ENTRY: 1. 2. 3.	STOP LOSS: 1. 2. 3.		TAKE PROFIT: 1. 2. 3.	TRADE GOAL:	
POWER POINTS: (WHAT WORKED) 1. 2. 3.			END EMOJI:	+, - PIP$/PROFIT$		ACTUAL LOSS/PROFITS	

TRADING JOURNAL

ACCOUNT:			DATE:	SESSION:		TIME:
PAIR:	START EMOJI:	ENTRY TIME FRAME:	TRADE TYPE:	RISK TO REWARD RATIO:	RISK % LEVEL (%/$1000)	BALANCE:
ENTRY CONFIRMATIONS: 1. 2. 3.	ENTRY: 1. 2. 3.		STOP LOSS: 1. 2. 3.		TAKE PROFIT: 1. 2. 3.	TRADE GOAL:
POWER POINTS: (WHAT WORKED) 1. 2. 3.			END EMOJI:	+, - PIP$/PROFIT$		ACTUAL LOSS/PROFITS

ACCOUNT:			DATE:	SESSION:		TIME:
PAIR:	START EMOJI:	ENTRY TIME FRAME:	TRADE TYPE:	RISK TO REWARD RATIO:	RISK % LEVEL (%/$1000)	BALANCE:
ENTRY CONFIRMATIONS: 1. 2. 3.	ENTRY: 1. 2. 3.		STOP LOSS: 1. 2. 3.		TAKE PROFIT: 1. 2. 3.	TRADE GOAL:
POWER POINTS: (WHAT WORKED) 1. 2. 3.			END EMOJI:	+, - PIP$/PROFIT$		ACTUAL LOSS/PROFITS

ACCOUNT:			DATE:	SESSION:		TIME:
PAIR:	START EMOJI:	ENTRY TIME FRAME:	TRADE TYPE:	RISK TO REWARD RATIO:	RISK % LEVEL (%/$1000)	BALANCE:
ENTRY CONFIRMATIONS: 1. 2. 3.	ENTRY: 1. 2. 3.		STOP LOSS: 1. 2. 3.		TAKE PROFIT: 1. 2. 3.	TRADE GOAL:
POWER POINTS: (WHAT WORKED) 1. 2. 3.			END EMOJI:	+, - PIP$/PROFIT$		ACTUAL LOSS/PROFITS

TRADING JOURNAL

ACCOUNT:			DATE:	SESSION:		TIME:	
PAIR:	START EMOJI:	ENTRY TIME FRAME:	TRADE TYPE:	RISK TO REWARD RATIO:	RISK % LEVEL (%/$1000)	BALANCE:	
ENTRY CONFIRMATIONS: 1. 2. 3.		ENTRY: 1. 2. 3.	STOP LOSS: 1. 2. 3.		TAKE PROFIT: 1. 2. 3.	TRADE GOAL:	
POWER POINTS: (WHAT WORKED) 1. 2. 3.			END EMOJI:	+, - PIP$/PROFIT$		ACTUAL LOSS/PROFITS	

ACCOUNT:			DATE:	SESSION:		TIME:	
PAIR:	START EMOJI:	ENTRY TIME FRAME:	TRADE TYPE:	RISK TO REWARD RATIO:	RISK % LEVEL (%/$1000)	BALANCE:	
ENTRY CONFIRMATIONS: 1. 2. 3.		ENTRY: 1. 2. 3.	STOP LOSS: 1. 2. 3.		TAKE PROFIT: 1. 2. 3.	TRADE GOAL:	
POWER POINTS: (WHAT WORKED) 1. 2. 3.			END EMOJI:	+, - PIP$/PROFIT$		ACTUAL LOSS/PROFITS	

ACCOUNT:			DATE:	SESSION:		TIME:	
PAIR:	START EMOJI:	ENTRY TIME FRAME:	TRADE TYPE:	RISK TO REWARD RATIO:	RISK % LEVEL (%/$1000)	BALANCE:	
ENTRY CONFIRMATIONS: 1. 2. 3.		ENTRY: 1. 2. 3.	STOP LOSS: 1. 2. 3.		TAKE PROFIT: 1. 2. 3.	TRADE GOAL:	
POWER POINTS: (WHAT WORKED) 1. 2. 3.			END EMOJI:	+, - PIP$/PROFIT$		ACTUAL LOSS/PROFITS	

TRADING JOURNAL

ACCOUNT:				DATE:	SESSION:			TIME:	
PAIR:	START EMOJI:	ENTRY TIME FRAME:	TRADE TYPE:	RISK TO REWARD RATIO:		RISK % LEVEL (%/$1000)		BALANCE:	
ENTRY CONFIRMATIONS: 1. 2. 3.		ENTRY: 1. 2. 3.	STOP LOSS: 1. 2. 3.			TAKE PROFIT: 1. 2. 3.		TRADE GOAL:	
POWER POINTS: (WHAT WORKED) 1. 2. 3.				END EMOJI:	+, - PIP$/PROFIT$			ACTUAL LOSS/PROFITS	

ACCOUNT:				DATE:	SESSION:			TIME:	
PAIR:	START EMOJI:	ENTRY TIME FRAME:	TRADE TYPE:	RISK TO REWARD RATIO:		RISK % LEVEL (%/$1000)		BALANCE:	
ENTRY CONFIRMATIONS: 1. 2. 3.		ENTRY: 1. 2. 3.	STOP LOSS: 1. 2. 3.			TAKE PROFIT: 1. 2. 3.		TRADE GOAL:	
POWER POINTS: (WHAT WORKED) 1. 2. 3.				END EMOJI:	+, - PIP$/PROFIT$			ACTUAL LOSS/PROFITS	

ACCOUNT:				DATE:	SESSION:			TIME:	
PAIR:	START EMOJI:	ENTRY TIME FRAME:	TRADE TYPE:	RISK TO REWARD RATIO:		RISK % LEVEL (%/$1000)		BALANCE:	
ENTRY CONFIRMATIONS: 1. 2. 3.		ENTRY: 1. 2. 3.	STOP LOSS: 1. 2. 3.			TAKE PROFIT: 1. 2. 3.		TRADE GOAL:	
POWER POINTS: (WHAT WORKED) 1. 2. 3.				END EMOJI:	+, - PIP$/PROFIT$			ACTUAL LOSS/PROFITS	

TRADING JOURNAL

ACCOUNT:			DATE:	SESSION:		TIME:	
PAIR:	START EMOJI:	ENTRY TIME FRAME:	TRADE TYPE:	RISK TO REWARD RATIO:	RISK % LEVEL (%/$1000)	BALANCE:	
ENTRY CONFIRMATIONS: 1. 2. 3.		ENTRY: 1. 2. 3.	STOP LOSS: 1. 2. 3.		TAKE PROFIT: 1. 2. 3.	TRADE GOAL:	
POWER POINTS: (WHAT WORKED) 1. 2. 3.			END EMOJI:	+, - PIP$/PROFIT$		ACTUAL LOSS/PROFITS	

ACCOUNT:			DATE:	SESSION:		TIME:	
PAIR:	START EMOJI:	ENTRY TIME FRAME:	TRADE TYPE:	RISK TO REWARD RATIO:	RISK % LEVEL (%/$1000)	BALANCE:	
ENTRY CONFIRMATIONS: 1. 2. 3.		ENTRY: 1. 2. 3.	STOP LOSS: 1. 2. 3.		TAKE PROFIT: 1. 2. 3.	TRADE GOAL:	
POWER POINTS: (WHAT WORKED) 1. 2. 3.			END EMOJI:	+, - PIP$/PROFIT$		ACTUAL LOSS/PROFITS	

ACCOUNT:			DATE:	SESSION:		TIME:	
PAIR:	START EMOJI:	ENTRY TIME FRAME:	TRADE TYPE:	RISK TO REWARD RATIO:	RISK % LEVEL (%/$1000)	BALANCE:	
ENTRY CONFIRMATIONS: 1. 2. 3.		ENTRY: 1. 2. 3.	STOP LOSS: 1. 2. 3.		TAKE PROFIT: 1. 2. 3.	TRADE GOAL:	
POWER POINTS: (WHAT WORKED) 1. 2. 3.			END EMOJI:	+, - PIP$/PROFIT$		ACTUAL LOSS/PROFITS	

TRADING JOURNAL

ACCOUNT:			DATE:	SESSION:			TIME:	
PAIR:	START EMOJI:	ENTRY TIME FRAME:	TRADE TYPE:	RISK TO REWARD RATIO:	RISK % LEVEL (%/$1000)		BALANCE:	
ENTRY CONFIRMATIONS: 1. 2. 3.		ENTRY: 1. 2. 3.	STOP LOSS: 1. 2. 3.			TAKE PROFIT: 1. 2. 3.	TRADE GOAL:	
POWER POINTS: (WHAT WORKED) 1. 2. 3.			END EMOJI:	+, - PIP$/PROFIT$			ACTUAL LOSS/PROFITS	

ACCOUNT:			DATE:	SESSION:			TIME:	
PAIR:	START EMOJI:	ENTRY TIME FRAME:	TRADE TYPE:	RISK TO REWARD RATIO:	RISK % LEVEL (%/$1000)		BALANCE:	
ENTRY CONFIRMATIONS: 1. 2. 3.		ENTRY: 1. 2. 3.	STOP LOSS: 1. 2. 3.			TAKE PROFIT: 1. 2. 3.	TRADE GOAL:	
POWER POINTS: (WHAT WORKED) 1. 2. 3.			END EMOJI:	+, - PIP$/PROFIT$			ACTUAL LOSS/PROFITS	

ACCOUNT:			DATE:	SESSION:			TIME:	
PAIR:	START EMOJI:	ENTRY TIME FRAME:	TRADE TYPE:	RISK TO REWARD RATIO:	RISK % LEVEL (%/$1000)		BALANCE:	
ENTRY CONFIRMATIONS: 1. 2. 3.		ENTRY: 1. 2. 3.	STOP LOSS: 1. 2. 3.			TAKE PROFIT: 1. 2. 3.	TRADE GOAL:	
POWER POINTS: (WHAT WORKED) 1. 2. 3.			END EMOJI:	+, - PIP$/PROFIT$			ACTUAL LOSS/PROFITS	

TRADING JOURNAL

ACCOUNT:			DATE:	SESSION:			TIME:
PAIR:	START EMOJI:	ENTRY TIME FRAME:	TRADE TYPE:	RISK TO REWARD RATIO:	RISK % LEVEL (%/$1000)		BALANCE:
ENTRY CONFIRMATIONS: 1. 2. 3.		ENTRY: 1. 2. 3.	STOP LOSS: 1. 2. 3.		TAKE PROFIT: 1. 2. 3.		TRADE GOAL:
POWER POINTS: (WHAT WORKED) 1. 2. 3.			END EMOJI:	+, - PIP$/PROFIT$			ACTUAL LOSS/PROFITS

ACCOUNT:			DATE:	SESSION:			TIME:
PAIR:	START EMOJI:	ENTRY TIME FRAME:	TRADE TYPE:	RISK TO REWARD RATIO:	RISK % LEVEL (%/$1000)		BALANCE:
ENTRY CONFIRMATIONS: 1. 2. 3.		ENTRY: 1. 2. 3.	STOP LOSS: 1. 2. 3.		TAKE PROFIT: 1. 2. 3.		TRADE GOAL:
POWER POINTS: (WHAT WORKED) 1. 2. 3.			END EMOJI:	+, - PIP$/PROFIT$			ACTUAL LOSS/PROFITS

ACCOUNT:			DATE:	SESSION:			TIME:
PAIR:	START EMOJI:	ENTRY TIME FRAME:	TRADE TYPE:	RISK TO REWARD RATIO:	RISK % LEVEL (%/$1000)		BALANCE:
ENTRY CONFIRMATIONS: 1. 2. 3.		ENTRY: 1. 2. 3.	STOP LOSS: 1. 2. 3.		TAKE PROFIT: 1. 2. 3.		TRADE GOAL:
POWER POINTS: (WHAT WORKED) 1. 2. 3.			END EMOJI:	+, - PIP$/PROFIT$			ACTUAL LOSS/PROFITS

TRADING JOURNAL

ACCOUNT:			DATE:	SESSION:			TIME:	
PAIR:	START EMOJI:	ENTRY TIME FRAME:	TRADE TYPE:	RISK TO REWARD RATIO:		RISK % LEVEL (%/$1000)	BALANCE:	
ENTRY CONFIRMATIONS: 1. 2. 3.		ENTRY: 1. 2. 3.	STOP LOSS: 1. 2. 3.			TAKE PROFIT: 1. 2. 3.	TRADE GOAL:	
POWER POINTS: (WHAT WORKED) 1. 2. 3.			END EMOJI:	+, - PIP$/PROFIT$			ACTUAL LOSS/PROFITS	

ACCOUNT:			DATE:	SESSION:			TIME:	
PAIR:	START EMOJI:	ENTRY TIME FRAME:	TRADE TYPE:	RISK TO REWARD RATIO:		RISK % LEVEL (%/$1000)	BALANCE:	
ENTRY CONFIRMATIONS: 1. 2. 3.		ENTRY: 1. 2. 3.	STOP LOSS: 1. 2. 3.			TAKE PROFIT: 1. 2. 3.	TRADE GOAL:	
POWER POINTS: (WHAT WORKED) 1. 2. 3.			END EMOJI:	+, - PIP$/PROFIT$			ACTUAL LOSS/PROFITS	

ACCOUNT:			DATE:	SESSION:			TIME:	
PAIR:	START EMOJI:	ENTRY TIME FRAME:	TRADE TYPE:	RISK TO REWARD RATIO:		RISK % LEVEL (%/$1000)	BALANCE:	
ENTRY CONFIRMATIONS: 1. 2. 3.		ENTRY: 1. 2. 3.	STOP LOSS: 1. 2. 3.			TAKE PROFIT: 1. 2. 3.	TRADE GOAL:	
POWER POINTS: (WHAT WORKED) 1. 2. 3.			END EMOJI:	+, - PIP$/PROFIT$			ACTUAL LOSS/PROFITS	

DAILY ACCOUNT SUMMARY TOTALS:

DATE:	+ 0r -	WEEKLY	MONTHLY	6 MONTH	YEARLY

TRADER'S THEME SONG

"You gotta know when the trend is up,
know when the trend is down,
know the best lot size,
know when to take profit.
You nev'r count your money
when you're at the trading table,
there'll be time enough for countin'
when the tradin's done."
--Adapted Song by Kenny Rogers